THE BLOG OF WAR

Front-line Dispatches from Soldiers in Iraq and Afghanistan

Matthew Currier Burden
"Blackfive"

SIMON & SCHUSTER PAPERBACKS

NEW YORK · LONDON · TORONTO · SYDNEY

SIMON & SCHUSTER PAPERBACKS
Rockefeller Center
1230 Avenue of the Americas
New York, NY 10020

First Simon & Schuster paperback edition 2006

For information about special discounts for bulk purchases,
please contact Simon & Schuster Special Sales:
1-800-456-6798 or business@simonandschuster.com

DESIGNED BY PAUL DIPPOLITO

Manufactured in the United States of America

3   5   7   9   10   8   6   4   2

Library of Congress Cataloging in Publication Data

Burden, Matthew Currier.
The blog of war : front-line dispatches from soldiers in Iraq and
Afghanistan / Matthew Currier Burden.
        p.   cm.
Includes index.
1. Iraq War, 2003—Personal narratives, American. 2. Afghan War, 2001—
Personal narratives, American. 3. Soldiers—United States—Weblogs.
4. United States—Armed Forces—Biography. 5. United States—History,
Military—Sources. I. Title.
DS79.76.B87 2006
956.7044'3092273—dc22
[B]
2006044361

ISBN-13: 978-7432-9418-8

For My Brothers:

U.S. Army Major Mathew Earl Schram
JANUARY 25, 1967–MAY 26, 2003
Killed in Action

U.S. Navy Lieutenant Kylan A. Jones-Huffman
APRIL 20, 1972–AUGUST 21, 2003
Killed in Action

U.S. Army Captain Sean Patrick Sims
AUGUST 27, 1972–NOVEMBER 13, 2004
Killed in Action

U.S. Army First Lieutenant Erik Scott McCrae
NOVEMBER 1, 1978–JUNE 4, 2004
Killed in Action

U.S. Army Sergeant Arnold Duplantier II
JUNE 3, 1979–JUNE 22, 2005
Killed in Action

U.S. Army Specialist Robert Allen Wise
AUGUST 6, 1982–NOVEMBER 12, 2003
Killed in Action

U.S. Marine Corps Corporal Jason L. Dunham
NOVEMBER 10, 1981–APRIL 22, 2004
Killed in Action

U.S. Marine Corps Lance Corporal Chance Russell Phelps
JULY 14, 1984–APRIL 9, 2004
Killed in Action

U.S. Marine Corps Lance Corporal Eric Scott Freeman
AUGUST 2, 1984–JANUARY 3, 2005
*Killed in an automobile crash on his way to report for
duty for a third tour in Iraq*

CONTENTS

THE BLOG
OF WAR

INTRODUCTION

Yet all experience is an arch wherethrough gleams the untravelled world.

—ALFRED, LORD TENNYSON, "ULYSSES"

Memorial Day is like any other day when you're in an army at war.

On Memorial Day, May 26, 2003, at approximately 7:00 A.M., Major Mathew E. Schram was leading a resupply convoy in western Iraq near the Syrian border. Major Schram was the support operations officer for the 3rd Armored Cavalry Regiment, a unit out of Ft. Carson, Colorado. He had responsibility for organizing the regiment's logistical arm, ensuring that the cavalrymen never ran out of food, fuel, or ammo.

Normally, Major Schram would not accompany the convoys as his responsibilities kept him at the main resupply point. However, due to the attacks on supply convoys, he decided to lead this one. He also decided that there was a side benefit to the ride: he would be able to talk with the field commanders and troops that he supported. Major Schram wanted to make sure that his customers were happy. Anyone who knew Mat Schram knew that he was obsessive-compulsive about making sure "his soldiers" were taken care of; that's why he was one of the top logistical officers in the U.S. Army.

The convoy was headed north from Al Asad Airbase–Forward Operating Base (FOB) Webster along Route 12 to FOB Jenna. After delivering supplies at Jenna, the convoy would continue on to Al Qaim, where the 1st/3rd Armored Cavalry was based.

At 7:15 A.M., Major Schram's convoy approached a wide ravine where the bridge had been destroyed during the invasion. The convoy had to go down the embankment, into the ravine, and back up the other side to get back onto the highway.

Once the lead vehicle started up the far bank of the ravine, the convoy came under intense fire from rocket-propelled grenades (RPGs), machine guns, and small arms. It was an ambush. Thirteen Iraqi insurgents had been waiting by the ravine.

An RPG hit the lead tanker vehicle, disabling it in the kill zone. It was a perfect ambush. If the insurgents could knock out the first and last vehicles, the entire convoy would be stuck in the kill zone. Bullets flew from insurgents on both sides of the ravine. The insurgent grenadiers were trying to concentrate fire on the last American vehicle to bottle up Major Schram's convoy in the ravine. The attackers would then be able to kill the Americans at will.

Major Schram ordered his driver, Specialist Chris Van Dyke, to accelerate from their position in the convoy into the insurgents' positions. Major Schram sent a message to Headquarters for help and began returning fire out of the Humvee. The Iraqi grenadiers recognized the threat and shifted their fire from the rear truck to Schram's Humvee, HQ-12.

Multiple grenades exploded at the front and rear of HQ-12. Specialist Van Dyke was blown out of the vehicle. Once he stopped rolling on the ground, he got up and ran back to HQ-12. He got back in and drove the Humvee out of the kill zone.

When he turned to get orders from Major Schram, Van Dyke realized that his major had been killed. Even though he wore body armor, two 7.62-millimeter rounds had gone through Schram's armpit (where there is no body armor coverage) and struck his heart, killing him instantly. But Major Mat Schram had accomplished what he set out to do: he broke up the ambush.

The Iraqi insurgents fled after they fired their grenades at HQ-12, which was heading for them at full throttle.

I was at my desk at work on Tuesday, June 3. The phone rang.

It was John, a friend of mine and Mat Schram's. We had all served together in the Army years ago and had stayed in touch. He told me to sit down. He told me that Mat had been killed in Iraq.

After I composed myself, we finished our conversation and I promised to see John's wife, Patti, at Mat's funeral. John had to be at Special Operations Command and couldn't make it.

I shut the door to my office, sat back down at my desk, and wept.

At the funeral, Mat's family displayed the last letters and e-mails he had sent. Not surprisingly, all were strong, positive messages. Mat believed in what he was doing—freeing Iraq from Saddam Hussein.

Major Schram's convoy had been followed by a car transporting a reporter. Once the action began, the reporter and his driver turned and got the hell out of there. If it weren't for Mat's charge up into the ambushers, they never would have made it out of there alive. The reporter never wrote a story about my good friend, Mat, the man who saved his life. That wasn't news.

It took a few weeks to figure out what to do with the story that I knew, the news that I felt should be out there. On June 18, I started *Blackfive*, a blog.

The blogging phenomenon began in 1999. In those early days, Web logs (better known as blogs) were mostly online diaries and home-pages, but they've evolved into portals about current events, politics and economics, law and medicine, travel stories, movie reviews, celebrity gossip, and more, including the military.

Like everything else, blogging changed after September 11, 2001. The United States and its allies were officially declaring a war against terrorists worldwide. Soldiers were being deployed in massive num-bers to the Middle East. The world was rapidly changing. People were nervous and curious about what was going on with the government and the military—curious beyond their nightly or cable news. In Afghanistan and Iraq, technologically adept young soldiers were mak-ing sure they didn't lose contact with family and friends back home. Blogging was the perfect way to maintain contact, to tell their stories. And those blogs—soon known as milblogs (military blogs)—were ideal for filling in the gaps that both the media and the military left out of the war. Now anyone with an Internet connection had the ability to find out what was happening overseas from the soldiers themselves.

Currently, there are three kinds of combat reporting. The combat correspondent (embedded with troops or not) reports directly from the area of conflict. Press releases come from the Department of Defense, highlighting what the DOD wants us to know from the combat zone. And, finally, soldiers tell their own stories.

This last reporting method has, in past wars, been the slowest and most censored of the three. Typically, soldiers would write letters home, which would then be censored by the military and sent on. It wasn't until years after a war that veterans would recount their entire experiences in interviews or books. By that time, some of their memories may not have been as clear, emotions would be more subdued or altered by time, and the impact of their words was somehow lessened.

But now military men and women have access to the same communication tools as the media. Today, with digital cameras, Web cams, cell phones, and Internet access readily available, the letter home has taken on an entirely new form, with a new honesty and urgency. The soldiers are telling their stories through blogging, instantly publishing expert on-the-ground accounts from the war zones. I began blogging because of a tragic but heroic event. Others blog to chronicle their experiences, and many blog to keep their families informed about them and to stay in touch.

That's what military bloggers are doing today—offering unfettered access to the War on Terror in their own words. The public does not have to wait weeks or months to hear what's happened. They don't have to settle for the government's approved messages to the public.

Never before has this occurred: real experiences flying unfiltered to anyone with an Internet connection and an interest.

This is the power of the military blog.

And millions of people are reading them.

I decided that a blog was the best way that I could focus on the good, the bad, the ugly, and the humor of military life. For a name, I decided on an old call-sign of mine, one that I was proud of, one that was universal for the second in command: "Blackfive" is the generic call-sign for the executive officer making things happen behind the scenes.

Blackfive.net is a lot like Blackfive the XO—just trying to make things happen and bring focus where it needs to be.

Mat Schram would have liked the title.

Throughout the past few years, I've had the immense privilege of knowing many of the military men and women fighting the War on Terror. Through my blog, I've learned what really happened during combat in Fallujah and Sadr City, been reconnected with friends fighting the war, and mourned a few who gave their lives in Iraq or Afghanistan.

As you join me for this adventure, I'm hoping that you will discover a new way to view the military and the war as you get an uncensored, unmediated, intimate, and immediate view of the reality of this conflict. For everyone on both sides of the computer screen, the military blogs have been an experiment in putting lives that are on the line online. Now, by pulling together these voices into a choir, by giving the ephemeral Internet bits and bytes a permanent place to live between these covers, I hope to pay lasting tribute to those men and women who have opened this window into their lives and to convey a better understanding of what it's like to be in the war zone.

CHAPTER ONE

SOME MUST GO TO FIGHT THE DRAGONS

Day by day, fix your eyes upon the greatness that is Athens, until you become filled with the love of her; and when you are impressed by the spectacle of her glory, reflect that this empire has been acquired by men who knew their duty and had the courage to do it.

—THUCYDIDES, "FUNERAL SPEECH OF PERICLES"

"Pack your bags. You'll be gone eighteen months. Good luck."

Finding out that you are heading to a war zone for longer than a year and leaving your life behind can be like getting punched in the gut.

Soldiers who receive notice of their deployment to a hostile land will tumble from the routine life they knew into a world of uncertainty and danger.

"Tying up loose ends" has a lot more meaning for someone heading to a combat zone. Those ends can be anything from a to-do list to make sure everything at home is good before you go, to last-minute good-byes over the phone. Some may just want to say goodbye; some want to say the things they haven't said in case they don't make it back.

I've lost three good friends in the War on Terror. I have more than a few friends over in Iraq and Afghanistan today. I wish they were all home. They wish they were all home. But we all know that they have an important job to do. And now, I have another good friend heading into the breach.

Chief Warrant Officer Stephen Arsenault wasn't always my friend or a warrant officer.

A few years ago, I was company commander of a group of Military Intelligence linguists, analysts, interrogators, and counterintelligence agents that augmented the 101st Airborne Division. My previous first sergeant (the commander's right arm) had been promoted to sergeant major and, due to his elevated rank, could no longer fill the position.

To replace the former first sergeant, HQ sent me Steve Arsenault. Steve was a tough New Englander and Boston Red Sox fan who couldn't hide his immense irritation the moment he saw my Yankees hat on a shelf in my office—an ominous beginning to our relationship.

It took us some time to build a rapport. Sometimes, we rubbed each other the wrong way. Sometimes, we worked together like we were best friends and family. It was a learning experience for both of us.

We worked like hell, into the night, day after day, through weekends, and we created something great. After seven months, we had one of the best companies in the division. That was something that not even my former first sergeant and I had accomplished in over a year.

After my command tenure was over, I took an assignment at another unit, and Steve and I became friends. Good friends. We spent many nights at the VFW, backyard BBQs, and ball games. A few years later, after Steve was moved to Missouri and I had left the service, he would occasionally fly to Chicago, where I work and live, for a weekend. I would meet him in Kansas City for Chiefs games and to see his family.

I also strongly encouraged his decision to attend the Warrant Officer Course. He's now a chief warrant officer (CW2) heading out for Iraq. Tikrit, to be exact. We've talked a few times about what Steve needs to do, what he needs to focus on.

We talked one last time before he was to head down range, mostly about how his kids were going to handle his absence.

Steve said, "Madelyn is trying to be a big girl about this. Danielle won't look at me when I tuck her in at night. Right now, she's angry with me for leaving. And Nick is really too young to know what's happening."

Steve has three kids and one more on the way. The baby will be born in January. Can you imagine being Steve's wife, Sue, with a job, three kids, a baby coming, and your husband in Iraq? It's something our military men and women and their spouses and families deal with every day.

I tell him, "I'll fly out and see Sue and the kids during Christmas."

"Sue would love that."

"What about the baby delivery? Do you have that covered?"

"Yeah, our neighbors are going to help out. I think we'll be okay as long as there aren't any complications. They are really great people."

"Okay, I'll call Sue and let her know that I can fly there at any time and that I have a lot of vacation days saved up, so it'll be no problem if I need to stay to help out for a while."

"That'd probably help relieve some stress."

"Consider it done."

Pause.

We're just dancing around the reason for the call. I know what is coming and am making small talk to avoid it. We both know where Steve is headed. The company he's replacing received seventeen Bronze Stars and a ton of Purple Hearts.

"Matt, I have to say this."

Shit! I knew he was going to do this!

"If I don't make it back . . ."

I interrupt him, raising my voice, rattling off reasons in a staccato manner. "Thinking like that might get you killed. You know I'll take care of your family. No matter what happens. You get your ass over there and forget about us. Focus on the mission. Keep your soldiers alive. We'll always be here for you."

Then I launch into all of the organizations that can help get comfort items to his unit, letters to his troops. I even try to rile him up by telling him that I'm sending four hundred Yankees hats to his battalion.

I try to change the subject, but Steve won't have any of it.

"Just promise me." Long pause. "Just promise me that if I don't make it back, you'll take care of Sue and the kids."

I can barely say "Of course I will. You have my word."

"Thank you." Two simple words, but I can hear how much they mean.

Another pause. He's relieved. I'm worried about him. We're emotional. So I say the only thing that I can think of to bring us back to reality.

"Go Yankees!"

"Fuck you, Matt."

"Hey, just remember what George Patton the Elder said: 'When you're sitting around the fireside with your grandkids, and they ask you what you did in the war, you won't have to say, "I shoveled shit in Louisiana!"' Stay in touch, you big lug."

"You, too, pal."

As the phone clicks, I whisper an empty toast. "To better days . . . until better days."

Steve leaves for Iraq two days later. Though he'd rather be home with his wife and kids, he's not shrinking from his service, and he knows the stakes of this war.

Into the Breach. Heading Downrange. Into Harm's Way.

I will introduce you to some of the men and women fighting the War on Terror by beginning with the motivations of someone who knew his duty and had the courage to do it. Stephen Wilbanks, one of the bloggers at *Red State Rants,* was already a Marine veteran and, at thirty-five, thought himself a bit too old to reenlist. But September 11, 2001, changed all that for him. Wilbanks contemplated his life and what he wanted for his family. He decided to "Go Green, Again":

My efforts began on September 11, 2001, when the news about the terrorist attacks in New York City came over the radio. I immediately drove to the recruiter's office to inquire about reenlistment options. My advance was rebuked, however, due to an ankle injury that I'd sustained two months previous, one which eventually landed me on the surgeon's slab six months later. Running, and therefore staying in shape, was a painful proposition for nearly a year thereafter. Then my wife and I decided to start our family, a decision that I in no way second-guess, but one which further altered my plans.

As I watched the kickoff of Operations Enduring Freedom and Iraqi Freedom from the sidelines, I couldn't stand the fact that Marines were out there doing what Marines do, and here I was, a man of eligible age, riding the bench. The final straw came on the day that my brother, a career Marine until a back injury put him out of active duty after 15 years, emailed me a photo of himself being sworn back into the Corps as a reservist. That was simply more than I could stand.

I got off my ass, got back in shape, and got on the phone with the prior service recruiter. Skipping all the sordid details of a paperwork nightmare, a little more than a year later, on July 10, 2005, I stood before a Captain with the 4th Marine Division, raised my right hand, and took the oath of enlistment for the second time in my life, sworn in as a 35-year-old Corporal of Marines (reserve) as my wife and son looked on.

I'd been off active duty for almost 10 years, but as we walked out of the HQ building at the Navy/Marine Corps Reserve Center and passed a Colonel, the salute that I snapped felt just as natural as it ever had, and the uniform I wore felt like an old friend. I straightened my back, poked out my chest just a little, and stepped more smartly. God, it felt great to be green again!

I give the reader all of that to answer a question many people have asked, including the worshipful Red State Rant blogmaster and my life-long friend, Lance: Why? After all, I've already served my country, "paid my dues," or "done my time," as some say.

To that, I have this to say: Serving my country is not a 4-year contract. It is a lifelong commitment. Nor is it a "due" to be paid like some cheap membership fee. It is a deeply personal obligation. And it is certainly not "time" that has to be "done" like some felony prison sentence. It is nothing short of an honor that I hold in the highest regard, an honor that I must prove worthy of, an honor that must be earned every single day.

Many people have shaken their heads in disbelief, sometimes I think in disdain, when they learned of my plans. I'm a family man now, after all. Why would I volunteer, when there is a very real possibility of a combat deployment? Don't I care about my family?

Without question, my family is the single most important part of my life on earth. But just exactly what sort of husband and father do I want for my family? What kind of man do I want my wife to devote her life to? When my children are grown, what is the picture of their father going to look like in their minds? I'll tell you: I want my beloved wife, to whom I am utterly devoted, to go through her days without a shadow of a doubt that the man she married is a man of honor and commitment, a man that knows there are things in life worth giving one's own life for, if necessary. I want her, as she looks out upon all of the world's deception, falseness, infidelity, and evil, to know that her husband is on the right side of things.

I want my children to have a father that they can unwaveringly look up to as an example. I want them to grow up, not with an attitude of entitlement, but with a sense of duty, obligation, and reward. I want to teach them that we don't always say, "Let the other guy do it." Instead, I want them to learn that there are times that we must ask, "If not me, then who?" I want to be the best father I can be, and I can think of no better lessons to teach them than the value of honor, integrity, dedication, perseverance, and selflessness. I can offer no better example for my family than to strive to live those values every day in my own personal life.

All of that is a way of life for United States Marines.

In addition to all of that, throw in any applicable clichés regarding patriotism, fighting for our country, etc. They're all no less true for me than anyone else who has said them, but they have become overused to the point that they have begun to lose effect. I will add one: Revenge. I make no apology for wanting to kill the bastards that want to kill us.

I harbor no illusions about saving the world, being a hero, or altering the course of events. It's simply that at no time in my life have I been more proud and satisfied with what I was doing than while serving as an active duty Marine. My decision to leave the Corps, if I had it to do over, likely would have been different. I want to at least partially amend that decision while I am still young enough (barely) to do so. I love being around fellow Marines, doing what Marines do: training, fighting, working, sweating, cussing, bitching, adapting, improvising, overcoming, accomplishing the mission, and taking care of each other.

Lastly, these are historic times for our country and for my Marine Corps. For me, it's decision time—sit on the sidelines and merely be an observer, or step up and be a participant.

I'm stepping up.

Semper Fidelis

, , ,

Reservists all over the country were being mobilized in late 2002 and early 2003 for the eventual invasion of Iraq. Phone calls and letters arrived to inform the recipient of impending deployment to Southwest Asia.

Navy Reserve Lieutenant Scott Koenig, known as the popular blogger *Citizen Smash—the Indepundit,* went to a routine weekend Reserve drill that turned out to be not so normal as he discovered that he would be going "Somewhere Dangerous":

, , ,

It was only supposed to be a planning meeting for a weekend exercise, just like the ones we held before every other reserve drill weekend. That's how it started out, anyway. All of the officers and chief petty officers were gathered around the conference room table, and the executive officer went over the schedule of events. But this meeting was different.

We always held the meeting on the Friday evening before a drill weekend. The civilian working week was over, and the meeting usually had a very casual, laid-back feel to it. Sometimes we brought pizza. Once or twice, we even had beer. We'd normally chat about our lives, work, and our families for a while before getting down to business.

But not this time. The commanding officer and executive officer both seemed a little tense this evening. The XO was going over the schedule very thoroughly, stressing the importance of getting each event completed safely. He asked if we had any questions or revisions to the schedule. We didn't. Then the CO dropped the bombshell.

6 December 2002—"Somewhere Dangerous"

"We're being mobilized," said the Commanding Officer. He gave us a few seconds to absorb the news.

"Go ahead and tell your civilian employers that you expect to have orders by the end of next week. Tell your families that you won't be home for Christmas."

The assembled officers and senior enlisted personnel looked around at each other, not certain how to respond. The news was not a complete surprise, but nobody had expected it to be so soon.

Someone managed to ask the first question that we all wanted answered. "Where are we going?"

"I can't say."

We had, in theory, been expecting something like this to happen. Ever since that terrible Tuesday morning a year earlier, we had been waiting for the word. All of our exercises had been building up to this possibility. On paper, we were ready. But nothing can really prepare you for the day that you learn you will be deploying to a potential war zone.

It was a sobering moment, but also exhilarating. I knew that the coming months would not be pleasant. I was not looking forward to being separated from my wife, our family, and our friends. I was anxious about the real possibility that some of us might not come back. I knew that a war, if it came to that, would bring with it pain, suffering, and loss for many people—maybe even some people that I cared deeply about.

But at the same time, I felt a little thrill. This wasn't just another exercise, or a routine deployment. We had a mission. We were about to perform the tasks that we had trained so long and hard to do. And if it came down to it, we were going to help rid the world of one very nasty tyrant.

Telling your wife that you won't be home for Christmas isn't easy. When I arrived home that evening, the first thing I did was give her a big hug.

"I'm sorry, I'm so sorry." I told her, holding on a bit longer than normal.
"Why are you sorry?" she asked, dreading the answer.
"I won't be home for Christmas this year." She went limp in my arms.
"Where will you be?"
"I don't know yet."
"Will it be local or . . ."
"Overseas. And when I do find out, I probably won't be able to tell you—at least not right away." We both knew what that meant. This wasn't going to be a pleasure cruise.

I was going somewhere dangerous.

She didn't kick me out.

,   ,   ,

Prior to departure, the final gatherings commence to send off the soldiers. In spite of the inherent seriousness of deploying, family and friends try to lighten the mood, but, sometimes, these last-minute parties can turn slightly macabre, when everyone tries to hide their fears and smile like they mean it. *American Soldier*, an Army sniper, writes about his send-off party and the strength he gathered from his family:

,   ,   ,

I had my family and some close friends over last night for a little good-bye gathering. It was so nice to have everyone over. The evening started off with the kids coming back from their grandparents. The wife and I needed some time together alone, so we shipped the kids away for a few days. The children were happy to be home. The oldest is obviously aware that the days are numbered before I depart. It wasn't any more than 15 minutes before he started to get sad and cried a little. I picked him up and wrapped my arms around him and told him it was ok and I understood why he was sad. I know that at this point, telling him not to cry isn't fair. His life and his little world full of happiness and day-to-day routine will soon be drastically changed. So I held him close and tried to change the subject towards something he would be excited about. He showed me some hockey pucks that he got from a hockey game he had attended the night before.

My parents showed up a little while later. I had a very comforting feeling come over me when I saw the two of them arrive together. My parents have been divorced for well over 24 years. They have remarkably become close in the last couple of weeks. I can't exactly put my finger on it, but whatever it is, it makes me very happy to see them together and actually happy around each other. I look at it like companionship has kicked in for the both of them. It was always there, but they each had gone their separate ways for years. I told my mother that it feels good to see the both of them together. I just hope that the two of them can manage to see the light that has been clouded over for so many years. Mom & Dad, I love you both. I can only hope the two of you find what was lost so many years ago.

Two of my cousins from my father's side showed up. Always making light of the situation, my one cousin was cracking jokes no more than 5 minutes after he arrived. Funny of course! For example, hoping that I don't think camels and their humps begin to look good after a few months. LOL!

Aunts & Uncles and bears oh my! Soon enough my house was filled with people. Everyone was having conversations, from politics to work. My one uncle, who is an architect, wanted to see my house. He had never been over. I gave him the grand tour and tried my best to explain the various dimensions of different rooms and how the house was designed. I have always been fond of this uncle. I used to tell him I wanted to be an architect when I grew up, just like him. I didn't exactly become an architect of homes but rather of networks. His eye is for the aesthetic angle; mine is for the aesthetic design of data & voice communication routes.

I wandered from group to group. Enjoying the time well spent. Including myself in various conversations. Some would ask me about how I felt about going to war. I got the sense that people thought this was beyond my control and was being forced upon me. It was at that point that I wanted to talk to everyone and lay it all out on the table. I didn't want anyone second-guessing what I would be doing and where I may find myself.

I wanted to wait till my grandmother left. Her health has not been good lately. What I wanted to say was the truth. I knew that some things would be hard to explain, or accept rather. It wasn't that I wanted to keep it from her, but I was confident that my relatives would explain it to her when she was feeling better.

As the night went on we took many pictures. Of course I was in every one of them, so my face began to look like The Joker. Behind the smile was some sadness though. You know, it's weird when people look at you as if it were the last time they would see you. It's very eerie! The feeling that they want to confide in you, because they fear the unknown. I didn't let this get me down. I was just so happy to be in the company of so many that love me. I assured them that I would be ok.

My grandmother gave me a big hug and told me that she was so proud of me. I told her that I would be ok and would send plenty of pictures.

A little while after she left I decided that I would talk to everyone. With my command voice I managed to get everyone's attention. I told everyone that I wanted to talk to them all and if they had any questions to not hesitate to ask. I gave them an overview of where I would be going for the time being. The post that I would be training at and what parent unit I would be going with. I explained that my unit was going to be equipped with all uparmored humvees. The body armor was top of the line and I had a very confident and well-trained command structure. I then told them that the role that I would be doing is that of a Sniper. I hesitated after I said that to look at everyone. I then went on to explain that the role of a sniper was very much in demand over there. The war is essentially urban combat and snipers helped greatly in eliminating targets that could pose a threat to soldiers fighting on the streets. I told them that I had a variety of training while I was in the Army. I had a conventional job in the Army and then an unconventional role that I had trained for back when I was on active duty. A lot of my family only knew that I had work in communications. So I didn't want them to think that I was doing anything other than what I was very proud to do.

I got a lot of "We are very proud of you" comments and such during my makeshift open forum discussion. One of my uncles expressed his concerns about helping and having others help if need be while I was gone. He was very adamant about ensuring that I make people aware if anything needed to be done. I assured him that I would do that.

When the discussion was done, I felt very relieved. It felt good to tell them about my role and in the end I feel very embraced.

For the rest of the evening I laughed and talked with my family. Almost forgetting that soon all this atmosphere of love and sincerity would be replaced with hardship and danger. The closest to family will be my fellow soldiers whom I will lead into battle. I will surely miss this feeling and will not forget it.

I looked at all the pictures later on that evening with my wife. I thought to myself that I looked different. Maybe it was the way I was smiling. Or maybe it was how my family hugged me tighter. I didn't want to analyze it too much. When the evening was all said and done, I was happy.

One thing that I will take from that evening is the look that one of my cousin's children gave me. Earlier in the evening my cousin told me that she was trying to explain to her daughters why they were coming over to my house. She tried to relate it to when, on Veterans Day, she and her daughters go and place flowers on fallen soldiers' graves. She said that her daughters think of those soldiers as heroes. My cousin told me that she told her daughter that I was going to go fight in a war and I would go there to help other people.

She said her daughter said, "He's a real-life hero, Mommy!"

It was the look that she gave me before she left. The look of how a child would see a superhero in the flesh.

It was a good night.

,   ,   ,

Bloggers live in the electronic world of bits and bytes, where communication with family and friends via their blogs is second nature.

Some who depart for Iraq or Afghanistan leave messages for their loved ones on their blogs, giving them the opportunity to interact and communicate immediately from afar. Jay Czaja, "Caelistis" of the *Makaha Surf Report,* heads to war again. This time, however, he takes the opportunity to publish a good-bye letter to his family on his blog with a special message for his sister, who is against the war:

Well it's time to go and do what I have been called to do. Today I head to the war for the third time and I have some things to say. To me this is a blessing, a calling from God to do what I can to help our brave men and women in uniform. Also this post is for my family, as some of them still don't understand why I am on my third trip to Iraq. First of all:

K, you have been the best sister a brother could ever have. You and I had some good fights when we were kids, but you were always there if I truly needed you. We don't see eye to eye on anything political, and you are one of those people calling for our troops to come home now. I love you, but you are wrong in this count. You have three boys and if we don't do this right, it will have to be done again and it could be your boys next time. When I'm in Iraq, I think about my three nephews and how I don't want to see them in DCUs [desert combat uniforms or desert camouflage uniforms] in the next decade. I want to fight our enemies in their country until they either surrender or become so ineffective they aren't a threat to any of us. I don't want my nephews fighting a fight that I couldn't finish. I want them to go to college or play professional soccer, or be beach bums. However, if they choose to become soldiers I would be proud to be in the same chain that links all military personnel past present and future, the chain that holds America together. That being said I would prefer they not have to fight the war I have seen, I would prefer they not lose any friends like I have and I wish that they would never lose their innocence by having to kill another human being. War takes so much out of a person, it changes us in ways that are almost never positive and I would not want your boys to have to go through what I have. I hope one day you understand, that I don't do this for the money, that Bush is not Hitler, and that the people of Iraq deserve as much a chance at a better life as we were given. You and G and the boys will be on my mind the entire time I am in Kirkuk.

Mom, I was the baby of the family and I know you still view me as that little boy that wouldn't eat his green beans and only wanted peanut butter. I am still that little boy inside, but I am so much more now. I am a husband and a veteran, and now a successful man with my own family. I chose to go back to Iraq this time, because I believe in a better world. At 30 I am more of an idealist now than I was at 20. I believe one person can make a difference. I know you will worry about me the entire time I am gone, but you won't tell me how scared you are. I just wanted to say it's ok, I am on the path that brings me the greatest happiness. No matter what happens to me, I am doing what I believe is my destiny. I come from a family of warriors, your family and Dad's were all warriors, it's what they knew. I am a product of their collective service to nation. This isn't about adventure or money or some death-wish, it's about doing the right thing. The men and women and especially the children of Iraq are worth fighting for. When I see them I know that any sacrifice I can make is worth it. What kind of man would I be if I refused to help someone in need? How could I live my life knowing that someone was being tortured and I stood by and sipped my latte and refused to get off my ass? I don't know if you will ever understand what drives me, Mom. Just being able to help one Iraqi is worth my life. People on this planet are so hell-bent on persecuting others, they are so concerned with appearing strong that they prey on the weak and the helpless. Mom, the people of Iraq were helpless and being crushed by a petty clone of Adolf Hitler. Now they have hope where before they had none. Iraq is a mess, but it is a mess because freedom is messy, we had to fight a Civil War that killed more than 600,000 of us just to make all men and women free. Iraq is already having to fight a soul-searing conflict with itself to find itself. How could we abandon these people to this chaos? I will continue to support this cause until we win, we lose, or I am knocked out of commission. I cannot call myself a man and abandon the men, women and children of Iraq to brutal butchers. I've made my choice. You'll be in my heart every day.

Dad, you are my hero. I don't know if I've ever told you that, but you are. You served in Vietnam and came back and made a life for yourself and your family. You did everything you could to provide for K and me, you worked extra hours to make sure we never went without. You never took sick time even though you were out in the elements every day. You are the definition of what a man is. I hope one day I am half the man that you are. I think you understand what drives me and why I have to keep doing this job. When you were here in Hawaii to visit me and you told me you were proud of me was a moment I'll never forget. I can't let the people of Iraq suffer without doing something. I know I am only one person, but you were only one person and you did so many things in your life. I want to be like you, but I want to do so much more. I know I'm not going to "save the world," but every day I can do a good deed, whether in Iraq or in Hawaii, is a day that I feel like I have done my job as a man and an American. I know you understand!

Jan, my wife, my love, my life, this has got to be the hardest on you. This is the third time I have asked you to take a leap of faith and believe that no harm will come to me in Iraq. Three times I have left you and our puppies behind to pursue some quixotic belief that I can make the world a slightly better place. Three times I have left you behind to pay the bills and manage the house and so many other things that no one should be forced to do by themselves. I have not been with you for 3 of our seven anniversaries because of my commitment to this. All I can say to you is thank you! I will always love you for your patience and your support of me and my ideals. I know that I make your life hard with these deployments, and for that I am sorry. I wish that it were easier to be away from you, but it's not. In fact, each deployment it gets harder and harder for me to say good-bye. I've lost friends now and had a few close calls myself, but I can't quit doing this. You know why, you more than anyone else understand why. You and I both believe it is our destiny to do whatever we can to make the world better. We are two tiny fish in the enormous universal ocean, but we both know one person can make a difference. When I am in Iraq I know you are in my heart at every moment and that our faith and love protects me. I firmly believe God has a plan for both of us. We are his instruments to do what we can to make the world better. So don't worry about me this time, I am doing what I was meant to do, and I have never been happier. So go and find my molly-molly and give her a scratch behind the ears.

For anyone that reads this: Yes I am a 30-year-old idealist. At 20 I was a cynic, but now I have a mission in life and a purpose. I found God, but I am far from a religious fanatic. I found a God that inspired me to do good deeds just for the sake of doing good. I can feel his presence in everything around me, the sunset, the waves crashing on a Hawaiian beach and even in the evening breeze that is laced with plumeria. I would call myself a soldier of God, but not in any way that says he favors me or my cause. I am a soldier of our lord because I choose to serve the side of good. Good is opening a door for a stranger, or helping your neighbor empty his trash can, or going to Iraq because you want to help a people find their voice and feel what we feel when we think of our freedoms. The most fundamental question I ask myself every day is: If I have the chance to do good, even if there is a terrible price to pay, why wouldn't I? I wish more Americans would ask themselves this question. If you can do good, what on earth would stop you from following through?

Finally I just wanted to state one more time, Iraq is the whole bag of marbles. If our ideas win there, then militant Islam will wither on the vine and eventually die. If we lose in Iraq, the world will become a much darker place where the evils of the past such as slavery and holy wars will become the norm. I ask the people of America this question. We are the last hope for this planet to realize its potential, the Europeans are too weak to do it, what kind of world do we want for our children to live in? I made my choice, and now I leave to do what I believe is my duty. God bless my family, God bless our brave men and women in uniform, God bless all Americans and God bless America.

Caelestis

P.S. Love you my hummingbird

　　　　　，　　　，　　　，

While deploying soldiers write letters to their families to ease anxieties about their long separations, friends also try to find the right way to say good-bye. One of the first military bloggers, U.S. Navy Hospital Corpsman Sean Dustman of *Doc in the Box*, writes of his friend Wonda Baugh and her tribute to him before deploying to Iraq:

，　，　，

I was out at my mom's house one weekend and ran into this dislocated and disoriented girl that looked to be going through some shell shock from her transplant from San Francisco.

She seemed a bit lost and depressed. This is a totally understandable reaction for having just moved to a very small town.

The town has to be absorbed in steps. Prescott is on Route 66 and is full of odd characters and all the tackiness implied with that. Won was a fish out of water so, being the knightly figure that I imagined myself being, I placed her under my wing and took it upon myself to introduce her to the dark side of Prescott nightlife, which included our Thursday night jaunts to the poetry reading.

All she needed was a finger to point her in the right direction and she was off on her own. When Won read her poetry, people sat up and listened. After the first time she read there, she owned the place. Soon, we were all hanging out all the time and just passing time.

Then 9/11 happened and it made me take a hard look at my life. I had a talent for helping people and nothing I was doing at that point in my life was helping anybody. I was coasting and, when you're coasting, you're going downhill. So I made a visit to our local recruiter and signed back up. And our last weekly trip together to the poetry reading, Won wrote this poem for me.

After she was done reading it there wasn't a dry eye in the house.

I say that he is joining the Navy
Or that he is moving away
Or that I'm helping him pack
I avoid saying
That he is going to war
And that I am scared
I avoid saying

That my heart is breaking
A thousand times all over again
I avoid saying
I cannot take one more
Of my friends dying
I avoid screaming at God
How come you can't
Just leave me alone for a while
I try to put on my happy face
But I fail
I am proud of him
I love him
He is no longer sensitive ponytail man
He has been shorn into a beautiful
Monk, ready to sacrifice
Ready to jump to help the helpless
I admire him, but I still don't want him to go
I avoid telling him that my heart is breaking
A thousand times all over again
I am learning to pray ceaselessly to a deity
I'm not sure I really believe in
Keep him safe keep him safe keep him safe

I left her and my friend Larry behind. Our friendship hasn't lessened but that chapter of our life was over.

Don't worry Won, it's not the end of the story. Love you.

Parents leaving for a battle zone have a whole different set of concerns. They need to ensure not only the physical care of their children but their emotional well-being as well. Greyhawk of *The Mudville Gazette* writes a message for his beloved children about why he must leave them to go to war:

I awoke in the quiet watches with my youngest in my arms, wondering what I might say to her and her brother and sister and their mom and knowing I was done with sleeping for this night.

Here is why: *Some must go to fight the Dragons.*

And if you think such things don't exist then it must be I read you the wrong sorts of stories when you were young.

If you ask only why *I* and not some other, then I can tell you this.

Listen

We choose to go to the moon. We choose to go to the moon in this decade and do the other things, not because they are easy, but because they are hard, because that goal will serve to organize and measure the best of our energies and skills, because that challenge is one that we are willing to accept, one we are unwilling to postpone, and one which we intend to win, and the others, too.

The President of the United States said that when I was very young. Now some will tell you that such thinking is out of fashion these days and that the causes we turn our energies to are unjust. I can tell you only that I don't think so, and that I'm quite certain the dragons themselves would raise such concerns were we to give them voices.

This is for us all: Have faith, not fear. Trust God. Stand fast, be strong.

For me the time is here to leave precious things behind for just a while, and that cost is not too great to bear. After all, what things could be called precious if not worth any price?

For you it's simply time to be brave, as so many of your friends have been. Think about this: Without *bad* there could be no *good*. Hard times pass. Be kind to one another in every possible way; lift the burdens that others bear and I think you'll find your burden's lighter too.

Worrying helps nothing, try not to do it. Don't feel bad when from time to time you do. And please do fun things and enjoy doing them— you owe me nothing more than that.

And never tell me anything's too hard.

Take pictures.

Write.
Smile.
See you soon.

,   ,   ,

The day for departure arrives. Spouses and families face the stark reality that their loved ones are headed toward danger. Sarah Elizabeth Walter, whose blog is *Trying to Grok,* writes about the day her husband, an armor officer in the 1st Infantry Division stationed in Germany, left for war—the day she fully realized he was gone:

,   ,   ,

But I stand my ground
And I won't back down . . .

It's the lyrics behind our favorite Armed Forces Network commercial: *Every generation has its heroes. This one is no different.*

I did really well this morning. I didn't cry at all. Until I sat down four hours later and I started playing this song.

Yesterday morning my husband got promoted to First Lieutenant. I got to go to morning formation and pin his new black bar on his DCUs, and then the Company Commander "watered" his rank with champagne to "help it grow" in the future. He stood in the cold doused in champagne, and the countdown began.

We had less than 24 hours.

We went home and I did all that sewing, he packed and unpacked and repacked and shuffled stuff around and tried to figure out how he could get enough stuff for 14 months into one duffel bag and one rucksack. We went to bed sad but promised each other we'd wake up strong.

He had to report at 0430, but I didn't have to be there until 0800. When he came back into our room to kiss me good-bye and I saw the pistol holster on his thigh, I knew it was for real. He left the house, and when I woke back up to get ready to go, I knew he wouldn't be back home for over a year. How long should I leave his dirty clothes sitting on the bedroom floor? When will I feel like cleaning up all the extra brown t-shirts and sunscreen that wouldn't fit in his ruck?

I went up to the gym to find an entire battalion of soldiers complete with Kevlar, IBA [interceptor body armor], and M16 rifles, plus mountains of duffels and rucks in the middle of the floor. We played the Army hurry-up-and-wait game for hours, but I must say that I was mighty impressed with how organized everything was run. Report here. Line up here. Get weighed here (he added 100 pounds with all his gear). Show your ID card here. Line up for your bus here. Sound off in alphabetical order as you get on the bus. And they were gone.

The First Sergeant was giving us a hard time this morning. "Both of you are going to cry like babies when it's time to go," he teased. So we were determined to prove him wrong. I got a kiss on the forehead and the husband headed to the bus. On the way out, another wife whose eyes were red commented on how strong I looked. Her four-year-old son said, "I'm being strong too." We both agreed that he was a brave boy, and he said, "Yeah, Mom, you're just a big crybaby." It was the comic relief we needed. The hardest thing I did this morning was watch two little daughters start to cry when their daddy's name got called for the bus. How could I feel sorry for myself after seeing that?

On the way home, I got stopped at a red light, and a row of buses crossed my intersection. I counted: Bus One, Two, Three, Four, FIVE, and honked the horn. And there he was, waving to me out of the window of Bus Five. And like that, he was gone.

It's hard to really imagine how long a year is. One year ago this weekend the husband and I were eating our nasty old wedding cake and celebrating our anniversary (four years ago this Sunday was the day we decided to make the leap from being good friends to being a couple). When you realize we've only been married 2 years, it makes 14 months seem like it will never end. But we're lucky to have so many advantages on our side.

We live in a military community, where everyone is going through the exact same thing. All but one of the men on my street are now gone. Even my co-worker's girlfriend is gone. Everyone around me is in the same boat, and we can take care of each other and help each other through this.

We also have the advantage of being optimistic about our country's military goals and mission. My husband and I support our President and this war in Iraq, we believe the War on Terror is very real and very important, and we think that his service to our country is an honor and a duty that he is proud to fulfill. I can't imagine what this year would be like if we didn't believe that we were sacrificing for something as important to us as our country's future.

And finally we both know that the real news from Iraq is not what you see on the TV. We know that progress is being made every day, progress that leads us one day closer to a democratic Iraq and a more secure future in the Middle East. I know where to read the real stories from soldiers, through blogs and the *Stars and Stripes* newspaper, and I have my own personal eyewitness on the ground right now to provide me with an honest opinion of our presence in Iraq.

As I watched the soldiers get ready to go, I couldn't help but think about how amazing they are. They are about to spend a year of their life doing a job that might bring lots of danger and only lip-service respect, yet you could feel the excitement in the air. There were some tearful good-byes with families, of course, but I didn't hear any grumbling at all. I saw smiles, heard jokes, and shook lots of hands as I said my good-byes. I'm so proud of every last one of these young men that my heart could burst.

Every generation has its heroes. This one is no different.

CHAPTER TWO

LIFE IN A WAR ZONE

For the first time in decades, after an invasion, our bases that were used as temporary shelter have turned into permanent Forward Operating Bases that are being improved over time.

Originally built as small tent cities with minimal amenities, FOBs now range in size from small fortresses to sprawling complexes covering dozens of square miles, complete with gyms, dining facilities, recreation areas, small airfields, and movie theaters.

Some of my friends in Iraq and Afghanistan joke that they've seen more movies than Roger Ebert because watching DVDs is all they can do in rare off-duty moments. Others have told me that the day-to-day life on an FOB makes them wish they could go out on patrol. Sometimes, the friends that go out on patrol or on raids would rather stay back at the FOB.

Routine business in the middle of a combat zone may seem strange to some. For others, it brings about a sense of stability in an otherwise unstable environment.

Then again, nothing is routine in a combat zone.

Most soldiers in Iraq and Afghanistan are not infantry soldiers. However, everyone in Iraq and Afghanistan is in harm's way. Specialist Alex Barnes's blog, *Blog Machine City,* describes his experiences as a Minnesota National Guardsman radio communications specialist. Alex writes about the sky falling in Iraq:

, , ,

Today, around 1500, a yellow-brown cloud of dust descended on us, turning the sky a strange color. It made no sense to me—how could there be any dust in this goddamn mud pit after raining for two days?

I walked to the DFAC (dining facility) for dinner tonight, slogging through the ankle-deep water and equally deep sucking mud (thank the maker for Gore-Tex). I crossed the street into the "parking lot" which is a giant open area between the DFAC and the motor pool; just as I crossed between the rolls of concertina wire, I heard a distant "whoomp." The Paladins [155mm self-propelled artillery guns] had been firing all day so I knew it wasn't them—this came from the opposite direction and was clearly distant, maybe beyond the wall. An instant later I heard the sickening descending whine (well, more like a whoosh) of an incoming mortar round.

I felt a stab of fear as I assessed my situation. First, if I could hear it, it must be close. Second, I was standing in an empty lot, with nothing resembling cover for maybe 100 meters in any direction. Third, I had the strange thought that once that whoosh sound ended there would be an explosion and I could be in the middle of it.

All this thought occurred in the second or two that the round was incoming—I tensed, expecting a blast somewhere, nearby or otherwise, but I heard nothing. I shrugged, looked around, and continued into the DFAC.

What made it frightening was the sense of impending doom, the foreknowledge and inevitability of the round's trajectory. This was in contrast to yesterday, when I was chatting merrily away until a blast rattled the trailer. My roommate and I dropped to the deck, just before I heard the sound of airborne mud splattering the trailers nearby. I reached for my body armor and slapped it on while my roomie did the same—we looked at each other, agreeing that some shit had just blown up. He said he thought he heard someone call for a medic.

I hastily put on my shoes and dashed outside to see what the situation was (probably stupid, given the circumstances, but . . .). Luckily the only casualty was the base's collective dignity and common sense, as a fair crowd of gawkers gathered around the four-foot hole in the road. People on the scene recovered a giant piece of shrapnel, about the size of my forearm; luckily the previous day's rain had made the ground so soft that the round just burrowed in before exploding.

There was no time or opportunity for fear—it was just "wham" and then "What the fuck?" A little adrenaline, sure, but no real sense of danger. Maybe even a little exhilaration—as in "That blew up and nothing happened!"

Sure enough, this happens right after I post about how I think we're not going to get mortared . . . Murphy's Law is in full effect, it seems.

,   ,   ,

Staff Sergeant Fred Minnick of *In Iraq for 365* is a military journalist. His team is responsible for filming, photographing, and telling the stories of our military in Iraq. Fred describes where he and his sergeants hang out to have a few laughs, "NCO Alley":

,   ,   ,

Every night, we meet in between the row of trailers. Sometimes, there's just two sitting in the red plastic chairs that would snap in two if Roseanne Barr sat down. Even though our job requires us to leave the camp a lot, normally the majority of our NCOs are present in the alleyway covered with cigarette butts and gravel. We call this place "NCO Alley." It's our refuge . . . where we get away from all the crap and just dump our brains for the night. And since we can't enjoy an ice-cold beer made in Milwaukee, Wis., we get drunk off of laughter.

Joe is always the first one there—we call him the "King of sleep," because he goes to bed early and wakes up late. The next to walk down the alley path are Sammy—he's a little chubby, 40+ and laughs at anything; Tommy—he's toothless; Johnny—Mr. Punchline; and then me.

We sit in a circle, talking about the strangest things imaginable. Oh, man, if hunks of rock and sheet metal could talk, we'd be in trouble. I won't lie; we can be quite vulgar. As we open the latest issue of *Stuff* or *Maxim*, "God, did you see her rack?" (Sammy laughs) When we talk about an "active" girl on post, "It would be like throwing a hot dog down a hallway." (Sammy laughs) Of course what good would a group of NCOs be if they didn't talk about officers or their Joes' shenanigans? "Yeah, I didn't agree with that decision." (Sammy laughs) "You know what I'd do if I were you, sergeant? I'd smoke her." (Sammy laughs)

We also have our own little ritual or initiation per se. Most people would find this absolutely sick, but I assure you that nobody's ever been hurt physically or emotionally. Joe, Johnny and I grab Sammy when he's in the middle of one of his chuckles (he's a big boy so it takes three), throw him to the ground and hump him from three angles, like a coyote ravaging a house cat. I don't know why we do this, but it is hilarious. I even admit, it's sick, but that ritual has gotten me through some tough days and made me laugh so hard that I once slobbered on myself. And no I'm not gay (but Sammy might be, because he seems to like it), not that there's anything wrong with that. Sad thing is, this ritual is practiced in most combat arms units . . . so, we're just carrying on a tradition of what I like to call "Stuck in a Foreign Country Fighting a War" (SFCFW) humor.

The jovial conversations and SFCFW humor are only broken up when somebody we don't like walks up or when mortars fall. Tonight was the final gathering in NCO Alley. We have packed our bags and moved out of the trailers. FNGs [fucking new guys] will be moving in soon, as we have relocated to temporary housing (military for the projects) as we just count down the final days.

Because we wanted to share our joy, we gave somebody an honorary membership today and just sat there rehashing the past year. "Hey, you remember when so and so lost her weapon?" "Yeah, that was ate up." We also humped Sammy. Even the honorary member understood . . . he laughed. Sammy, the oldest, baldest NCO of he group, laughed too. "Sammy, one of these days, Haji's going to hear your damn laugh and hit us with mortars." And just a split second after this sentence was completed, I kid you not (I swear this really happened), we heard whistling and saw flashes. Bullets were whizzing by our heads. I heard the ricochet of some pretty high caliber rounds and felt the wind of them flying by. We hauled our butts to the bunkers. Tommy's ears were ringing. "I saw a flash in front of my face. I can't hear." We checked him for entry or exit wounds. None. The bullet must have flown right by his ear, completely missing him, thank God.

"Everybody OK?" A near unanimous yes echoes off the bunker. "We told you they'd find us if you kept laughing, Sammy." He started laughing and so did everybody else. "Well, I guess that's the end of NCO Alley." We all thought about that statement for a second. Many good times were shared between the five of us, some of which got us through some difficult days. It's really a bittersweet ending to a beautiful thing—NCO Alley.

'   '   '

You'll find that discussing the weather in Iraq or Afghanistan is an important topic for a soldier. The weather can be both a boon and a detractor to missions; wet weather might help dampen IED detonation cord and make it unable to fire, or it may make it impossible for helicopter gun ships to protect your convoy. Weather also reminds the soldiers of home.

First Sergeant Jeffrey Nuding of *Dadmanly* is the senior noncommissioned officer in a company of New York National Guard soldiers. He writes of finding a "Cooler Breeze" in Iraq:

'   '   '

The heat here has definitely tapered off. I think we've actually had a high this week that was like 99 instead of over a hundred, and at night or in the morning it has actually dipped into the 60s once or twice. Cool breezes, very very nice for a change. Not as much air conditioning. The only downside is, now the bugs are coming back. I hadn't realized, but the heat here completely kills almost anything that stays out in the open, so they don't. You never see an ant, unless food is like right there in front of their hole, then poof, they're all over it. Take the morsel away, and they disappear. Same with mosquitoes. The surface water here reaches such a temperature, the larvae are killed off. No mosquitoes at all during the summer, but now they're coming back.

That is a funny thing about the water; we are connected to city water, but it flows in through these reservoir tanks (black, go figure), so that there's water if the city water goes out. (Like the electricity, but we are lucky and have a generator that kicks on.) Anyway, throughout the summer, the cold water was actually hotter than the hot water (unless the hot is set to highest heat). The bathroom I use for showers (the females in our building use that one too, no funny business but it's next to my room), the hot water heater went out sometime in July. I thought someone intentionally turned it off. So here's how I took a shower. While I brushed my teeth and shaved, I turned on the cold water tap in the shower and let it run. By the time I get in, it's hot. I then used the "hot" water to cool it down. (With the hot water heater off, it acts like a giant cooling tank, it's inside and the tank is white.)

The air quality might be improving, too. At night, some of the troops have said, "Man there are a lot of stars." I look up, and I think two things. One, this guy's never spent much time in the Adirondacks, and two, that's something we just got used to. You don't see a lot of stars, not because of night illumination (there's not a lot of that), but there's always sand or dust or haze, or even just junk in the air, and you never see much by way of stars. But perhaps we are seeing more than we had.

On a cool morning, or later at night, you can almost be lulled into believing you're back home, somewhere in the old familiar places. A cool night, late summer hanging on, or an early fall, no crispness yet. Breathe deep, make the illusion last. And then there's some boom way off, and the reverie is broken and you're back in the sandbox, wondering if that was off the FOB or if a rocket or mortar landed somewhere down by the river. Curious, but not with any real concern. Just wondering. Were those last two counterfire?

Praying it's like every other night, and the Soldiers of the FOB are safe. No injuries, no wounded, no medevacs, no casualty reporting.

And we can go back to look at the sky, thinking it's supposed to be the same one that the folks back home are looking at.

, , ,

While everyone misses something about home, some soldiers write of the American things that they find in Iraq. Taylor Allen Smith was an Army Reservist and college student studying foreign languages when he was sent to Iraq as a sergeant. On his blog, *American at Heart,* Taylor describes what life is like on his base:

, , ,

Sorry for the delay, but I've got another story and a few pictures for you. I told you I'd write about our FOB here, and that's exactly what I did . . .

What is an FOB? Well, it stands for Forward Operating Base. It's a collection of things, and life can vary quite a bit depending upon which FOB you are residing on. As for my FOB, we have a good life. Our FOB is about 50 square miles. It's quite large. We have a major "airport," a large chow hall, and lots of soldiers. There are both Army and Air Force personnel stationed here. We are separate, but equal. We have both an Army and an AF gym. We have a PX which stocks all sorts of things: groceries, snacks, shoes, clothing, personal hygiene supplies, magazines, books, DVDs, electronics, video games, minor appliances, just about anything you could need. The foreigners on base operate a massage parlor, a beauty parlor, a barbershop, a rug shop, and a miscellaneous shop. Once a month we have what's called a "bazaar." I'm not sure what the word means, but they allow Iraqis on base to sell us things from the market place. You can find anything and everything. We have a Burger King, and a Pizza Hut for when you tire of the DFAC (dining facility). *Most* of the soldiers avoid those places and opt for a nutritional meal, but some people have jobs where health isn't an issue. If I ate burgers for lunch every day, I think I'd keel over and die in the heat on a hot day. The weather here is cooling down. Our 140-degree days have been replaced with 110-degree days. Now, I have been here for quite a while, 110 here feels like 85 back home. It's hot, but not unbearable. It's getting cooler and my time here is getting shorter, so I think I can put up with anything. When it gets really hot on our off days, we like to swing by the pool. Yeah, that's right, there is a pool here. Chlorinated and clean, we swim almost once a week. For the brief couple of hours at the pool, you "almost" feel like a civilian again. Guys here will do all sorts of crazy things so that they don't forget they are human. One of my roommates and I each have a pair of comfortable sweatpants from Old Navy. We wear them frequently when in our room. I also like to put on a baseball hat and forget that I should be wearing a Kevlar helmet. It's the little things that keep us sane. I like to clean my own clothes as well. KBR [Kellogg, Brown and Root, civilian contractor providing services in Iraq] has a laundry service, but the mass laundry system just isn't for me. There is a do-it-yourself laundry nearby, so I like to walk there and relax while my clothes are cleaned by "mountain fresh Tide." And the "Snuggles" dryer sheets keep my clothes smelling just like Mom used to do them.

Everyone likes to keep in touch with their families and friends, so we are provided with a couple of "internet/phone centers" on the FOB. You can use calling cards and talk to your family and friends, or you can log onto the computer and type an email, or check out some milblogs. Technology is something I'll never take for granted after this experience. Like I've said before, we do a lot of odd things to pass the time. Lighting things on fire, playing with knives and swords, and causing all sorts of destruction and mayhem. We are just like a bunch of schoolyard boys.

There are two separate hospitals here. The EMEDS [Expeditionary Medical Support] clinic is run by the Air Force and is top notch. I've read it all over the blogosphere, and I can't argue, the US military has the greatest surgeons we could ever ask for. It's a relief, if not a small comfort to know when we go out, that if something bad happens we can rely on the people waiting here to care for us. It makes our job just a bit easier. Besides, the AF techs are a bunch of cuties, and what can numb pain better than a pretty face?

Speaking of that, there are not many females here. It's tough as a male, because the lack of females and the rules against hanging out with them deter us from seeking relationships, yet they are here, so we can't parade around naked and do all the "macho guy" things we'd like to do. It's a catch 22. There are worse things, though, so we don't think about it too much.

, , ,

Driving transport vehicles used to be regarded as a relatively safe position in the military. Not so in the combat zones in Iraq and Afghanistan. Sergeant Elizabeth A. Le Bel, known as SGT Lizzie on her blog, writes at *New Lives* about waking up the day after her truck was hit by an improvised explosive device (IED):

So my little war story:

We left early this morning from camp, enroute to Baquba (ba-kuba) to drop off troops and pick others as well as equipment up. Hence the reason we were driving an LMTV (also known as a big freaking truck). Most of the drive was uneventful, and we pulled onto the long stretch of highway towards "quba." I was seated with my back to the driver, parallel to the door, keeping an eye out for anything bad. I heard a very loud bang and looked to the windshield and surmised that we had just been hit with an IED as our windshield was shattered. In that split second I thought we were fine and then realized that we were barrelling full tilt towards one of those barriers that sits in the road. I vaguely remember rolling, but the next thing I clearly remember is looking and realizing that I was (1) good and truly stuck, and (2) hanging upside down, and (3) I was alone.

I started to scream bloody murder, and one of the other females on the convoy came over, grabbed my hand and started to calm me down. She held onto me, allowing me to place my leg on her shoulder as it was hanging free, until the medics arrived some 30 minutes later. It took them a while to pry me out, using the Jaws of Life, but finally I was free and was placed into a C collar and rolled over onto the stretcher. I remember lying there, looking at the sky, and realizing that I could actually breathe easy and this was a good thing. Of course the whole time I was trapped and then being pulled out, my ever present humor was out in full force.

While I was under the truck, I thought that my face had been blown off, so I made the remark that I wouldn't be pretty again (trying to laugh). Of course, the medics all rushed to reassure me which was quite amusing as I know what I look like now and I don't even want to think about what I looked like then. Oh, by the way, it was a COLD morning. I was ready to swear I would never be warm again, especially since they literally cut ALL the clothes off of me. They got me stabilized and into the Blackhawk. (Goes to figure I finally get a ride in the Blackhawk and I can't quite enjoy it.) From there we flew to the base where I am now at, and they wheeled me into the emergency room, where I was worked on by a very nice Australian, and a bunch of very nice AF doctors. The Aussie had a good time jibing me about the fact that I was wearing matching panties and bra (The old adage, always wear clean underwear), and helped me out a lot. By the time he was done with me I was mimicking him back perfectly and had quite the accent going. They wheeled me into the ward where I was staying and the dentist came to see me, and actually ended up putting me into a truck and taking me to the clinic to work on my teeth right then and there. (I am missing my front left tooth now FYI.)

When they brought me back (oh and I have never had better drugs, I don't remember them working on me at all), my command group was there to see me. The other command group of the MI BN [Military Intelligence battalion] up here had previously been to see me, and had brought a phone, but seeing faces I knew was great. I think I actually fell into one or the other of them crying. I then learned that the driver of my truck had indeed not made it through, and that is a very tough thing for me. Thankfully, it was quick, I am told.

It was interesting in the ER as when I rolled in I was still cracking utterly inappropriate jokes and keeping myself upbeat and not letting myself think about my injuries. While the facial doctor was working on me though, for some reason it all of a sudden hit me that I was alive and that I would make it through. All I have is a face full of stitches, and a couple of nice gashes on my legs. I was telling the doctors that I have never had stitches or a root canal before, and here I have had both on the same day. Funny. Okay, not so funny, but is okay.

It was while not quite great lying out there under the sky, I had my LT there encouraging me, another person was holding my IV bag, and I think I will ever love him for not wincing at the sight of my face, and just everyone out there on that convoy was really helpful in keeping me up and alive. I think at one point I rolled my head and asked my BC [battalion commander] if everyone out there would be recognized please. Then I got my CSM [command sergeant major] to laugh when I pointed out that this was probably the only time I would get away with totally screwing with the uniform (I am wearing PT [physical training] shorts, black long sleeved shirt, black fleece jacket, black socks, and for the topper, my bright pink shower shoes). One of my comrades went through my gear and packed up my ruck for me, so I have a few things of my own, including the all important TIGGER!

Well, I am going to hobble back to my bed, and see if I can't drift off some more. Have a good day all.

,   ,   ,

First Lieutenant Micah Bell is a Michigan Army National Guard officer stationed in Iraq. His blog, *Courage without Fear,* describes his role as the mayor of the FOB, the soldier in charge of all of the day-to-day operations supporting the soldiers living on the base:

,   ,   ,

Well I've received a new title, and along with it a bunch of new and exciting duties. I'm the Mayor. Not the Mayor of Baghdad, but of my own, highly defended and fortified Forward Operating Base. Yep, I'm the FOB Mayor. What does it mean to be the FOB Mayor? Well, everything that happens here that is not directly related to our mission falls on me. From chow, to the computer center, to cleaning the crappers, it's my job to make it happen. I don't exactly have to cook the food, pay the Internet bill or scrub toilets. But I do have a good bit of coordination to do. Luckily, I have a small staff, 1 other person. And we do have contractors who do much of the work.

I'm assisted in my endeavors by SGT Jeff Hawkins. In his former life, SGT Hawkins was a member of my Maintenance Section. But now, he's my right hand man. Most of his day is spent with our crew of 30 Iraqi workers.

The Iraqis do most of the maintenance, much of the general upkeep of the FOB, and serve the food in our mess hall. We have about 30 Iraqis total. Some Shia and some Sunni. For those that don't know, Shia and Sunni are the 2 major religious sects, and they don't always get along.

Since I've taken over the Mayor duties I've done a few interesting things. I've paid my workers two times so far. That consists of the contractor bringing in about $2,500 in US currency to my office and us passing it out to all the workers. Some of the guys shake our hands and smile; others just sign their name on the pay sheet, pocket the money and walk away.

I also had to fire a worker. That was interesting in several ways. This particular worker had been a pain for some time, but the previous Mayor didn't want to do anything about it. So after refusing to do as she was told (yes, it was a female) and being a general troublemaker, I told her she had to leave. It took about 5 minutes of me talking to her through a translator before she realized I was firing her. Then the tears came. Ugh. I had 2 soldiers escort her to gather up her things, and then we all piled into a Humvee and drove out to one of the checkpoints. I collected her ID badges that let her into the International Zone and then we escorted her on foot through the checkpoint and out to the Red Zone.

I've never fired anyone before. Even when I was a supervisor for a large security company in Chicago, I never fired anyone. This was weird. We just walked her out, took her ID cards and that was it. I felt like someone who drove out into the country and dropped off a pet they didn't want anymore. I know that's a strange analogy, but it's how I felt. I feel better about it now. It was the right thing to do. Now we'll hire a new worker who actually wants to earn his money. There is a waiting list to come and work in the IZ. So I just gave someone else an opportunity to succeed. And I'll probably be getting more out of your tax dollars that we pay these workers with too.

Due to my dealing with so many Iraqis every day, I've been picking up more sayings and customs. A handshake in Iraq isn't the same as one in the States. In the US we use a firm grip to show the other person how strong we are and that we mean business. Here it's more of a gentle squeeze. Often times the handshake is followed by the gesture of placing your hand over your heart as a gesture of friendship and respect.

Since taking over as Mayor, we've kept the workers pretty busy. Several of them have completed a good deal of work on our new MWR [morale, welfare, and recreation]/Internet Cafe (see my previous post on that). We've also been able to clean the place up quite a bit. I mean literally picking up trash. I guess we just have different standards than the previous Mayor had. We've completed a number of concrete projects and are currently working to improve the living spaces in the buildings recently vacated by the other unit that lived here. I'm glad I can keep the workers busy. Honest work, honest pay. And when we someday turn this FOB over to the Iraqi Army or whoever, it'll be a nicer place than when we got here.

,　,　,

As much as hiring and firing employees can sound mundane, there's nothing routine about getting mortared before your first cup of coffee in the morning. Sergeant Joshua Salmons of *Talking Salmons* is an Army journalist in Iraq. One day, he goes for an early morning jog that doesn't quite go as planned:

,　,　,

Five o'clock Friday morning smacked me in the face.

Sitting up in my bed, the room dark, I reached over to quiet my alarm clock before my roommate woke up.

After a minute or two of rubbing my eyes, I started my little morning ritual of changing in the dark. When living with someone on different work schedules in a tiny room, you get quite good at operating in darkness—finding shoes, keys, stepping over bags and clothes.

I locked the door as I stepped out. It was cold—damn cold. Just as I had begun to grow used to fierce heat, now the fall was bringing a new aspect of arid life. I stopped for a second and thought about putting on a jacket, but figured I'd warm up after starting the run.

Friday was chest/triceps day. I had started a nice little six-day weight workout plan from a while back. Although the gym was very crowded by 0530-ish, I didn't mind squeezing a little more sleep out of my night versus a few fewer bodies in the weight room.

Forgoing most of my stretching routine, I started my mile-or-so jog to the nearest gym. I heard there were three in the general area of my gym, but had never bothered with finding them. This gym was the biggest and was right next to a huge dining facility—easy to find.

I made my way on the gravel paths through the clusters of trailers that housed everyone from aviation personnel to cooks. Some were sound asleep, other clusters showed the beginnings of life. A smattering of runners gave me a few people to say "hello" to.

Down the street and around a few corners, I finally came to the gym itself. It wasn't until I reached for the door that I realized I had forgotten my ID card back in my trailer. Without it, nada on the weight room. You needed it to get in, and the civilians who run the place are cold-hearted bastards when it comes to exceptions.

Oh well, I thought, and started along the normal route I use on run days. Rounding the nearby PX and heading south put me near the fence that slides along the south-western edge of the camp. An Iraqi village was beyond the fence. Apparently there were two villages nearby: a friendly Shiite one to the south, and the not-so-friendly Sunni town next to the fence.

After finally finding my pace, there was this boom that happened off beyond the fence. Then this sort of whine—like a police siren spinning down. Just hearing that, I thought a police car outside the gate had just been hit with an IED. Strange that the police siren hadn't been going off before it was hit.

Then there was a louder boom to my left. This explosion had more of a cracking sound and was definitely on camp.

Thus went my education on mortar attacks. The thumping sound was the launch. The whine was the shell arching into the sky. The cracking explosion was the shell hitting.

No mortar alarm sounded, so I kept running. I was heading home anyway and figured I'd make it back before another hit came.

Two minutes later I was almost home when the alarm finally went off, signaling everyone to head to the bunkers.

Another thump came from my right. You could barely hear the shell's whistle over the siren. Small arms fire started up in the distance—apparently some of the guards saw who was shelling us.

Then a flash off to my left, some 150 meters away. The shell had burst in the air, leaving a small cloud hanging in the sky like a July 4th firework. Wow, close one, I thought.

Veering off the road, I headed to a nearby bunker and huddled in the concrete and dirt shelter with some sleepy Mississippi National Guardsmen. A first sergeant nodded at me as I came in.

"Air burst?" he asked.

"Roger, top, close as hell," I said.

A few minutes went by before the choppers started up. Watching them from the bunker, they flew low over the camp toward the offending village, searching for our attackers. An unmanned aerial vehicle took to the sky as well, putting more eyes on the now still and quiet row of shacks beyond our border.

And that was it. Soon we got the signal saying we could leave the bunkers. I said my good-byes and made it back to my trailer. Just another attack. No biggie.

Retelling the story later to a sergeant first class in my personnel office, she said, "With it that close, you could qualify for a combat action badge. All you need is two eyewitnesses."

Not that I was gunning for the award, but no dice—I was alone, I told her. "Oh well," she replied.

Regardless, it was an interesting start to the day, and the convoy I was scheduled to go on that night would make the day's close just as eventful. Our main supply routes are very interesting places, full of suspense and adventure. Damn insurgents love sending us little bombs to keep us on our toes.

Thank God it's Friday just doesn't have the same sparkle as it does in the States.

,   ,   ,

First Sergeant Patrick Cosgrove, the top noncommissioned officer in his artillery battery, blogs at *Six More Months* and writes about missing his kids and being a "Dad Interrupted":

,   ,   ,

On Friday, my Wife and I celebrated our 16th anniversary. It was the third anniversary we have spent apart, and each time I promise that this will be the last time. Somehow that hasn't worked out yet. 8,000 miles and 9 time zones is a long ways apart, but we managed to spend some time together anyway. It was early evening here, late morning there, the kids were at school, and I was done with work for the day. We chatted, flirted, and blew each other kisses on the web cam. We smiled and laughed. We talked about the past and the future and pretended that the present wasn't real, like we were on a date, enjoying dinner and each other's company. Keeping a marriage going is tough under any circumstances, but we are pretty much a statistical miracle. 3 deployments, and 9 years working in a prison, nights weekends and holidays, working Christmas day or Thanksgiving evening, it amazes me still that she stuck with me. What the hell is she thinking? Well, whatever keeps her from tossing me out like yesterday's trash, Thank God for it!

Missing another anniversary reminded me of all the other moments I have been missing. A couple of weeks ago, school started. Our oldest daughter (the Artist) started high school. Our middle daughter (the Athlete) started middle school. And our youngest son (the Jedi) started second grade, his first year of being "alone" at school, without the burden of a big sister running around the school creating oh so unreasonable expectations for him. The Artist is keeping my absence a secret from her teachers to avoid any special attention it may bring, because talking about it with people who lack a mutual perspective just doesn't help her deal with it. She made me very proud the other day when she told me that she doesn't like her government teacher because "Dad, she is really liberal." I get the feeling that if this particular teacher knew that The Artist spent Election Day 2004 waving a Bush/Cheney sign over Highway 10, it may cost her a few points on the final. She is currently scheming to create the perfect moment to inform this teacher that "My Dad's in Baghdad and he says wishing failure on his mission does not support him!" She chuckles with glee when she talks about this, and at the same time feels bad that I am not there to share the fun. Her confirmation is next spring, and I will be home.

The Athlete doesn't share too much with me about how she feels, until it is time to say good-bye, then the emotion comes surging to the surface. She has always been the fiery one, tough as nails and determined, but still a little girl when faced with a father going to war for what seems a lifetime. The single most painful moment of my life was in 1996, as I was leaving for Bosnia, when my name was called to get on the bus. The Athlete, who had been tough through the whole thing, asking questions and taking in answers with little comment, watched me turn to climb on the bus and screamed, as only a 3-year-old can, "Daddy Noooooooo!" as I walked away. How I climbed onto that bus I don't know to this day. Subsequent good-byes have gotten easier, sort of, if only through repetition and familiarity. Hockey tryouts start in 2 weeks. I won't be there.

The Jedi, named that because he is 7, and what else could a 7-year-old boy be? While I was home on leave, we saw *Revenge of the Sith* together. It was all he would ask me before I came home. "Dad, are we going to see *Star Wars* together?" As far as he was concerned, once we checked that box, it was a successful vacation. The rest was icing. His current plan involves building a clubhouse in the backyard together when I get home. The plans are elaborate, as they should be. When I asked him how we would build the clubhouse in the middle of winter, when I get home, he applied perfect 7-year-old logic: "We can build it in the garage, and then move it when the snow is gone." As far as I am concerned, it is a perfect plan. A few minutes a day of sweeping snow off of cars and scraping windows is an insignificant price to pay. Cars come and go; clubhouses last forever in a son's mind.

Four more months. I get to be a real Dad again in four more months.

,   ,   ,

Sometimes a sense of humor helps to ease the pressure of being in a war zone—even at the expense of your officer. Staff Sergeant CJ Grisham is a Military Intelligence analyst for a combat brigade in the 3rd Infantry Division. Grisham's blog, *A Soldier's Perspective,* portrays his experiences during the invasion of Iraq:

,   ,   ,

Part of my job is that I exploit enemy documents for any intelligence value. During the war, it was my distinct pleasure to search dead for any information they may have been carrying on them. As soon as a battle was over, I'd take a team and go through the pockets, personal effects, and buildings of the enemy trying to establish an identity, affiliation, and/or who else was involved. I'm not your run of the mill intel nerd. I'm a tactical intel nerd. I am on the front lines fighting the fight with whomever I'm attached to at the time. For the first week of the war I was with 3/7 Cav as they blazed a trail for the rest of the 3rd ID. Then I moved to 4/64 Armor battalion for a feint operation to draw the Iraqi military from Karbala and Hilla. Then I moved to 1/64 Armor for the "Thunderruns" into Baghdad. Once in Baghdad, I was attached to 3/15 Infantry to cleanup and regular presence patrols. I stayed with them when we transferred to Fallujah.

When we got Baghdad, there was no shortage of information to sort through. The worst part was searching the guys that had obviously been dead a while. You cannot understand the sights and smells of combat until you've been through it. The smell of a decomposing human body is one that will never leave my nose. The sight of one will never leave my mind. Picking through the pockets of one to find out why he was shooting at us or why he had so many RPGs in the trunk of his car is an experience I hope I never have to relive.

After every mission, the leaders would bring my team and me whatever documents they thought were of intelligence value. One day, I got an urgent call from the S2 (battalion intelligence officer) that some maps had just come in and I needed to go over them immediately. I rushed up to the makeshift office, took whatever information they had, and went back to my area to begin the tedious process of going through hundreds of papers and maps. I went immediately to the map in question and stopped cold as I began to open it up. For those that aren't too indocrinated about how the Army works, officers are commissioned after completing college degrees. Usually, they are commissioned through military academies or ROTC programs. Sometimes, they branch over from enlisted guys to officers (a program called green to gold). So, the majority of second lieutenants (the lowest officer ranking) are children, no older than 22 years old most of the time. As soon as they graduate college they are placed as platoon leaders in charge of anywhere between 15–40 soldiers. It's the job of the platoon sergeant to properly train the platoon leader on military matters and assist with leadership decisions. At times, we also help change their diapers.

The story goes that as the patrol was clearing an area a man took off running. As he ran from the patrol, he dropped a map. The platoon leader picked it up and brought it in for me. I looked at the map and instantly began formulating how I would deal with this "important" information. I went back and told the S2 what we had and asked if he could get the Lieutenant (LT) to come in immediately. He was on patrol but would be able to come in about an hour. As we waited, I got my team together and briefed them on their jobs during the meeting: We needed someone to take detailed pictures of the map, someone to agree profusely and sternly to everything I said, and someone to apply the pressure. I would ask the questions.

When the lieutenant was brought it, I assembled my team, the S2 and the S3 (operations officer). I laid the map out on the table and asked the LT if he recognized it. His eyes lighting up, he answered, "Yes, that's the map that guy dropped as he ran off."

I asked him to tell me in exact detail where he was when the map was found. Where was the guy running from? Where did he think he was headed? What did the guy look like? Did he have any other maps on him that he could see? How old was he? Would he be able to get there again? Were there other people around? Did they see the man drop the map? Does he know what this thing is?

He answered everything he could and I pulled out one of our tactical maps and laid it beside the map he brought in. I showed him how certain lines on his map corresponded with our entry routes into the city. One box represented Baghdad International Airport (at the time, we called it Bush International Airport after removing Saddam from the name. That didn't last long.). Some of the circles around the routes represented underground bunkers where chemical munitions were being stored. I explained the significance of all the markings on the map he gave me. Then I said, "And the one thing that really told me exactly what we were dealing with is this." I unfolded the top righthand corner that I had previously wanted hidden during my oration. Unfolding the corner, I read "Pattern #326" and the name of the dress pattern for a little girl. After I wasted about 35 minutes of the LT's time explaining what he had brought me, his face turned bright red as he realized that his "map" was actually a sewing pattern!!

Everyone in the room burst into laughter, something you could tell everyone was trying hard to avoid throughout my entire presentation. And we made sure that we got it all on film.

,   ,   ,

For many combat soldiers in Iraq, everyday life sometimes includes a patrol or a raid on a suspect's house or place of business. Sergeant Michael Durand of the California Army National Guard was stationed in Iraq with the famed 3rd Infantry Division. His combat experiences have placed his blogs, *This Is Your War* and *Paint It Black,* as the premier soldier experience blogs. His call-sign is "RedTwoAlpha":

,   ,   ,

I couldn't believe we were lost! . . . well . . . actually, I could.

With this unit anything can happen.

"Typical," I said to myself, adjusting my Night Vision Goggles so I could see better through them. Driving around without headlights through an area that Charlie Company had never been in before tonight didn't help either. I had only seen this neighborhood in grainy black-and-white aerial photographs. Seeing something from the air is totally different than seeing it from the inside of a moving Humvee.

This was another raid, but instead of kicking in doors Charlie was on the outer cordon. Our mission: block off certain key intersections and don't let anyone in or out until the 3rd Infantry Division units conducting the operation were done. It was after curfew, 2300 to 0500, so traffic should be nearly nonexistent. Throw up some strands of concertina wire, cones, chemical lights, and wait until the mission was over.

Easy.

Until we got lost.

In the dark, my squad overshot its turn after dropping off Corporal Karr and Specialist Montoya where we thought they were supposed to be, but they weren't because we were in the wrong place. Shit happens.

I was in the trail truck, anyhow, so I was following Harvey. Even if I had had a map, which I didn't, it wouldn't have mattered since we were moving in the pitch dark to begin with.

The squad stopped and picked up Montoya and Karr, found where they were supposed to be, dropped them off, and raced to our intersection, the joining of six roads—two of which were dirt. One side was bordered by a walled-in warehouse complex, the other side houses. Along the long axis—what would become our 12 and 6 o'clock—the main road shot through our perimeter. To the 12, houses flanked the road on the left and right as it faded into the night. Nearer to us on the left front was a walled-in grove of palms, behind was open for 500 to 600 meters—a wide dirt median separated the north- and southbound lanes of the main street.

Back at camp SSG Harvey and I had discussed my concerns for laying out the traffic control measures. Starting 275 meters out from the center of our perimeter were to be signs:

WARNING REDUCE SPEED TO 5KMH
YOU ARE APPROACHING A MILITARY CHECK POINT
DIM LIGHTS
OBEY ALL COMMANDS

The signs are in English and Arabic. At the 250-meter mark were orange cones marked with red chemical lights and reflective tape. The spike strip was placed there as well. The final barrier was a strand of concertina wire. Again, red chemical lights would be hung from the wire like decorations on a sadist's hedge.

Harvey was concerned with the time crunch setting everything up would take.

"We need to get it done fast." He wanted both trucks and crews to operate independently, setting up their own obstacles.

"I'll do whatever you tell me to, you know I will, but how about this? We with Keo on leave still, Jones still on profile with his ankle, both our trucks are short a body. That's only two guys dismounted setting all this shit up, in the dark, and in an area where we are not liked much. This isn't Karradah anymore, man."

"So, what are you thinking?"

"Using both trucks. One crew sets up the wire and stuff and the other provides overwatch. Just in case, you know?"

He went with my idea and I felt better.

As soon as the two trucks rolled into the neighborhood lights began coming on in houses. Edges of curtains pulled away from window frames and faces appeared, the features in shadow. I wondered how many figures were pressing buttons on phones, how may unseen eyes were wishing us ill and looking for weaknesses.

It felt like it took forever for Gilbert and me to set up our barrier material. Carrying anything in full gear is awkward but I especially hate dealing with concertina wire when I have to carry my rifle, wear a vest, helmet slipping to cover my face—front heavy from the goggles—the lip banging into the bridge of my nose and making my eyes water and sting. No matter how careful you are with concertina wire you will always get cut and snagged. Pulling away and struggling won't help either. It just makes it worse. You have to stop and find where you are hooked up and then free yourself, probably getting nicked in the process. I have a nice double scar on my right kneecap, the result of charging full speed into the razor sharp stuff on an assault one night years ago.

Standing on one end of the wire, I looked around me—checking rooftops and shadows—as Gilbert jogged backward with the other end, spreading it across the road, the metal coils sounding like a chain-link fence as they bounced and scraped against the pavement. A huge jagged slinky. The urge to get back to PROJECT MAYHEM and the illusion of safety it provided was strong as we cracked the chemical lights and hung them in the wire. They swung from 550 cord lanyards as we turned and sprinted back to the truck.

The concertina wire was the last line before we started shooting.

First a warning shot above the oncoming vehicle when it made contact with the wire. Once it punched through it was on. A mad minute would commence until the vehicle was stopped. If it was a vehicle-borne improvised explosive device (VBIED), I hoped we would be alive to fire. Two hundred meters is well within the blast radius of a vehicle packed with explosives. Two hundred meters can be covered in seconds by a car traveling at speed. If anyone got that far they wanted to be there, it was no mistake, no drunk driver, not a case of pure stupidity.

With the trucks and guns positioned, engines were shut off and we settled in to wait and watch. Night dogs began to creep out of the shadows, closing in on us, sniffing the air for food or danger or weakness.

I watched them when I wasn't watching everything else, noting which windows stayed lit and which turned out. The people inside returning to bed or continuing to watch us from the dark.

The dogs came in much closer than they had ever done before, nose to the ground and eyes never leaving us. Always tracking our movements.

I like the dogs. I respect their ability to survive, their skill. Somehow I feel safer when they are around. I watch them for clues and danger signals. They are neither for us nor against us. I know they wouldn't hesitate to take one of us down if they smelt fear or weakness. They just are. They were here before me and will be here long after I am gone. Somehow that thought comforts me.

I watched a woman on her back porch. It was after midnight and she was working on something outside under the single floodlight above the door. Fluttering white dots circled and dove on the bright bare bulb, making just audible clinking sounds. Moths orbiting the light like planets orbiting a star.

The woman's house was inside our perimeter. As I watched her I became concerned, first for my squad, then for her. What would happen if shooting started? She could be hit.

"Hey, Staff Sergeant Harvey, can you send the interpreter over here?"

The interpreter and I walked over to the fence line. "Ask her what she's doing."

"She is baking bread." Just then she moved to where I could see her better. She was slapping a disk of dough between her hands, making flat bread.

"Oh." I felt foolish, embarrassed. "Oh, ok, tell her to go inside when she is done. Tell her it's for her safety."

"She says ok."

Time stretched and compressed as we watched and waited, listening to the other units take down objectives and capture wanted individuals or coming up empty.

Charlie's third platoon happened upon five males sleeping in an abandoned house armed with seven to ten AK-47s, a spotting scope, pictures of Zarqawi and Al Sadr, several thousand dollars in cash, and more trucks than they could drive.

I was bored, but it was nice to not be on the sharp end for once, to play observer this time. Bradley fighting vehicles and M-1 tanks roared and squeaked in the distance. Overhead two Apache gunships prowled the dark, their tail booms like scorpions poised to strike.

The VBIED thought made me remember when I had gone with Sergeant Silver to see the truck Watkins was killed in. The shattered body of the truck was hidden in a far corner of the battalion motor pool, tucked behind a crumbling mud brick wall. It had been brought in on a flatbed HEMTT [heavy expanded mobility tactical truck], strapped to a scarred metal and wooden pallet, the wood smooth and silvered with age and wear.

I had seen plenty of car wrecks. This was not like any of those. This was not the result of another vehicle colliding with the truck. This one had been blown apart. The hood rested upside down where the back hatch was supposed to be, stacked with jagged scraps of metal and fabric. The roof was buckled upward, armored windows shattered and blackened. In the driver's compartment, the floor had been pushed up, like a freeze frame photograph of a bubble just as the surface tension gives and the first break appears. There was a drip of dark blood, like chocolate syrup, already dried near the door. I resisted the urge to wet a fingertip and wipe the blood away. On the lip of the roof "Lil' Flip" had been written in black pen. Oil, antifreeze, and power steering fluid leaked from the engine block, pooling together and dripping off the sides of the pallet, dropping to the dusty ground with audible pops.

As Silver and I walked away three Soldiers came over to the remains with thick white sheets of plastic tarp.

"VEHICLE!" Gilbert cried out. "Twelve o'clock! See the headlights?"

Everyone shifted, rifle stocks were seated into the joining of shoulder and armpit, turrets traversed to get a better shot. I wedged myself behind the driver's door and brought my M-4 up, the safety flipping off with a snap.

"Is it a Humvee?" somebody asked.

"No, the lights are too close to the ground," Gilbert reported from behind the gun.

The car approached slowly, weaving around the obstacles, and stopping just short of the wire. No one moved, fixed on the lights. Doubt crept in. Who was out there? Harvey and I played our lasers over the car, his green, mine red. For an instant I heard one of Darth Vader's lines from *Return of the Jedi* in my head: "I see you have constructed a new Light Saber."

The car's headlights blinked out then came on again. One was brighter than the other.

What the hell is going on out there?!

I was tensing up, expecting a blast or the ripping burst of automatic weapons fire. The rounds would kick up clouds of dust and spark off the doors of PROJECT MAYHEM sounding like rocks thrown from a car tire. It could be a drunk, or somebody that just doesn't give a damn about the curfew or it could be full of AK-wielding bad guys. Or a fucking bomb.

The lights went off again and stayed off. Nobody shot. Our ROE [rules of engagement] dictated we could shoot but everyone held their fire. Waiting.

"Red Six, Red Two, over."

"Go for Six."

"Roger, I've got a car outside the wire. It's just stopped there with the headlights off. I'm going to fire a warning shot. Over."

"Roger."

Harvey's rifle cracked once, the report echoing down the street and back to us.

Nothing.

Time seemed to stretch out forever. We were frozen in this moment. There was no Back Then and no Later. Only Now. I kept trying to see into the dark, trying to feel what was out there. Willing my senses to tell me something.

Just as I was reaching for my night vision goggles, the lights came back on. Here we go again. Were they using the lights and darkness to cover their movement? Emplacing a bomb or booby-trapping the wire?

Finally, the interpreter used the bullhorn to call out, his voice bouncing off all the flat surfaces and coming back to my ears as if he were everywhere and nowhere at once. He called out twice more before a faint voice came from behind the lights.

A male voice.

"He says he has a sick woman and needs to get to hospital."

"My ass," I muttered and tightened my grip on my rifle, settling behind the sights, readying for a shot.

"I got him. Just say the word."

"No. Fuck that," I heard Harvey say. "Tell him, 'too bad.' This place is locked down and I'm not sending anyone out there. He's just going to have to find another way. Tell him."

There was another exchange of Arabic. One amplified through the bullhorn, the other sounding faint. Finally the car began to back up and turn. Making its way back out to the street. You could almost hear everyone let out a breath.

As Harvey filled the Lieutenant in I vented my fear and frustration. "What the FUCK! Are these people born stupid? It must be something in the water or food or air. Two motherfucking years we have been here. Two fucking years and they still don't get it. We have fucking signs on all our trucks saying 'stay back or we'll shoot your ass' but they just don't get it! It's like . . . it's like dealing with retards. Fuck!"

"They know," the interpreter put in, "that the Americans, they sometimes make exceptions."

"Oh, great. So now our weakness, our lack of resolve, is being used against us. It's bad enough when we have to fill out reams of paperwork on every warning shot we fire. And that's IF you don't get fried by your own chain of command. You get in more trouble here if you kill a bad guy than you would if you killed an American. Bullshit."

For every shot fired we have to fill out sworn statements outlining exactly what we did, hoping that someone that never leaves the safety of the wire of the FOB, Fobbits we call them, thinks you acted and performed in just the right manner. If they don't, you can find yourself up on charges, if you're lucky. On your way to Leavenworth, if you're not.

"Were gonna lose this war because of paperwork."

◢   ◢   ◢

Major Brian Delaplane blogs from Afghanistan on *Fire Power Forward*. His role as executive officer (second in command) of a task force places him in the Tactical Operations Center (TOC)—the nerve center of the task force—where he monitors events in Afghanistan. On Mother's Day 2005, Major Delaplane witnesses Marines calling for a Medevac miracle:

◢   ◢   ◢

Sundays are usually a pretty slow day around here. There are no morning meetings, troops get a little extra rest, and both the message traffic and the workload are usually pretty light. Understand, this is for the FOB where you can usually find most of the support personnel. The combat units are still out and about. We are acutely aware that the cave-dweller doesn't take Sunday off.

This past Sunday wasn't shaping up to be any different than most of the others we have experienced here. I had slept a little later than normal, then stopped in the TOC after breakfast to catch up on a few things and check the message traffic. It was a hot clear morning, then the thunderstorms rolled in and by early afternoon it was raining pretty solid. The comforting patter of light rain gave way to an increasingly heavier downpour, and when the wind began to shake the heavy canvas and make the metal poles creak, it became downright ominous.

When the hail started, I stopped what I was doing at my desk long enough to peek outside and make sure it wasn't big enough to cause any damage. I had just gotten back to trying to concentrate on my work when LT Mahoney, my operations officer, came by and said, "Sir, we're tracking a TIC with Trinity. They're sending a 9-line."

TIC is an acronym for "Troops in Contact" and Trinity is the call sign for the 3/3 Marines who had just moved off the FOB last week after being relieved by 82nd Airborne units. They had established operations in another area and were continuing to do what they do best, take the fight to the cave-dweller. TICs are more common than we would like them to be but that isn't what caused the sense of urgency. A 9-line is a standard radio format to request medical evacuation. The big flat-screen television in the operations center resembles a teenager's computer monitor with multiple text chat message windows open at any given time, and even though they are all encrypted and secure, most of the time the messages that flicker across are just as benign. Not this time. I read the last message.

"TRINITY: Stand by for 9 line."

We in the LTF [logistical task force] aren't in the medevac business, and, no longer supporting Trinity, we had no part in this operation, but the people gathered at the screen because we had worked with these guys for the past 3 months and we had made a lot of friends. Absolutely powerless, we stood and waited for the next message to pop up.

"TRINITY: Line 1—##A, AA, ########." The series of numbers and letters that popped up reflected the grid coordinates of where the marines wanted the medevac to land.

SPC Stogner copied the coordinates and began to plot them on one of our wall maps.

As we waited for the following lines, I scrolled back through the messages to see what had brought them to this point.

Having taken some fire from a hillside, the marines had pursued and seen the attackers disappear into a cave. Close air support was called, but the A-10s aren't built to flush thugs out of a hole in the mountain. Nothing is, except Marines.

"TRINITY: Line 2—####, Trinity." It was the radio frequency and call sign of the Marines at the landing site.

The smoke cleared, and of course the Marines had to go in. The firefight ensued, the TIC was reported and soon after word came that there were 2 US WIA [wounded in action]. 9 line to follow.

"TRINITY: Line 3—2 critical." Now I was worried. This line was supposed to be the number of patients by precedence.

It wasn't only the word "critical" that concerned me, but the fact that they had used it. There are only five different words that should be used here, each with a specific meaning to the medics as to the severity of the injuries. "Critical" isn't one of them. It was a break from protocol and uncharacteristic of the consistently professional, by-the-numbers behavior I had always witnessed from these guys. I could only imagine what was happening on the ground, and I prayed that it wasn't a sign of panic.

I looked to the map where SPC Stogner was plotting the coordinates. My heart sank. The dense contour lines around the point he had plotted indicated a viciously rugged terrain.

I returned to the monitor and waited. The minutes stretched. In another break from precedence, higher headquarters had already approved the medevac. Normally, all 9 lines of the request are received and the mission is evaluated before the approval is given. Two critical marines was analysis enough in this case, but I also knew that the helicopter couldn't take off until at least 5 lines had been received. The crew needed at least that much information to know if any special equipment would be required and how to configure the cargo area. The minutes continued to stretch and I tried not to think about what was happening on that mountainside.

"TRINITY: Line 5—2 non-ambulatory."

"Where is line 4?" I asked to no one in particular. I scrolled up and checked again. It hadn't been sent. I looked at the time stamps on the messages: 20 minutes and some change. The pilots would be in the aircraft and the blades would be turning. They would be looking at maps trying to find the best approach and calling for the weather. The crew was configuring the patient area to accommodate 2 patients on litters, but they couldn't go until they had line 4. Higher headquarters broke in with the weather: "Broken000, wind 35G55, thunderstorms and hail."

I looked from the big screen to the computer terminal and back hoping I had misread this. I hadn't, and a wave of resignation swept over me. A broken ceiling with 000 meant that the clouds were coming down to the ground in places. The wind had a sustained speed of 35 knots and was gusting to 55, near the limitations of the aircraft. Throw in the thunderstorms, hail, and mountains, and it was a recipe for disaster. There was no way they were going to fly.

"MEDEVAC: Send line 4." I stared at the screen with a bizarre mixture of awe, pride and disbelief. They might die trying, but they were going to go after these marines and they needed to know what special equipment was needed. The minutes ticked by.

"TRINITY: Line 4—Ventilator. 1 Marine isn't breathing." My mood turned to despair again in the time it took me to read the message.

I watched the other 4 lines gradually pop up on the screen as I tried in vain not to think about these Marines lying in the mud with their life slipping away. No sooner had the Marines sent the 9th line than they followed up with "Please advise when medevac is wheels up."

Even from my disassociated vantage point, the minutes seemed to stretch interminably. It was impossible for me to fathom what it was like on that muddy hillside with marines trying everything they possibly could to save the lives of their comrades, waiting for help that would take a veritable eternity to arrive, if it came at all.

"MEDEVAC: Send patient status . . . update vitals."

We waited, staring at the immobile screen as if at a telephone that refused to ring. I remembered talking to Trinity's executive officer a few weeks prior. They were entering the home stretch of their deployment and the fact that they hadn't lost any Marines up to this point made him proud, nervous, and hopeful.

"TRINITY: 2 US KIA [killed in action]."

And just that quickly, all of our hopes vanished.

Overcome with frustration and helplessness, I stepped out the back door to collect myself. The rain had stopped and the wind had died down where we are, but the mountains in the distance were still obscured by storm clouds.

I wondered who those Marines were, if they were someone who I had passed any number of times on the FOB, or seen laughing with their buddies in the chow hall. Were they part of that ever present group of Marines on the volleyball court or in the gym? I wondered what their plans had been upon their redeployment which was at hand, and I wondered about their families whose perception of Mother's Day would be changed forever.

I felt my eyes well up. I said a prayer, then went back to work.

It didn't seem to make much difference later, when we saw the reports that the Air Force AC-130s and A-10s had caught remnants of this group of attackers in a nearby valley and gave the Marines 19 less to worry about the next day. The whole incident didn't seem to make much of a difference to the world in general as the Reuters report was barely longer than the 9 lines it took the Marines to call for a miracle that wouldn't come.

CHAPTER THREE

THE HEALERS

My business is staunching the blood and feeding fainting men; my post the open field between the bullet and the hospital.

—CLARA BARTON, NURSE FOR THE UNION ARMY, 1863, AND, LATER, FOUNDER OF THE AMERICAN RED CROSS

Among the words you can hear on the battlefield, one of the most horrifying when screamed out is "Medic!"

And among the best sounds that you can hear is the footsteps of the medic racing to the wounded, yelling "Medic up!"

One group of soldiers that receives an enormous amount of respect are the healers—doctors, nurses, medics, combat lifesavers, and chaplains—who fight on the battlefields and the operating rooms to save lives. Some medics are integrated into the combat forces, storming enemy-held objectives and dodging bullets to save their comrades, others wait for the wounded to arrive and begin fighting for their lives on operating tables. Chaplains heal in ways different from the medical professionals. They wage spiritual warfare, caring for the soldiers' spiritual and mental well-being.

U.S. Navy Lieutenant Commander Heidi S. Kraft was stationed at a naval combat hospital in Iraq, where she wrote a good-bye poem about leaving the war zone called "The List" that was featured on *Blackfive.* "The List" is about the things that were good and were not so good about her tour. She writes of comforting Marine Corporal Jason Dunham, who was wounded and dying. Dunham threw himself on a grenade to save his brother Marines:

,   ,   ,

Greetings all from hot, hot, hot Iraq.

We are short indeed . . . although not quite as short as we had originally thought . . . our flight home has been posted and is showing up 3 days later than planned. The good news is that we leave in the middle of the night and arrive (all admin complete, including turning our weapons in to the armory!) around dinnertime at Pendleton on the same day we leave (11 hrs time difference). The other good news is it appears we've got commercial contract air carriers taking us home . . . so we don't have to worry about sleeping on the cold steel deck of an Air Force C-17.

So . . . we turned over authority of the surgical company last week to our replacements, who had a serious trial by fire here in multiple ways, including multiple traumas, surgeries, increased risk to their personal safety, power outages, water outages, and camel spiders in the hospital . . . all in their first 4 days. But a few days ago, we heard the helicopters coming and knew they were dealing with multiple traumas, several of which were going to the OR . . . and we sat in our barracks and waited for them to call us if they needed us. They never did. Last week was the ceremony to mark the official end of our role here. Now we just wait.

As the days move very slowly by, just waiting, I decide that one of the things I should work on for my own closure and therapeutic healing . . . is a list. The list would be a comparison: "Things That Were Good" about Iraq and being deployed with the Marines as one of the providers in a surgical company, and "Things That Were Not Good." Of course, it's quite obvious that this list will be very lopsided. But I thought I would do it anyway, hoping that somehow the trauma, the fear, the grief, the laughter, the pride and the patriotism that have marked this long seven months for me will begin to make sense, through my writing. Interestingly, it sort of turned into a poem. To be expected, I guess.

Most of all it's just therapy, and by now I should be relatively good at that. Hard to do for yourself, though.

So here goes . . . in reverse order of importance . . .

THINGS THAT WERE GOOD

Sunset over the desert . . . almost always orange

Sunrise over the desert . . . almost always red

The childlike excitement of having fresh fruit at dinner after going weeks without it

Being allowed to be the kind of clinician I know I can be, and want to be, with no limits placed and no doubts expressed

But most of all,

The United States Marines, our patients . . .

Walking, every day, and having literally every single person who passes by say "Hoorah, Ma'am . . ."

Having them tell us, one after the other, through blinding pain or morphine-induced euphoria . . . "When can I get out of here? I just want to get back to my unit . . ."

Meeting a young Sergeant, who had lost an eye in an explosion . . . he asked his surgeon if he could open the other one . . . when he did, he sat up and looked at the young Marines from his fire team who were being treated for superficial shrapnel wounds in the next room . . . he smiled, lay back down, and said, "I only have one good eye, Doc! But I can see that my Marines are OK."

And of course, meeting the one who threw himself on a grenade to save the men at his side . . . who will likely be the first Medal of Honor recipient in over 11 years . . .

My friends . . . some of them will be lifelong in a way that is indescribable

My patients . . . some of them had courage unlike anything I've ever experienced before

My comrades, Alpha Surgical Company . . . some of the things witnessed will traumatize them forever, but still they provided

outstanding care to these Marines, day in and day out, some-
times for days at a time with no break, for 7 endless months
And last, but not least . . .
Holding the hand of that dying Marine

THINGS THAT WERE NOT GOOD
Terrifying camel spiders, poisonous scorpions, flapping bats in the
    darkness, howling, territorial wild dogs, flies that insisted on
    landing on our faces, giant, looming mosquitoes, invisible
    sand flies that carry leishmaniasis
132 degrees
Wearing long sleeves, full pants and combat boots in 132 degrees
Random and totally predictable power outages that led to sweating
    throughout the night
Sweating in places I didn't know I could sweat . . . like wrists, and
    ears
The roar of helicopters overhead
The resounding thud of exploding artillery in the distance
The popping of gunfire . . .
Not knowing if any of the above sounds is a good thing, or bad
    thing
The siren, and the inevitable "big voice" yelling at us to take
    cover . . .
Not knowing if that siren was on someone's DVD or if the big voice
    would soon follow
The cracking sound of giant artillery rounds splitting open against
    rock and dirt
The rumble of the ground . . .
The shattering of the windows . . .
Hiding under flak jackets and kevlar helmets, away from the bro-
    ken windows, waiting to be told we can come to the
    hospital . . . to treat the ones who were not so lucky . . .
Watching the helicopter with the big red cross on the side landing
    at our pad

*Worse . . . watching Marine helicopters filled with patients landing
at our pad . . . because we usually did not realize they were
coming . . .*

*Ushering a sobbing Marine Colonel away from the trauma bay
while several of his Marines bled and cried out in pain inside*

*Meeting that 21-year-old Marine with three Purple Hearts . . . and
listening to him weep because he felt ashamed of being afraid
to go back*

*Telling a room full of stunned Marines in blood-soaked uniforms
that their comrade, that they had tried to save, had just died
of his wounds*

*Trying, as if in total futility, to do anything I could to ease the
trauma of group after group . . . that suffered loss after loss,
grief after inconsolable grief . . .*

*Washing blood off the boots of one of our young nurses while she
told me about the one who bled out in the trauma bay . . . and
then the one who she had to tell, when he pleaded for the
truth, that his best friend didn't make it . . .*

*Listening to another of our nurses tell of the Marine who came in
talking, telling her his name . . . about how she pleaded with
him not to give up, told him that she was there for him . . .
about how she could see his eyes go dull when he couldn't
fight any longer . . .*

And last, but not least . . .

Holding the hand of that dying Marine

Sergeant Michael Durand of *This Is Your War* is an infantryman on patrol around the city of Baghdad. On one patrol, the usual steadfast medic that accompanies his squad is hospitalized and his squad is assigned a new medic straight out of school:

Nearly two hours later, my patrol was back at the scene of the event, the only evidence of the drama that had unfolded there were the still bright puddles of blood and a few scraps of plastic from the battle dressings and Kerlix we had used.

Everything else was gone.

The blood soaked flannel shirt and T shirt I had cut off the man I was working on. His jeans, well, those had been carried off seconds after I had pulled them off the man by a woman in a black abaya, the half empty water bottle, the car the men were riding in, blood-splattered interior, the windows frosted and crazed by bullets, the door skins pockmarked with more strikes.

I shouldn't have been surprised but I was.

Iraq is like that.

Every time I think that I have finally seen it all—seen everything that there possibly is to see—that my capacity to be shocked or amazed is over, Iraq will show me something else.

Just to prove me wrong.

Today's events did just that . . .

The patrol was just into its first hour on the street, my first daylight patrol since returning from leave. I was in a good mood, happy to be back out on the street, images of the sun rising behind the gray clouds above the chow hall fresh in my mind. Rays of light spread across the sky like spokes on a wheel, the edges of the clouds burned a neon orange red.

On the edge of the built-up area kids were going to school, the girls dressed in white long-sleeved shirts, bib type dark blue dresses reaching down to their ankles. The boys in white polo shirts and dark pants, backpacks slung over their shoulders, the girls pressing their books to their chests, arms akimbo. Just like school girls back in The World.

The boys yelled at our Humvees as we rumbled by. Some strutting and looking hard at us, the younger ones holding out hands and shouting.

"Mister! Mister! Chocolate!"

The girls ducking their chins down but following us with their eyes. Some smiling shyly at the gunners. Ski, my gunner, was throwing handfuls of Jolly Ranchers to some groups.

"Only the ones that don't ask for anything."

He thought for a minute. "And the cute girls . . . the rest of 'em can go fuck themselves."

Crossing a dirt and trash strewn open area between roads and houses, high-tension towers above, Ski was the first one in the truck to hear the firing.

"SHOTS! Off to the five o'clock, about three hundred meters!"

The LT called up to the lead truck, SSG Bull and his crew. Bull's gunner, Rio, had heard them as well. Random shooting is nothing out of the ordinary in Iraq. The Iraqis like to shoot. They shoot into the air at weddings, birthdays, when their soccer teams win, when someone dies. Sometimes when they just feel like it. The IAs [Iraqi Army] and IPs [Iraqi Police] shoot when they are bored or scared or want to get through traffic jams. Whatever.

The patrol thumped over the curb and onto the street when a second burst of fire ripped the air off to my right front.

"Where THE FUCK is that coming from?" I wondered.

I didn't see anyone running but it sounded close. Through the Humvee windshield I saw a metallic gray car lurch to a stop and three figures tumble out. Two men and a woman. The woman was wearing a red dress with large tropical-looking flowers on it. I watched her stagger forward, like someone carrying a great weight on their shoulders. Bent at the waist, she was clutching her arm to her midsection. The two men were just behind her; one had his arms raised above his head, and the other lurched forward. The woman finally went to her knees then rolled onto her back. Like it was a signal for the two men they all stopped, the trailing one crumpled to the roadway, loose jointed, head bobbing, like a machine slowly breaking down.

By then the Soldiers in the two lead trucks were dismounted or in the process of doing so. I had just popped my door when the hated cry reached my ears. "MEDDDDDDDIC!"

Fuck. Here we fucking go, man.

"LET's GO DOC! They need you up there!" Turning around in my seat I looked at our current medic. A 19-year-old Asian kid from our Brigade. Our normal platoon medic and my roommate had been out of the game for a while with whiplash to his back and neck. The result of an IED that blew our female translator's face off back in August. Doc A, my buddy, had worked on her, saving her life. I had seen him save other lives. I had seen Doc A bring people back from *Death*. He had worked on Iraqis and Soldiers, putting the pieces back together, elbow deep in blood, but Sara was just too much for him. He had seen too much, taken too much pain inside himself, looked too deep and long into Horror. Sara lived just under twenty-four hours. The doctors had reconstructed her face with what was left of her feet but we all agreed that she had just given up. With both her feet gone and her face the way it was, I don't think she tried very hard to hold on.

Doc F was his replacement until Doc A got back on his feet again. Doc F was fresh from medic school at Ft Sam Houston. Out from Camp Anaconda on a war safari, doing his time "in the shit." Well, he found it with us. Here the war is 24/7. It never goes away. And people get hurt in terrible ways.

I grabbed one of his bags, slinging it over my shoulder, M-4 in one hand, while Doc F shouldered his aid bag. "I'll go with him."

I don't know why I wanted to go. I have seen the damage that bullets and shrapnel do to a human body. I had done some of the damaging myself.

Run up with Doc or leave him alone?

I wondered what I was going to see, and for a second, for one step, I hesitated.

Do I really need more images of rent flesh, of people in pain to have dreams about?

Those nasty little flashbacks that come at unexpected times. No, but it was too late to go turn back now.

The three people were close together, the two on the ground lying a few feet away from each other. Throwing the aid bag to the ground, I scanned over the people and stopped again. What I had thought was a woman in a red dress with flowers on it was actually a man in what had been an off-white Dish-dasha, the Haji man-dress that many men wear. The red was blood, the flower pattern the white portions on the material. The blood was already specked with the dark bodies of flies that raised and fluttered like clouds.

Well, you're fucked, I thought, turning to pull near security at the corner of the nearest Humvee. The exhaust flashed warm across my face.

Glancing back one more time at the fellow in the flannel shirt, I watched a thick stream of blood spurt at least four inches out of his neck. There was already a pool of blood under the man's head, running down his arm, soaking his clothes. His pants were dark with it. The hot copper smell hung in the air mixed with the old locker room smell of sweat.

Shit.

I slung my rifle and tore my flight gloves off. No way I was getting those all fucked up in Haji blood. The words Hepatitis A, B, and C flashed in my head. At the same time I was attempting to dig into my leg bag and aid pouch—the leg bag for a roll of Kerlix, the aid pouch for my latex gloves. I needed more hands. Finally, I got the gloves on and began tearing at the wrapper of the Kerlix with my teeth when the smell hit me again and I realized I was going to have to put my hands in that mess. I gagged, saliva pooling in my mouth. God I was going to be sick. I tasted the hash browns and bacon I had eaten for breakfast again.

Shit! I am NOT going to vomit. Get a hold of yourself, man.

I knelt down and pressed the white gauze to the guy's neck. He was moaning and crying in Arabic. The roll of gauze was rapidly soaking up the dark blood still pumping out of the Iraqi's neck.

"Doc! I need you over here. This guy is shooting blood all over the fucking place!"

Doc picked up and moved over to me. I scanned the man's body over, looking for more wet spots, more wounds.

Right. This guy's entire clothing was soaked and dark with blood. Coagulated chunks of blood had pooled in the wrinkles of his jeans, showing up bright against the dark material.

I dry heaved again. Old memories beat against the insides of my eyes like the dark wings of a trapped bird.

Pull it TOGETHER! Get control! NOW!

"Doc, hold this while I cut his shirt off. This dude's so covered in blood I can't tell if he's hit anywhere else." I reached for my shears and felt Doc's hand press down on mine. Letting go, I pulled the shears free and reached for the edge of the guy's shirt just as he spit out a mouthful of blood, splattering my knee and boots.

I tasted bacon again and fought down the urge to puke once more. Puking on the wounded will definitely not earn me any cool points.

Cutting his shirt away I pulled another roll of Kerlix out of my leg bag. At this point in the deployment I carried more medical gear than I did ammo. I wiped away the blood on his side and began counting holes.

One, two, three, four, five . . . Wait, let me do that again. One, two, three . . . Five. Five holes in the side of this man's chest.

Not big holes, not like you see in the movies, torn and gaping, just little innocent-looking things no larger than a big zit. They weren't even bleeding. Little gouges in his skin, black purple, and beginning to swell. What was happening inside? He was breathing, gasping for air and talking.

I have seen sucking chest wounds before, the side with the deflated lung sunk in, the wounded struggling for air and in great pain.

Yet this guy had been shot five fucking times. Five times and was still moving around.

Goddamnnnn.

"Ahhh . . . Hey Doc, this fucker's got FIVE goddamn holes in his chest. You might want to look at this, man."

I looked at Doc F. He was working but overwhelmed, focusing on the still bleeding neck wound.

"Doc. Doc, look at me." My voice was calmer than I felt. Doc found my eyes. "Hey! We need some more help over here!"

Mac came running over and held the soaked Kerlix while Doc put a bandage on the worst of the chest wounds, feeding the little latex hose into the hole.

The third Iraqi was wandering around. I snagged him.

"Hey! You're his friend, right?"

The man looked blankly at me. I couldn't remember the Arabic word for friend.

"Look," I said pointing to the wounded man and making opening and closing motions with my hand, like a mouth, "talk to him, ok? Make sure he stays with us."

I was afraid of the guy going into shock, of fading out on me. Giving up.

Fuck that.

I was not going to let this son of a bitch die on me. The man fired off rapid Arabic. There was a woman in a black abaya standing nearby, crying and putting her hands to her face.

"Someone get her the fuck out of here!"

There were people everywhere. Soldiers, Iraqis, kids on bikes. Fuck, the entire city had turned out to watch the show. Better than what's on TV. Life and death in your front fucking yard.

"Sgt D! Hold this!"

Mac was digging for a fresh roll of Kerlix. I replaced his hand on the guy's neck just as he spit out another mouthful of blood. At the same time I felt a warm syrupy stream of blood splatter against my palm. And gagged again.

With the new roll placed I threw the old one away. It landed heavily in the dirt a few feet away. It sounded like a wet dish rag.

I began to cut the guy's pants off, trying to cut through his leather belt with the Harley Davidson logo in the buckle.

Blood was pooled in the low spots of the brass-colored oval, bringing the letters and the motorcycle into stark relief.

I was singing a goddamn Anna Nalick song to myself. The weirdest shit goes through your head out here at these kinds of moments. Lines from movies, images, memories that have nothing to do with the current situation. Sometimes you wonder if you're losing it a bit . . . Ok, more than just a bit.

I ended up just pulling the guy's pants off, with his help. Shot five times and the guy is helping me take his pants off.

"Hey, dude, just lay back, ok?"

I flung them aside, noting the overlarge billfold in his pocket. His ID would be in there. I turned my head back, doing a quick scan of his legs. When I looked back for the pants the woman in the abaya was making her way out of the press of Soldiers with the pants under her arm. Ah, well . . . Fuck it. He really didn't need them anyhow.

With a wounded man, a wounded anybody, standard procedure is to cut EVERYTHING off the person. The Iraqi male I was helping to treat had knee-length blue shorts on under his pants. They looked like soccer shorts or something to me. There was no visible blood on the shorts, no wet spots, unlike another Iraqi that Doc A and I had treated on the shoulder of Route Downfall one evening.

That male had been hit by an IED—either an innocent bystander or the trigger man—my first sucking chest wound. He had pissed himself, and there was blood coming out of the end of his penis, staining his white undershorts. In the orange light of the setting sun the blood took on a rust color.

I tugged at the elastic waistband of the shorts. I was aware of the Muslim squeamishness toward nudity and I asked myself if I really wanted to see this guy's junk. I decided to leave his shorts on him.

During the entire process, cutting clothes, trying to stop the bleeding, the man had been moaning and talking. I find it interesting, with wounded Iraqi children—little bodies with jagged chunks of metal in them, holes in their heads—I have never seen them cry. Instead, they just look at you, expecting you to help them.

The adults, however, will roll and thrash around. Crying out, asking for water—one time an Iraqi that had been shot six times asked Doc A for juice—demanding treatment.

This guy kept pointing to his mouth and talking. "Look dude, I can't give you any water, man," I kept telling him.

Finally Mac poured a little water into his mouth and discovered another wound.

"Holy shit! This guy was shot through the mouth! The bullet entered his mouth and came out the back of his neck! GodDAMN!"

We rolled him over and began strapping him to one of the plastic backboards that are strapped to every vehicle in the company. The boards are just a bit over six feet long and resemble surfboards. They were yellow until Keo and I spray painted them black. I left a yellow smiley face and a hippy-looking flower on mine.

Four of us carried the man to my truck and I stayed with him to monitor his condition while Doc assisted with the Evacuation of the other man in the dish-dasha. He had been shot in the arm, chunks of flesh removed from his bicep. It turned out that their other friend, the guy that had been running around, was shot in the arm as well. The last I had seen of him, Sgt A was helping him put a field dressing on his arm.

"Hey, let me help you with that, dude." Sgt A helped with the board.

I stood at my man's head looking into his eyes, trying to keep him with me. He was laid out across the wide body of the Humvee, his head behind the driver's seat. I would be the one driving him to the CASH [combat support hospital].

Clouds of flies, drawn by the smell of blood, were thick on his chest. I tried to keep them off but was losing the battle. I watched his eyelids flutter and he began to gasp for air. His eyes closed.

"Hey . . . HEY!"

I poked him in the forehead, hard.

"Stay with me, motherfucker. You're not fucking dying in my truck, ok?"

His eyes opened and focused, pupils big but not too big.

"Good. That's right, look in my eyes, ok? It's you and me in this together, man. Hold on."

My Arabic was failing me.

What was the goddamn word for hospital again? Do I know the word for hospital?

I couldn't remember.

Finally, after what felt like way too long, we loaded up and were on the way to the CASH up in the IZ, dodging snarled traffic. Doc F gave my man an IV in the back of a rolling and bumping Humvee. Not bad for a new Doc. Not bad at all.

In the end, we got both men to the CASH. The guy with the wound to the arm wasn't so bad after all.

My guy? He lived. He's going to live, too. He will spend a lot of time in the hospital but he will make it.

I'm glad, too . . . very glad, because next time, that could be me.

An Army nurse in Iraq who uses the pseudonym "Major Pain" posts messages at the blog *Magic in the Baghdad Café*. She writes about her role of being the head nurse in charge of an Army combat hospital:

,   ,   ,

I want my office back. My office here consists of a quarter of a foot-locker—just enough so I don't have to haul everything back and forth from my tent every day. Of course, I do haul my computer and fixings. (Some of my colleagues are sure I'm in an intimate relationship with my laptop—which they insist was confirmed the day I dragged the laptop into the bunker with me during a mortar attack—hey—it came in handy—I put a movie in it, *Gladiator,* and a bunch of us watched the movie until the all-clear.) Can't think of a better way of passing the time. Except sleeping, of course.

We haven't had an attack on Camp Anaconda in 2+ weeks now—maybe they ran out of mortars. Or are saving them for one big volley. Who knows?

We had some of the people from the CH-47 (Chinook Helicopter) SAM (Surface to Air Missile) attack come through here. About 7 of them—all of which got evac'ed to Germany almost immediately. To get to Germany they had to get transported to Baghdad. (I made sure the transport was not another Chinook.) Kinda sad—these guys were on their way to Qatar for a 3-day R&R.

Some soldiers from their chain of command came in looking for one of their wounded soldiers—the gunner of the 5-man Chinook crew. They had located the rest—the 2 pilots had been killed. One had been a master trainer pilot—one of the reasons the Chinook was able to land with, believe it or not, as little loss of life as it had. 2 others in the crew had gone to the other CSH [combat support hospital] in Baghdad. This was the one they were missing. The gunner had just come out of surgery and the nurse doing his recovery did not want any visitors as the ICU was crowded, busy, and the gunner was not awake anyway. We had 5 other wounded in the ICU from that crash. All were about to get loaded up on the flight to Baghdad in less than an hour. I came out to tell the rest of the crews that they couldn't visit. The CSH Chief Ward master was there and he gently pulled me aside to suggest I allow these guys in to see the gunner anyway, one at a time. Seems he saw the guys' faces when I said the patient couldn't have visitors. They NEEDED to see that their crewman was alive and "all right." I forgot, in the midst of this busy night, of the loss these soldiers were facing—they lost 2 men out of a 5-man crew, and had just spent many hours looking for the missing 5th. I returned to the ICU and told the recovering nurse that we were going to let these guys in—one at a time.

I am never so humbled as when I lose sight of the cost in human lives and human emotions. To me it was another mini-mascal (mass casualty), trying to ensure these guys get the best of care by stretching resources, staff and equipment. To them it was a man of their crew, whom they lived with and worked with for the last 6 months, and were responsible for. I overlooked that. I am so sorry, I wish I could apologize. I see so many come through here. Most leave from here alive and recovering. Some leave "critical" and "guarded" but expecting to recover. And a very few leave here through mortuary affairs. I can still name every one who left here that way on my shift. I met every one of them. When I can no longer remember the names, or care to, that is the time I need to get the hell out of this country.

Of course NOW is a good time to get me the HELL out of this country. If I ever volunteer for something again—somebody please shoot me. You'd think I woulda had enough of volunteering 17 years ago when I volunteered for the Army. Silly me. Should have learned better. Well, I keep telling myself—3 more years, 3 more years, then I can retire. And work at McDonald's or something.

I still haven't had a chance to leave Camp Anaconda—I really want to see Baghdad, or something other than tents and tanks. A few of our nurses go to Balad when we take civilians to the Balad hospital. It can be dangerous out there on the roads. The Iraqis have a new thing—they set up an IED, and then when the convoy stops—attack with small arms fire. Fortunately, this becomes increasingly deadly for the Iraqi ambushers. As one found out when a tank fired a round at an Iraqi's AK47. Which the Iraqi was holding at the time. Well, the shell did not explode when it hit the Iraqi's arm. Just kinda took it along with it down range. The Iraqi is in our ICU. He will live to go to the EPW [enemy prisoner of war] camp.

Went outside to watch the full eclipse of the moon, tripped over a sandbag and got a few more bruises for my trouble. Damn sandbags. But on a brighter note, the sand flies have decreased in number, and so have the welts from the bites.

, , ,

All of the military services have troops stationed in Iraq and Afghanistan. The Navy provides the Marine Corps with combat medics called hospital corpsmen. One such corpsman was HM3 James Pell, who had previously completed tours in Bosnia, Kosovo, and Iraq. His dispatches are posted at *Pull on Superman's Cape,* and this story is about his fight "One Day in Fallujah":

, , ,

After fighting in the city for a little over a week, it was again that time of day to start the push forward into uncharted territory. Every day so far had been a fight for every house, block by block. Every house in the city has a large front metal gate that is locked from the inside. There is no quiet way to breach the gates so the enemy inside is fully aware of our movement and is ready to fire the second we come in. Once inside the front gates there is a small yard with an outhouse—always an insurgent in the outhouse. First things first: put two rounds through the outhouse door. Next we move to the house itself. There are always two doors to choose from. One leads to the kitchen, the other into a large sitting room. I prefer the kitchen entry better, not as many places for the insurgents to hide. Also we have a present we can give the insurgents that can be made in the kitchen. It's called the house guest. We take the propane tanks from under the stove and mount a half block of C-4 [plastic explosives] to the spout and throw it down the hallway, then evacuate the house.

That's right, put the ladies and children to bed, we're in this for keeps. You never know how precious your life is until you have to willingly give it. The number one rule in the city is never expose soft flesh to the enemy when you don't have to. What would be the point of throwing Marines into a house with known insurgents inside? Instead, bring in the M1 Abrams main gun or better yet a D-9 armored bulldozer and level the house—insurgents and all. We use attack helicopters and artillery to prep the city blocks we are getting ready to move into. There are NO civilians inside the city limits. All have fled to the outskirt cities for refuge.

Moving to the next house, same routine. Gates go down, we pile into the yard, shoot the outhouse and immediately get massive fire coming from the sitting room windows. Shoot and move . . . get the hell away from the bullets . . . find cover! Nothing! No cover in the yard, we are pushed back outside the gates and use the wall as refuge. All is not lost, though, we have a foothold to work from. It's time to go to work. We start preparing the courtyard with grenades. It is answered by gunfire from the house. A round comes through the fence and strikes a Marine. He goes down falling into the line of fire! The first man behind him fearlessly runs into the open—shooting into the building trying to make it to the fallen Marine. He too falls into the dirt motionless, only he is dressed differently from the surrounding Marines, he is a local, part of the Iraqi Special Forces. And you read it right, he gave his life for a Marine. As a matter of fact the covering fire he set down gave others time to rescue the downed Marine. It actually took me a second to get over the fact that the ISF soldier had done what he did, no fear.

Grenade after grenade goes into the house—every time they are answered with AK-47 fire. These guys refuse to die. New plan: move to higher ground and snipe them. After the three are dead we clear the house and find needles everywhere. Then we find the adrenaline ampoule that they were using to load the needles with. Enough of this stuff and you're almost indestructible.

In the last room of the house my heart stops completely and I can feel death looking right at my soul and I know I'm as good as dead. The walls of the room are lined with 155mm artillery shells, hundreds of them, and I felt the trip wire break as I kicked the door open. But I'm not dead and time marches on. My first thought after I realized I wasn't vaporized was, "I wonder what idiot wired this room up, what a *putz*." Then slowly I backed out of the house and we all evacuated back to where we started that morning so the house could be control-detonated. The bad thing about going back is that now we have to re-clear all the houses we just cleared.

We come into a house that all the windows have been taped up, so it's dark. We break into smaller teams so we can flood the house. I hear one of my younger guys screaming gibberish. My partner and I run to his aid and find he has two insurgents cornered in the same room he is in and everyone is screaming at the top of their lungs. Insurgent number one meets the butt of my rifle with his face while my partner pins him to the floor.

Insurgent number two has a flashlight two inches from his face, attached to the flashlight is a loaded M-16. Both were cuffed and dragged outside to await pickup. Inside the house was a small weapons cache. My young Marine was lucky he was in between the insurgents and their weapons. The two can be seen along with myself and the young Marine running down the street on the Heroes of India Company video.

Two houses down India Company takes more casualties, this is Smith and Polock. Polock is shot all over and it's bad. He has to go right away. Smith is fading fast and doesn't make it out. I can't explain the coldness that took hold of my heart. I made sure I was the number one man into the next house. Retribution will be mine.

I kicked the kitchen door open and rushed into the house. The kitchen was empty so I moved to the next room, noting that the house smelled of dead something awful. First room I kicked the door in and rushed in. I was face to face with a man at least six foot three, and like everyone else he's screaming at the top of his lungs, but I can understand him, it's English. He claims to be a doctor. And, as I look around the room, I know he is not lying. There have to be at least twenty severely injured insurgents laid up in the room. Now I'm outnumbered and nervous. So I tell the doc that the first man that moves dies. And I start screaming for reinforcements.

All of the insurgent wounded are loaded into the back of military trucks and carted away. As soon as the last truck pulls around the corner the house across the street opens fire on us. No less than ten insurgents are firing down on us from the rooftop. We run into the house we cleared and pull the injured out of and headed for the roof so we could fight on the same level. As I come out onto the second-story deck I shoot the first insurgent moving across the other roof through his right eye and he goes down. Then I start to lay down covering fire so the rest of the team can make it into a cover position on top of the roof. Then they start firing at "targets of opportunity" on the rooftop across from us. As we engage the rooftop an assault element moves to the bottom of the house so they can clear up. They take a casualty and are shortly halted. Right about this time, the taller three-story house to the left of us that hasn't been cleared yet opens fire on the rooftop we are on. We have just become pinned down. Fire from across the street picks up and now grenades are landing on the rooftop we are pinned on. My partner starts to suppress the house to our left and I—using my 4 power scope—start picking off targets on the roof of the house across the street when I see that one of the guys still running and fighting is the first guy I shot. He is missing the right side of his head, but still throwing grenades at the Marines below. Something needs to happen fast or we will start to stack casualties. The India Company executive officer has made his way to the rooftop and makes the plan of attack to get us the hell out off the roof. It goes a little something like this.

Send a team with a nasty rocket across the street.

Fire the rocket into the building to our left.

My partner and I will then run across the roof and climb to the third story of the building the insurgents are in.

After the two of us secure the roof the rest of the Marines on the original roof will spill over and take the house.

So the rocket rips through the air, slamming right on target into the house. My partner and I run across the roof and climb up to the third story—throw a grenade and secure the roof. The first marine comes over the second-story wall, it's time to take the house down. Only I hear AK fire and then screams from the roof. I look over and see Shane on the ground screaming, he is trapped. The amount of gunfire from inside the house picks up and I yell to my partner that I'm going down to get Shane.

There's only one way down.

Jump.

Gear and all I must weigh over 200 lbs, body weight of 165. So no *Matrix* moves. I sit down on my ass to slide off and, right as I go, I feel my right leg go numb from the hip down. Then the left leg feels like someone smashed it with a 30 lb hammer.

And then it hits me: so this is what it feels like to be shot.

But it isn't slowing down—I take another round into each calf.

This guy is going to kill me, I have to get away from him and there is only one option, fall. Fall to the lower roof of the building next to me. Before I can shove off another round rips into my left foot.

Push off!!

I start to fall and the wind gets knocked out of me, then it feels like a donkey has kicked me in the groin. I land on a pile of bricks and dislocate my right shoulder.

Now, you will ask, what was the first thought you had, was it of death?

Or maybe you had thoughts of your wife? Parents, family, what?

The first thing I thought was that the insurgent is going to follow me over the edge of the wall and finish the job. I picked up my rifle, which was also damaged by rounds, and pointed it up to the top of the wall while my youngest Marine placed the tourniquets around my legs to stop the bleeding. Blood was *everywhere*.

I began to lose consciousness as Lance Corporal James Powers saved my life by stopping me from bleeding out. Marines rushed up to get me, their Doc, to safety.

　　　　　,　　　,　　　,

While medics, nurses, and doctors are critical to survival in a war zone, spiritual and moral support from chaplains can be just as important. Sometimes chaplains will accompany a combat mission, but more often will remain behind to wage a different kind of fight—ministering to our soldiers, comforting the wounded and survivors, and advising the commander about moral, ethical, and spiritual aspects of the soldiering profession. Chaplain (Captain) Brad Lewis at *Training for Eternity* writes about this duty in waging Spiritual Warfare:

,   ,   ,

I think few would argue with me when I say that the job of a chaplain is not necessarily a physical job. Oh, sure, we have our occasional display of superhumanity, such as when my heart continues beating even after running a few miles trying to keep up with the much younger and obviously better fit soldiers that surround me. But overall, I think, being a chaplain is not unlike being an armchair when it comes to actual motion in the performance of the job. But that's not to say it is an easy job. The difficulty of being a military chaplain during war comes not from the exertion of muscle and sinew, but from an altogether different kind of exercise. One that is unique to the chaplain, I believe. One that I have not seen explicitly addressed before.

In order to gain a clear understanding of the world of a chaplain you must understand that the chaplain is more than just a pastor in a pickle suit. The chaplain differs from the civilian clergyman in that he wears two primary hats: that of the pastor and spiritual guide and that of the staff officer and advisor to the commander. These two functions work in tandem with each other, the one making the other possible in a military setting. As a staff officer, the chaplain is part of the mission-planning process. He speaks with and advises the commander, prior to most missions, of the moral, ethical, and religious aspects of a given mission. As a spiritual leader, the chaplain reaches out to those men and women who will actually be conducting the planned missions to offer them a spiritual foundation upon which to build their actions during the mission.

One of the things I do, and enjoy very much, is to muster with the soldiers as they gather in preparation of an evening of fighting, patrolling, flying, etc. In a word, I see them off. However, this is not the "seeing off" of the movies. This is not the mother, with her hair in a bun and her ankle-length dust-covered skirt standing on the wraparound porch waving her hanky as her boys head off to war. I'm not there as an observer. I'm not there as a bystander. I'm there as a participant. Instead of a weapon and body armor, I carry a small bottle of oil. As my soldiers prepare for their mission, without interfering with their activities, I walk around and pray for them and with them. It is something spectacular to see an American Soldier, armed to the gills with pistols and rifles and all manner of explosive accoutrements, covered head to toe with Kevlar, and watch him bow to pray as I dab oil on his forehead and pray the protection and blessing of God on his life and his mission. Then to hear that same battle-hardened warrior, in a voice shaky from anticipation, adrenaline, and appreciation, say, "Amen" and "Thank you, chaplain." I then move from vehicle to vehicle, aircraft to aircraft, weapon system to weapon system, and like a cammie-clad prophet of old, pray for the success of the mission and the safe return of the soldiers. The sounds of clinking armors and snorting horses can be heard as the entire entourage loads up and moves out to the objective, by air, by land, by foot. If you've never seen bravery or courage, you're missing something. I see it before every mission.

Then comes the difficult part of being a chaplain in war. As the sounds of marching armies fade into the distance, the night closes in like a body bag and I'm left with the struggle that few others will ever experience. It is a fight with me and my theology. It is an individual free-for-all of the heart and soul. Alone in the dark, I hope and pray that my part was sufficient. I pray my life was what it needed to be for my prayers to be heard so that my boys would come home safely. Will someone die tonight because I didn't pray hard enough, or long enough, or sincerely enough? Did I use the right words or make the right motions? What in my life might cost someone theirs? This is the battle for the chaplain's heart. It is an almost nightly occurrence. And I believe it could crush Atlas himself.

It is here, in the middle of questions and questioning, under the weight of the burden of lives not my own, that out of the darkness comes a single simple idea straight from the Throne of Grace. I did my part, now relax and let God do His. I'm the chaplain, not the Lord. And until they return, I monitor the radio and continue to pray, believing that God can do incredible things in the lives and spirits of my soldiers.

So I may not have the most difficult job, but it is a struggle nonetheless. I may not fight with my men, but I certainly fight for them. And we will continue to fight, physically and spiritually, until the struggle is ended, the war is won, and we can return home to the smiles of our families or the judgment of our God.

,   ,   ,

Army Specialist Nick Cademartori is *The Questing Cat*. He and his friend, *The Jersey Cowboy*, blog about their experiences as infantrymen with the Big Red One, the famed 1st Infantry Division, in Iraq. Nick was cross-trained as a combat lifesaver, a soldier with more first-aid training than most soldiers but less training than a medic, to raise the chances of his platoon's survival in combat:

,   ,   ,

The army started a training system, a system to try and back up the combat medic. They call it the Combat Life Saver, or CLS. A line soldier is given just that extra bit of first aid training, so that if the situation calls, and there is no medic handy, they can leap into action and administer the most desperately needed care. Many soldiers, in the early stages of their careers, are required to go to the class to learn things like how to administer an IV, give first aid and assess a casualty. I first went to CLS Training in the National Guard, and it taught me a lot of handy things. Things you hope never to use.

My day started off so normal. I was attached as security detail to the civil affairs team as they toured the little town nearby to see how Ramadan was changing things. We walked the streets, talked to some people. Very rarely does any shit go down in this town. It is quiet and we like it that way. Our officers were in a meeting with local leaders, and after making the rounds we went into the building and started to relax a bit. Our Bradleys were outside pulling security with lots of Iraqi National Guards around. I took off my helmet and tried to get a little bit of air.

You want to know the most terrible moment of a disaster? It is that split second when it begins. When all of a sudden there is a bright flash that is nothing special except that it is the big break with reality to the fucked up world you are about to begin. A split second of bright light, and for the briefest second, there is no thought in your head, everything in you braces for . . . for what?

Glass and sound rain down on me . . . I know it was bad, I have NEVER heard anything so loud, and light debris is falling all around me. I get off the stairs, and get my fucking helmet on. Wouldn't it fucking figure, walk around ALL THE FUCKING TIME WITH THAT THING ON AND THE ONE TIME I MIGHT REALLY HAVE NEEDED IT, I WAS RELAXING.

What happened?

IED? VBED? [vehicle-borne explosive device; car bomb] Mortar? Rocket?

The local leaders are in a rush to get out that door. Everyone is trying to run for safety. Above it all, I hear my CO say, "It is safer inside than out."

"GET INSIDE!" I scream.

I am shocked to see everyone pause at this . . . look at me . . . the Civil Affairs chief takes up the call and begins shouting directions and we get everyone directed to a safe spot under the stairs . . . now we have to move out.

What the fuck happened?

We begin to move out, doing the infantry thing, moving between buildings and along walls to get back to our vehicles . . . everyone falls into sync as we try to get back to our vehicles, roll out and react. I make the dash for the Humvee . . . no one is firing. All the vehicles look to be where we left them . . . no one is rushing to attack.

What the FUCK happened?

"VBED!" goes around in shouts around our perimeter. "Casualties!" go around. Then MY name goes around. Our convoy has no medics and 3 CLS. 2 of those CLS are on the CO's Bradley crew. I'm the third.

Fuck.

My name is being screamed. Someone is hurt. You're on, kiddo.

Fuuuuuck.

I'm running . . . I'm trying to remember my training . . . and even as I move, some piece of me is awake and thinking without me. Some piece of me sees that I am going to a Bradley's driver's hatch. Some piece of me knows that "the Cowboy" was driving one of these Bradleys.

FUCK.

My mind feels like it can't grasp anything. This is a very shitty day.

The casualty is not "the Cowboy." But it *is* almost as bad. A 20-year-old kid from Tennessee who once asked me if I knew when our company would get "combustible" butt stocks for M249 saws. He meant "collapsible," so of course we gave him a huge ration of shit for it. But he took it in good humor. He wasn't always the sharpest knife, but he'd work hard. His face was a maze of blood . . . he quivered and we lowered him off the Bradley. But he could walk. Confusion is everywhere . . . we are in a dead spot for communications.

We need to move!

The first Humvee we load him into has room, but it has a flat tire from shrapnel. I steal their CLS Medical Bag, and cram into the other Humvee . . . we take off flying.

Well kiddo, you're on.

I rip off my Kevlar and slither across all the crap to start assessing the casualty. The casualty is a kid two years your junior and worlds apart from you in upbringing. He is a kid. So are you.

WAKE UP!

COMMON TRAINING TASK: ASSESS A CASUALTY: "RUB BIG BREASTS SLOWLY FOR BETTER HEAD"

RUB = R = *Responsiveness.*

I am talking to the casualty. He has to *BE* a casualty, not the kid with the funny accent from down south who is always cheerful. He is responsive, he can talk, but it hurts too much. He says he can't see.

"Casualty has imminent threat to eyesight."

"Casualty is an urgent surgical."

"Casualty needs immediate medevac."

I am sounding off with this information to the CA [Civil Affairs] Chief, and he is relaying it higher. Somewhere in all this shit, everyone is looking at me. You're on kiddo, break a leg.

No, fractures come later in the assessment of a casualty.

BIG = B = *Breathing.*

He is breathing—he is responsive.

BREASTS = *Bleeding.*

FUCKING BLEEDING!

Head to toe, he is bleeding all on his face. I pull out a roll of gauze and tell him not to open his eyes. CLS do not pick through the shit on a wound. They bandage it. Slow chance for infection; keep out dirt and other foreign matter. Slow bleeding.

That is all I can do.

I wrap gauze all around his eyes and face. This kid could go blind.

DON'T THINK ABOUT IT! HELP HIM!

I am talking to him, asking him to tell me where it hurts. It hurts in both shoulders, it hurts on his leg. Only once during the ride does he go limp . . . we all scream his name until he comes out of it and gives us the thumbs up. My heart can beat again.

FUCK! WHAT THE HELL HAPPENED TODAY?!

My voice is so calm I feel spooked. None of the shit I feel is there, I am just helping him, doing whatever I can.

Medevac is called; we have to get someplace they can land. I get on the radio briefly to directly relay the casualty's exact condition. I am surprised how concise I am. I usually have to plan my radio communications, but now it is just spilling out of me. Quick, to the point, what the fuck is going on.

That brave face I showed for my buddy in the hospital is on now. I am talking to him, giving him yes/no questions so he doesn't have to try and talk around his ripped-up mouth and gums. I can see the wounds are a little more complicated than I originally thought. Blood is seeping into his mouth and he has to keep spitting. The CLS bag is not mine really. I don't know where anything to pack his cheek with might be. I'm not sure it would be worth the damage I might cause . . . and the whole time, the Sergeant who took my spot on the gun is holding his hand, holding it tight to give him comfort.

Fucking Iraq.

We get to the dust-off [jargon for Medevac helicopter] point.

We get him out of the vehicle, I and a Staff Sergeant from California sit with him, and I am assessing him in my head, trying to figure out what is wrong with him. He can't lie down because too much blood is going down his throat. Probably too much blood getting into his airways, keep him upright. Urgent Surgical, lacerations to the face, possible loss of eyesight, lacerations left and right shoulder, shrapnel entrance wounds, scrape left leg. I am cutting away his uniform with a knife he gave me. Exposing his wounds, seeing how bad it might be. Other than on his face, none are terribly serious. His face scares the shit out of me. Out of my mouth are constant comfort and jokes and bullshit and anything I can think of. I am even telling him not to worry and telling him what I see. He is drowning and I am describing the water.

WHERE THE FUCK IS THE CHOPPER?

The CO drives up, he comes over, but even he stands back from this. This kid is in my hands. This kid who inherited a room I moved out of last night. Who was so FUCKING happy that I left all my beautiful women pictures still on the wall. So that when he moved in, they were all there all ready. He inherited the best room on the FOB, and he was so excited when I gave him the key. And now he is spitting out long bloody mucus spit. Trying not to talk and gripping my fucking hand like a lifeline . . . tightening against the pain.

He is thirsty . . . "Casualties exhibiting signs of shock should not be given water." I can't give him water, but he is dry and his mouth is full of blood. I give him water to rinse with and watch carefully that he doesn't swallow it. I don't even know what is coming out of my mouth. It is just a litany of comfort words. I just want to see him keeping nodding along. I just want to see this kid stay conscious. Blonde hair blue eyes. He looks at least 5 years younger than he is. How can I call him a kid? I've got two years on him. And somehow I have to save this kid, tell everyone how to save him.

CHOPPERS! FUCKING THANK GOD!

Dust-off coming in . . . Dust and shit blow all over him. The CA sergeant and I huddle together trying to block the wind off the casualty, try to keep the shit from getting in his wounds. Try to keep him safe.

Too late.

This is his dust-off and that is Iraq trying to get its last hit in.

Everyone is trying to move, to do something. Trying to get a hand in to help. They want to get him moving to the chopper right away. I tell everyone to wait; the flight doc will come to us to assess him before he puts him on. Inside of a minute I am trying to rattle off everything on the flight med. Trying to give him my burden. Finally, a trained professional, finally someone who can help, can save this kid.

HELP HIM!

My voice is more level than I could have ever guessed; I take charge of telling him what is wrong. The Doc looks at him for all of 5 seconds, nods, and starts to give the orders I crave, how to load this kid away on that life-saving bird. I leap to it. I feel almost vindicated because he seemed to accept what I said. I still have no idea exactly what I said to him. We pick up the stretcher and range walk to the chopper. He is loaded away, and with barely a parting glance the doors shut and we clear the bird to let it rise. When I load a casualty away, I always watch the bird fly. I am backing away watching it take off, squinting against the dust . . . and my stomach settles. All my emotions return. I am shaken and shaking.

Everyone is trying to say that I did a good job.

FUCK THAT!

Everyone is saying good work.

FUCK THAT!

Everyone is saying it is ok.

FUCK THAT!

Everyone is asking are you ok?

Yeah. I'm fine. I'm fine. I'm fucking fine.

NO I AM NOT FUCKING FINE!

I don't say that.

I say, "I'm fine. I'll be on the gun."

I'm so pissed. I kick the water bottle he was drinking out of across the yard. No one says anything to me about it. I am on the verge of tears. I'm fine.

I gather up that kid's torn DCU blouse and toss it in the Humvee. I'm not fucking fine. It is covered in blood.

I am not FUCKING FINE.

So much shit, on shit, on shit, on shit.

FUCK RAMADAN. FUCK SUICIDE BOMBERS. FUCK. JUST FUCK.

I ride the gun, because I want some time to think. I ride the gun so no one can look directly at me if I break.

I ride the gun, so if the opportunity presents itself, if there is a call, then I can cause the absolute maximum damage possible.

I want to cleanse myself in fire.

And yet the opportunity doesn't come. I want to make someone pay because that kid was 20 with a girlfriend younger than him.

Because, for all I know, he may never see again.

Because I had to be there.

Because I can see so many things I should have done differently.

Because his hand was holding mine, and that tears me apart.

Because there is so much shit on me.

Finally, I am back in my little cell. I am safe, relatively.

My command from highest to lowest is telling me "good job" and talking about an award (for me) and all I can think is that I fucked up somewhere and that he is paying. I don't know how exactly, but I am sure I did. I am not all right. But I'm not gone either. I'm still here. I'm not whole yet . . . but I'm not shattered. I want things simple, where I can go out and fight. Fight back against this. For most soldiers, there is no fighting for country. No fighting for money. No fighting for god. There is only fighting for each other.

Because we are all in this shit together.

I am back in the closest thing I have to a home. They tell me the kid will be all right. He will live. He will go back to Germany. He will see again. He took shrapnel to both eyes and his sinuses on one side. I don't know if I did all the right things, but at least he pulled through. But as for an award, I can't see it. I don't know what I could say to it. I can't really deal with the praise. I can't deal with . . . I don't know. I need to stay busy, and I think that is what I will be doing the next few days. Try to make sense of my thoughts.

But for now . . . I think I should just shower, and go to sleep.

, ⸴ ⸴

One of the greatest facets of the American military is its esprit de corps. It is a bond that American fighting men and women share: a sense of unity of purpose. It applies to many different kinds of battle-fields, including the combat hospital operating room. Below is an account that was published on *Blackfive* by an infantry battalion sur-geon, Dr. (Major) Kevin Cuccinelli, about how 113 soldiers struggled to save one of their own—"Saving Specialist Gray":

, ⸴ ⸴

While the daily headlines report that we need more soldiers in Iraq, I know one soldier that would disagree. For 22-year-old Specialist Roy Alan Gray, there were more than enough soldiers here when the task at hand was to save his life.

Specialist (SPC) Gray is a member of the 1-8 Infantry Battalion, 3rd Brigade Combat Team, 4th ID, otherwise known as the "Fighting Eagles." On September 8, 2003, he was part of a convoy delivering the coveted "hot dinner" [the one meal that was not an MRE] to his battal-ion's headquarters (HQ) area. SPC Gray had just returned to his truck when a mortar round exploded only 30 feet away. Shrapnel from the mortar pierced the truck's metal door and cut up through his left thigh. Smaller shrapnel bits lodged in his shoulder and ear. The leg wound, however, proved to be life-threatening.

At his location was the forward-deployed aid station for his unit. The medics acted quickly, called for an Air MEDEVAC immediately, and attended to his injuries while the helicopter was en route. The medics initiated this care as more mortars continued to impact around them. They started 2 IVs and began pouring fluid into him. His thigh wound still bled profusely even after their initial treatments so the medics quickly opted for a tourniquet, a common last-resort measure. The tourniquet stopped most of the bleeding by blocking all blood flow to his injured leg. While this greatly increased the chances that he would lose his leg, it stopped the more immediate threat of massive blood loss, thereby saving his life. The surgeons would later report that if not for the medics' immediate response, SPC Gray would have been dead on arrival (DOA) by the time he made it to the hospital.

Meanwhile, the MEDEVAC team from the 54th Medical Company, Air Ambulance (UH60, Blackhawk helicopter crew) was already en route to SPC Gray's location. From the time they received the call to landing at the site, they clocked 25 minutes. This includes the mandatory 18 minutes to prep the helicopter, chart their location, and load up. It was only a 5-minute flight, which means the crew was ready to go, from a dead stop, in less than 2 minutes. They did a quick assessment of the tight surroundings and set it down in the only open area, immediately in front of the HQ building. The medics quickly loaded SPC Gray onto the helicopter for the short trip to the 21st Combat Support Hospital (CSH).

The CSH (referred to as the CASH) is no ordinary hospital. Designed for field environments and quick mobility, it is comprised of numerous long insulated tents attached to one another to form a series of wings. Resources are minimal and cleanliness is a constant battle in the sand-covered country of Iraq. Less than 15 minutes after hitting the door, the ER staff completed a rapid assessment and SPC Gray was on the operating room table being treated and stabilized.

The medical staff knew all too well that death was imminent. They started the emergency medical board process, done to ensure that his family back in Iowa received maximum benefits. They didn't think he would live the 3 hours required to complete the board. He had lost almost all of his blood. Hemoglobin and Hematocrit, lab tests that measure blood levels, were at critical levels of 1.6 and 6.2, respectively. Normal levels are approximately 15 and 45. His blood pressure to perfuse his vital organs was unstable but being maintained with the initial IV fluid push.

Now the doctors and nurses began blood transfusions. They also cleaned out his wound and began antibiotics to help ward off infections. SPC Gray is now breathing through a tube hooked to a ventilator. He is receiving medicine for sedation and pain. He is then transferred to the Intensive Care Unit (ICU) wing of tents where he received round-the-clock attention from the staff, who managed all his medications, ventilator, fluid balance, blood transfusions, IV fluid replacement, wound care and labs.

Thus begins the intense monitoring of his status. Immediate lab results continue to reflect significant bleeding. The source of the bleeding is still unclear. Was it more open blood vessels or his body's reaction to the donated blood? At times his bleeding was faster than the replacement. The decision was made to again take him back to the OR for exploration as to the source of bleeding. While the wound left a hole in his thigh large enough for surgeons to fit their hands through, the largest artery, vein, and nerve were amazingly undamaged. His condition was tenuous.

SPC Gray's continued blood loss soon led to the problem of replacement. The hospital staff became concerned that they would not have enough. To make matters worse, the red blood cells and plasma he was receiving represent only a portion of all the substances in our "whole" blood. Platelets, another portion, which are necessary to clot blood, were not available in the blood bank. These levels had also dropped to critical levels.

As supplies ran low, the doctors began an impromptu blood drive. They simply walked from room to room in the hospital asking for personnel with O positive blood. Every available person with O+ blood capable of donating did not hesitate to do so.

Additionally, SPC Gray's company commander, CPT Kevin Ryan, rapidly mobilized the soldiers of his company, known as "Team Hammer." He and I returned from the hospital to brief the worried soldiers that were his co-workers and friends. They were notified that SPC Gray was likely going to die, but that the people taking care of him were doing everything possible to give him a fighting chance. This included the need for blood, which the hospital did not have enough of. Everyone with O+ blood was asked to go to the hospital and donate. We stay to answer some questions and return to the hospital less than 5 minutes later. To our surprise, we find 30 soldiers already lined up outside the lab ready to donate. This group also included members of the North Dakota National

Guard whom CPT Ryan had called for help. None of them knew SPC Gray personally. They simply knew what uniform they shared.

Now that a large source of blood donors was available and 12 more hours passed without improvement in his stability, he was taken to the OR for a 3rd time. It was only after a third trip to the OR that doctors were able to determine the source of the continued bleeding. They were less delicate this time, opening the wound wider to enlarge the exposed area. Tissue was sacrificed in deference to the ultimate goal. They finally located the source: a "pumper" coursing backwards, hidden behind the bone and buried beneath most of the tissue in his thigh. Doctors quickly tied it off. Other slow seeping bleed sources were cauterized (burned). And, as a final effort to stop the blood loss, doctors applied a new substance, called "Quick Clot," in a non-conventional fashion. They spread it over the surface to concentrate the blood seepage, thereby assisting with the wound's overall ability to clot. It is not typically used in this manner, but the surgeons wanted to take all precautions.

Two hours later, for the 1st time in 36 hours, SPC Gray's blood levels were stable without getting any additional blood products. The nurses continued to check frequently. The next lab results were even higher. His blood pressure was no longer falling and he did not need medication to maintain it. Other indicators of organ perfusion and function were also good. His clotting indicators improved and stabilized. His kidneys were working. A pink hue returned to his face. He required lower doses of medications. His blood pressure and pulse normalized.

In the early morning hours of September 11, the Air Force transported SPC Gray to Baghdad and shortly afterwards to Landstuhl, Germany. Still unconscious and reliant on a respirator, his condition remained critical. His parents were flown in to be by his side. The medical staff at Landstuhl continued his care and treatment, cleaning his wounds, treating infection and monitoring his condition until September 24, when he was flown to Walter Reed Army Medical Hospital in Washington, D.C. On September 27, he regained consciousness to discover all the fuss he caused. His broken leg will require further care. He still has much ahead of him.

A total of 47 units of blood products were given. Our bodies have about 6 liters of blood; therefore, this represents approximately 2 complete replacements of his blood supply. This does not include the 24 liters of IV fluid he received, representing another 4 total volume replacements. Sixty-one people were on the blood drive, including members of his unit, soldiers he didn't know from other units, medical staff taking care of him and others who just heard about the situation.

By all accounts, SPC Roy Gray should not have survived. Had he not been injured right next to his aid station, or his fellow soldiers and medics not raced out to his aid, or the helicopter not arrived in time, or the doctors not been able to find the source of his bleeding, or the blood drive not succeeded, then you would have heard that we lost another soldier on the evening news back home. Instead, by last count, 113 people took direct part in the care of SPC Gray from point of injury to his evacuation from Iraq. It took that many "cogs in the wheel" to accomplish this improbable save. There were many individual cogs, that if any failed, SPC Gray would have died.

Keep in mind that this count does not include the second Blackhawk crew that flew him to Baghdad, the C-130 aircraft crew that flew him to Germany, and his hospital staff there, or his final flight crew that returned him to Washington, D.C., so that yet another medical staff can nurse him back to health. This number does not include those who indirectly supported his care, such as hospital personnel who keep the hospital running, flight coordinators, supply personnel, etc. What about keeping all these people fed, sheltered and paid? Who made sure all the equipment in the ER/OR/ICU was stocked and available for use? Who kept all the vehicles involved in working order? Who is helping the families back home?

SPC Gray's case is representative of the esprit de corps of those in uniform out here in Iraq. There are many people involved in keeping us alive and working for freedom in Iraq that are never seen. The Army's doctors, nurses, medics, pilots, crews, lab techs, National Guard soldiers, and airmen are, more often than not, in a combat support role, much like SPC Gray. They too risk their lives, left their families and friends, and sacrifice. They are not likely to be the ones that find Saddam. They do not man the checkpoints or conduct the raids, but they do see the casualties. They understand truly that "Freedom isn't free" and witness its price. They can only stare at the daily horrors of the war and negotiate for a lower price. They spend all day, every day, attempting to get all the SPC Grays home to their families, alive and well.

Interestingly enough, on September 8, the national news back home reported "There was little action in Iraq today . . ."

The following persons saved SPC Roy Alan Gray's life:

1-8 Infantry, Forward Aid Station:
MAJ Wayne Slicton, 1LT Kyle Chowchuvech, SGT Steven Welch, SGT Sean Burns, SGT Curtis Driver, SGT John Gazzola (64th FSB), SPC Cory Sheldon, PFC Michael O'Shaughnessy, PV2 Earl Bennett

54th Medical Company, Air Ambulance, Blackhawk crew:
CPT Price, WO1 Walters, SGT McGovern, SPC Rafiq

21st Combat Support Hospital ER staff:
CPT David Coffin, CPT Emma, CPT Johnson, CPT Winn , 1LT Bishop, SGT Aquino, SGT Fisher, SPC Burrell, SPC Doetzer

21st Combat Support Hospital OR staff (3 shifts):
MAJ King, MAJ White, CPT Rathjen, CPT Ritter, 1LT Kosterbader, SGT Emerick, SGT Longfoot, SPC Ontivarios

21st CSH Doctors:
COL Kilburn, LTC Endrizzi, LTC Kim Kessling, MAJ Olsen, MAJ Doug Boyer, MAJ Matt Brown

21st CSH ICU:
MAJ Gorren-Good (GG), CPT Kate Carr, CPT Jen Florent, CPT Pulliam, 1LT Brandt, 1LT Krans, SGT Norman, SGT Troy Smith

21st CSH Lab:
SGT Stanley Taylor, SGT Larry Harrod, LT Reynaldo Torres, SPC Christian Chavez. SSG Antoine Smith. SPC Jordan Uzzo, SPC Mario Flores-Bautista, SPC Jason Williams, PFC Andrew Craig

1-8 IN Chaplaincy:

CPT Leif Espeland, CPT Dallas M. Walker (21 CSH), CPL Jesse Whitaker

Blood Donor Volunteers:

CPT Janice Follwell, 1LT Reynaldo Torres, SPC Jordan Uzzo, SGT Erick Cedeno, MAJ Douglas Boyer, COL Robert Lyons, PFC Thomas Watson, CPT Dallas Walker, SSG Raeby Malone, SGT Albert Juarez, Bryan Goff, 1LT Gregory Hotaling, CPT Kevin Ryan, CPL Simon Benkovic, SPC Matthew Harmon, SPC Shane Bartrum, PFC Kenneth Griffin, SGT Andrew Casebolt, Robert Henderson, CPL Chad Pecha, SPC Michael Marin, CPL Christopher OHearn, SPC Steven Haston, Brian Finney, PFC Ezra Davis, Jaime Martinez, SPC David Marron, SSG Ryan Miller, PFC Aaron Taylor, SPC Adam Gajewski, CW2 Wayne Fylling, Kevin Kerner, Charles Monson, Chad Vinchattle, Kevin Slagg, Cory Cavett, David Aldrich, Michael Gross, SPC Nicole Jochim, Vanessa Imdieke, David Drehn, SPC Curtis Petrick, SPC Derek Lennick, SGT Bracston Mettler, PFC Carmichael Gilespie, SSG Dwayne Hickman, CPL Jessica Larriba, CPL James Geah, SPC Jerry Nowell, SGT Tyler Berry, PFC Blondene Leys, SPC Lenroy Millet, SPC Dwayne Cooper, SPC Brandon Curran, PFC Adam Taylor, Carson Stringham, SPC Bullard, SSG Z Tumamad, PFC Jeremy Waldie, SPC Aenoi Phommachanh, SPC Richard Kern

CHAPTER FOUR

LEADERS, WARRIORS, AND DIPLOMATS

Leadership in a democratic army means firmness, not harshness; understanding, not weakness; justice, not license; humaneness, not intolerance; generosity, not selfishness; pride, not egotism.

—GENERAL OMAR N. BRADLEY

Of the vast array of weapons used in the War on Terror, most are corporeal and ominous. There are JDAMS, HEAT, and Hellfire, to name just a few bombs, tank rounds, and missiles. But there are also weapons that are not so deadly in name or function and not so pernicious in their delivery. However, they are just as effective and important in winning battles and the war.

"Small spheres of influence" are what today's combat leader wields in addition to firepower, teamwork, and training.

Every leader fighting the War on Terror must make many decisions, some that may seem small at the time, that will not only result in life or death, but will affect the outcome of the overall war effort. Combat leadership can be the toughest and loneliest job in the world. It can also be the most satisfying.

In every opportunity for contact with the civilian populations of Iraq and Afghanistan, positively influencing the conduct of the war can be as important as fighting and destroying the enemy.

Captain Danjel Bout, "ThunderSix" from *365 and a Wakeup*, served as a California National Guard battalion staff officer assigned to the

3rd Infantry Division before getting the chance to command an air assault infantry company in Iraq. He was a witness to Election Day in Iraq, where he saw democracy in action and the determination of American soldiers to save the life of a little girl:

, , ,

With dawn still several hours away the first stirrings of life appeared, the new day heralded by the collective groan of tired soldiers pushing aside dusty poncho liners. For most it had been a brief and quite unsatisfying sleep, more of a nap than anything approaching slumber. But the shared experience of suffering has a power all its own, and rather than roll over and get more rest our element moaned and bitched its way to wakefulness. After a few minutes the wry jokes settled into a dull murmur and we started packing our vehicles with the small mountain of equipment we had shuttled out with us. A few soldiers collected up our trash, collecting it in a small mound that they burned to ash. By the time they were finished all that was left as evidence of our brief occupation was a large pile of bottled water we left for the Iraqi police and soldiers.

Having finished our haphazard packing (if you have ever seen an Infantry unit pack a vehicle in the dark you might suddenly understand why everything is over-engineered) we rotated the security elements and waited for dawn. The election officials were supposed to arrive shortly after dawn, and as the sun climbed ever higher in the sky I started to wonder if they were going to arrive at all. The poll opening hour was rapidly approaching when a small white sedan plastered with election placards snapped around a corner. As the Iraqi soldiers checked the election vehicle our security elements pulled off station and we started mounting our vehicles. The poll workers were all men in their late 20s, neatly dressed in slacks and collared shirts, and as they approached they greeted us with wide smiles and warm English greetings. As the election officials started unloading the boxes of election material I walked over to my Iraqi security counterparts and once again gave them solemn assurances that we would not abandon them. I'm not sure if the bright, clear air of morning burned away their anxieties

or if our lengthy conversations the night before had bolstered their confidence, but I sensed some subtle change in demeanor. As I turned
away I was confident these men would give the last full measure to
ensure the election went smoothly.

We separated into two separate elements and took up stations several hundred meters from the election site. As the polls opened a
steady trickle of Iraqi citizens made their way towards the election site.
Since all vehicle traffic had been shut down to prevent VBIEDs they
came on foot, crossing the fields, weaving through the palm groves,
and loping down the vacant streets. They came in small smiling groups,
and when they noticed us in overwatch they waved with wide, open
smiles. There was no common feature that tied together these mean-
dering groups other than their common destination. Some were
dressed in the traditional Dishka as if they were conjured out of some
ancient Arabian fable. Others were dressed in neat western-style clothing that wouldn't have looked out of place in any American business.
And still others came out in jeans, sandals and gaudy American t-shirts.
Grandfathers walked with sons. Mothers came with children in tow.
Friends came in chattering groups brimming with bravado.

That was how we spent our morning, watching a steady stream of
Iraqis wave as they walked to the polling center, and then smile and hold
up their ink-stained thumbs as they returned. The entire area swam with
motion as Iraqis came from kilometers away to cast their vote. As the
sun reached its burning apex one of the Iraqi soldiers ran over with a
grave look on his face. He spilled a torrent of words, urgently motioning
for me to follow him. I took a small detachment to the outer perimeter, a
wall of concrete barriers a couple hundred meters from the polling site,
and was met with an anxious group of Iraqi soldiers. As I walked over
there I expected I would have to listen to pleas for additional ice, or
some other creature comfort. What they had to say took me by surprise,
and I felt embarrassed at my callous guessing game. The reason they
had called me over was to express concerns that one of the election officials was trying to sway the voters in the polling center. As they laid out
their case their eyes burned with passion and their voices trembled with
emotion. It was only then, seeing these soldiers aflame with a desire to

have a free and fair election, that I truly understood how committed these men were to their fledgling democracy. I had one of the Iraqi policemen collect up the election supervisor and the poll worker in question and as they arrived the soldiers let loose a heated verbal salvo. I motioned for them to stop for a moment, and as they lapsed into silence I explained to the supervisor how critical it was to remain impartial. The poll worker lowered his head in an obvious expression of shame, and the supervisor promised to keep a close eye on his staff. They walked back to the election building, and the soldiers seemed convinced that my impromptu civics lesson would cow the passionate poll worker into a semblance of impartiality.

As the afternoon heat flared I started seeing groups walk away with the water bottles we had left with the soldiers, and I walked over to the perimeter to see if everything was all right. They told me that they had plenty of water, and that they wanted to share it with the people who were walking great distances in order to vote. All of these soldiers were Shia, and all of the voters were Sunni, but that didn't matter to them. For on this day sectarian concerns faded away like the morning mist, and all the Iraqi soldiers could see was Iraqi citizens in need of a cool drink. For the second time in the day I was impressed and slightly humbled by these soldiers I had been so concerned about the prior evening.

The afternoon was no different from the morning, and voters continued to make their way to the polling site in spite of the oppressive heat. In our small position soldiers took turns on the heavy weapons scanning for threat that never materialized. And then it was over. The election officials packed the ballots into their small sedan and piled into it like it was a circus clown car. As they left the site we pulled out of our overwatch positions and reassembled on the election site. As I stepped out of my HMMWV [Humvee] I noticed an Iraqi soldier carefully cutting down the election banner. I snapped a picture of him holding up the banner and then watched him carefully fold the banner. Once he had done so he walked over and placed it in my hands saying "Take, take— thank you for you protecting Iraq democracy." His tongue stuttered on some of the unfamiliar consonants, but his message carried so much weight I almost staggered backwards. His words washed away all the miseries we had suffered over the last few days, replacing it with a deep sense of pride at what my men had helped accomplish.

As we waited for the armored vehicles to pick up the Iraqi soldiers the atmosphere burned with a sense of joy that is hard to express in words. American soldiers wrapped their arms around Iraqi soldiers and mugged for pictures. Iraqi soldiers let their American counterparts take pictures holding their AK-47s. One of the younger soldiers danced a clumsy jig in the empty street, flanked by Iraqi soldiers dancing to a tune only they could hear. Even the hardest of our NCOs had to crack a smile at this strange pageant.

A few minutes later the vehicles arrived and the Iraqi soldiers happily piled on. Our vehicles settled into formation and we started back towards the link-up site where we would meet the rest of our company.

At our link-up site the rest of our company was busy packing the last of their gear into their waiting vehicles, all traces of fatigue eclipsed by the tantalizing thought of returning to the FOB. The deliberate packing that had been slowly occurring all afternoon suddenly ended, replaced with an avalanche of boxes and bags hurriedly stuffed into the cargo bays of waiting M1114s [armored Humvees]. Finally, with all the material loaded into the overfilled HMMWVs the clamshell doors over the cargo bays creaked shut, and the soldiers scurried back to the sheltered alcoves of the main building.

The scattered conversations were suddenly muted by the sharp, angry bark of automatic weapons fire. The flat, ugly crack of AK-47 fire creased the night air, as if some monstrous rattlesnake had been stirred to wrath. But once the initial shock wore off most of the troops continued with their conversations. For all its fury this frenzied burst of gunfire was too far away to pose any kind of threat. As the firing was dying down, SPC Spartan heard a soft hiss, so gentle and short it seemed like an auditory phantom. He paused in midsentence, trying to get a bearing on the sound, but the night had swallowed the noise. On the other side of the building SSG Rock heard the same sound, followed in turn by another, and yet another. The sounds were so brief and so silent they barely reached the threshold of hearing. They were fragile unformed sounds plucked from the air before they were ripe—amounting to little more then a few sighs of air too weak to influence anything of substance.

As our soldiers finished their preparations to leave, a small Iraqi family a few houses away was settling around their dinner table to share Iftar. Iftar isn't just a dinner, it is the meal that breaks the daily fast required during the month of Ramadan. If you have ever gone without food or water for a day you have an idea of the joy, gratitude and kinship this single meal can bring rushing to the surface. Midway through dinner a stranger arrived, heralded by the same muffled hiss that had caught our soldiers' attention. It was the sound of a plunging bullet.

Far, far from this little table someone had raised their rifle into the air, switched the selector switch onto fire, and pulled the trigger. Whether their fire was celebratory, an angry warning, or a shot fired in anger we will never know. All we do know is that those deadly, arrow tipped rounds were suddenly rammed down the barrel of an AK-47 by the explosive expansion of propellant, and finding themselves in the open air they soared into the night sky. As the rounds clawed their way towards the black star-stained vault their momentum was bled away by the relentless tug of gravity, until they reached their bitter apogee and the implacable force jealously bent them earthward. As they hurtled back towards the ground they picked up some of their initial velocity, whipping through the air with deadly force. As the rounds crashed to earth they left soft hisses in their wake, as if the air in their wake was mysteriously transformed into a ghostly serpent. This gentle hiss was the sound that had caught the attention of a few of the soldiers, only to be shrugged off as some auditory hallucination.

The bulk of the rounds vanished into oblivion, the only trace of their existence the soft rustles of twisted air. But one solitary round left a more lasting memory—arcing down in an evil trajectory that brought it crashing down onto a roof. This simple, shoddy roof, designed to deflect little more then a mild winter storm, instantly yielded to the brute force of this fated projectile. And this is how a stranger arrived at this small celebration of Iftar . . . a stranger that tore into the happy, beaming face of a 10-year-old girl.

A ghastly scream tore through the darkness, a ghastly, painful cry plumbed from the very depths of a mother's heart. That shriek of terror and loss seemed to hang in the air for several seconds, only to be replaced with the hysterical sobs of the girl's family. All conversations came to an instantaneous halt, and in those terrible seconds security teams scanned the area for the origin of this calamitous, heart-wrenching sound. And then one of the sentries cried out "Medic!" Our two combat medics had already grabbed their gear, and the second they heard the cry they leapt into action. As they ran out front they instantly spotted the anguished father carrying his bleeding daughter outside into the street and sprinted over.

The father placed his daughter down, entrusted his daughter to our medics, and as he rose he revealed a shirt stained with bright, hot blood. The girl was dying right in front of them, her lifeblood pouring into the dusty street. Sizing up the enormity of their task SGT James T shouted out "Medevac!" and one of the Platoon Sergeants started making coordination over the net.

As this was all unfolding our convoy was steadily making its way toward the link-up site. As we approached we received an order to halt in place, and the radios crackled out an ominous message: "We need the medevac site clear." Any residual joy we might have felt bled away in the next heartbeat, and every soldier wondered just what the hell was going on a couple of hundred meters away.

The medics worked feverishly to stabilize the little girl, but her lifeless body was pumping out blood at a hideous rate. Their skilled hands worked feverishly to keep her crumpled body from pouring out any more blood, and in the next few minutes they managed to stabilize her frail form. This ghastly tableau was suddenly interrupted by the powerful growl of a Blackhawk helicopter on a crash descent. The rotors kicked up a tornado of dust as the bird settled down, and the medics used their own bodies to shield their patient from the sand blast. The second the medevac helicopter hit the ground the medics and the flight nurse picked up her tiny frame and loaded her into the chopper, and just as quickly as it had arrived it left. Leaving behind a tortured family, a shocked platoon, and two brave and blood-stained medics standing next to a pool of scarlet.

After a long pause the soldiers shook off their momentary daze and started to load into the vehicles—we still had to link up and make our way back to the FOB. Our convoy got the clearance to move, and we made our way to the rotor-scoured asphalt that had just served as a medevac site. The rest of the company finished loading into their vehicles and we started back to the FOB in one long, silent convoy. Our joy was tempered by the cruel twist of fate we had just witnessed, but not the pride. That still burned bright. I imagine it will for quite some time.

The little girl, Mala, survived long enough to make it onto the medevac bird, and then she left our protectorship. When the helicopter whisked her away at full combat power she disappeared from sight, but not from our memory. The minute we arrived back in the barracks the commander jumped on the line and made a call to the CASH (Army Combat Hospital) to find out if Mala was still alive. The nurse on the other end of the line told him that Mala was in surgery, and that we could call back at midnight to find out if she'd survived the surgery. The last couple days had worn us to the bone, but instead of succumbing to sleep the company leadership waited for the time to crawl by. The evening quietly slipped by, the small coffee pot set up in our command post straining to keep up with this sudden spike in demand. The coffee was hot and nourishing, but it did little to lift the tension that fogged the room. A little before midnight, unable to wait any longer, we made a second call to the CASH. In a cool, professional tone the nurse on duty told us that Mala was in ICU. Something about our tone must have hinted at the storm of emotion on our end of the line, and taking pity she added, "She is going to make it." As the news spread though the barracks everyone breathed a deep sigh of relief. Then, with our concern slaked, we all crawled into our bunks to get some desperately needed rest.

The next morning brought even better news. The bullet had broken her jaw and nicked her carotid artery, but despite the agonizing injuries she was awake and alert. Hearing this news we decided that, instead of our usual patrol, we would return to Mala's home and escort her family to the CASH. Although it was still early in the morning when we arrived at the small home, Mala's extended family told us her parents were already making their way to the CASH to see their daughter. We loaded into HMMWVs and made our way to the International Zone (IZ), hoping to link up with Mala and her family. As we entered the hospital there was no sign of the family, but when we got to the ICU ward we found Mala's family anxiously waiting for her in the hallway. They were as silent and grave as marble statues. That all changed the moment they recognized us. In an instant they had returned to life, and they started to shower us with blessings and tear-filled praise. We looked around sheepishly, uncomfortable with this sudden outpouring of praise. A few of the soldiers looked through the ICU door to see Mala for themselves, seeing instead her father anxiously signaling for us to join him. We walked over to Mala's father, and as we did Mala came into sight in the hospital bed behind him. She was awake, and as we walked up she gave us a tired, thin smile. We had brought some stuffed animals along to cheer up the antiseptic sterility of the room, and her eyes flared with joy when we placed them at the foot of her bed. As we were arranging the stuffed animals SGT James T., the medic that had worked so hard to save little Mala, came into the room. Although the young sergeant was making an earnest attempt to maintain some semblance of medical detachment, he beamed like a new father at the birth of his first child. Mala didn't recognize him, but he wasn't looking for praise or thanks. He just wanted to know that his little patient would survive her terrible wounds. We didn't want to tire out Mala by extending our stay, and, once we were convinced she was going to make it, we left the room. We said our good-byes to the grateful family, made our way to the vehicles, and returned to the FOB.

Ten years from now, our unit will have long since passed out of local memory, the desert swallowing any physical trace of our year in the Land of the Two Rivers. But there will be one living, beating heart that will bear testament to our company's mission and the good we tried to do. And right now that somehow seems enough.

, , ,

Colonel Austin Bay was a syndicated columnist, author, wargame designer, professor, and blogger at *austinbay.net* before being called up a reservist to go to Iraq. One of his routine missions was to travel between Baghdad's Green Zone and the airport along eight kilometers of road known to the military as Route Irish—a route, at the time of Colonel Bay's tour, some had dubbed the most dangerous road in the world. Colonel Bay calls the trip to and from the airport "Route Irish Racing":

, , ,

"Sergeant Carlson. Go through the rehearsal one more time."

"Yes sir." Brian Carlson spun the wheel of the Ford Explorer hard left, coming off the dirt connecting strip onto the airport exit road.

"If we make contact and we go down," he said, beginning his recap of the Route Irish pre-op mantra, "we'll attempt to roll through it, through the contact. If we get through, your position will be the right rear or non-contact side of the vehicle. Get down behind the wheel, the non-contact wheel. I'll be in the front, with the rifle and flares. We'll figure out if the ambush is front or rear and lay suppression fire for the trail vehicle . . ."

I listened carefully, as I always listened when we left Baghdad International. In Baghdad commuting is a combat operation, for both soldiers and civilians. Thank Saddam's henchmen and Al Qaeda fascists, the beasts who've made suicide car bombs their primary murder weapon.

". . . and continue to cover the extraction," Carlson said.

I checked my helmet strap, checked the seatbelt clamping my Kevlar vest. I swiveled, making certain I could quickly swing right, to cover my sector and shoot if our two-vehicle convoy tripped an ambush.

As we passed the First Cav Bradley on the left I checked my pistol's safety. Red—dead red.

Carlson pushed the accelerator and said something to me. The gist of it was "Oh yes, sir, and if there's trouble with the extraction from contact"—but I didn't hear all of it. At sixty-two miles an hour air blasting through open windows becomes audio chaos and puts a hard clamp on conversation. But contact, if contact were a euphemism for active ambush triggered by gunmen, wouldn't last more than thirty seconds.

If we popped an IED in our unarmored Ford or—Good Lord—were struck by a car bomb, there would not be a "non-contact side."

I glanced at the speedometer. Carlson had nudged up to sixty-five. I looked back at our trail. Sergeant First-Class Klante matched our speed, hanging back a hundred meters as Carlson jinked left into the fast lane then swerved right to pass a white sedan.

Baghdad, like Houston and Los Angeles, is built for wheels. Narrow side streets feed boulevards which feed expressways. Traffic moves day and night. This road net with a million vehicles is ideal terrain for an auto kamikaze. Roll up to a street corner and detonate—instant atrocity, instant headlines, with media coverage being the murderer's strategic goal.

"First overpass," Carlson shouted.

"Clear," I said, looking right for—for anything, a kid, a man, someone standing beside the wire.

The palm trees lining the freeway zipped by in a steady blur.

"Clear left," Carlson shouted.

I'd been up since oh-five-hundred, crashing on a project at Corps headquarters. We were heading for the US embassy downtown, which meant two heats of Route Irish racing, there and back via the eight kilometers of ambush expressway linking our base at Baghdad International Airport and the Green Zone. "The first heat's the easy one," I'd said a couple of days earlier, kidding one of our section's PFCs.

"Overpass," Carlson barked, jerking the wheel.

"Clear right," I yelled.

The SUV swerved from the center lane to the left lane, a move to frustrate any would-be rock or grenade hurler hiding on the overpass, a move to shake a could-be sniper in apartment buildings beyond the freeway's frontage road.

"Traffic right," I shouted. "Watch the squeeze."

Two sedans, one closing. Carlson goosed the accelerator and we hit seventy the same instant it came from the far right lane. A blue sedan with black side windows swerved towards us—the kamikaze targeting technique. Carlson floored it as I pivoted in the seat, pointed my pistol with a two-hand grip, started the squeeze but there is no space now this lane's too narrow—.

We shot past the sedan's enormous hood. In that short chasm—the broken second when I didn't pull the trigger—I absorbed the face of the sedan's frail driver: gray hair, gray mustache, hunched forward. An old man lost in a high-speed haze . . .

When heavily armed and armored men cram into Ford SUVs, jam the pedal to the floor and weave through freeway traffic at seventy miles an hour, film fans may think Road Warrior or the Keystone Kops. However, the Road Warrior's auto macho and the Kops' slapstick car chases are utterly misleading.

War in a sprawling, complex megacity isn't a movie that ends in two hours—it's a relentless experience where training, courage and discipline are constantly challenged by fear and adrenaline.

I didn't shoot. The right call—the right decision in trumps. Thank God.

But on Baghdad's streets the next Fiat or Mercedes may be a kamikaze. Or is it a family sedan, or that old man looking for an exit? As the car rushes forward the soldier—whose life is on the line—has a split second to decide.

,   ,   ,

Major E, a USAF Reserve Intelligence Officer assigned to the IED Task Force, was sent to Iraq and Afghanistan to hunt and destroy IEDs that plagued the roadsides. His dispatches as a combat correspondent have been posted on *Powerline*. Major E describes one of the quietest firefights ever to occur in Iraq and how one very wise sergeant utilized diplomacy in lieu of violence:

,   ,   ,

The last couple of days have been incredible. The elections went well and everyone seems excited yet exhausted. It is starting to sink in that yesterday's elections went really well, despite the best efforts of many.

The insurgents wanted desperately to terrorize voters on Election Day. Reportedly, their plan was to conduct probing attacks against various polling stations the night before the election, followed by attacks against the most vulnerable sites in the morning. Then, they would send video clips of those attacks to television networks such as Al-Jazeera, Al-Arabiyah and CNN, whose early Election Day broadcasts of the eye-catching videos might scare away many would-be voters—thereby depressing turnout and de-legitimizing the electoral process.

On the other hand, many were determined to see the elections through, including the Iraqi voters, the Iraqi police (IPs), and a US Army combat engineer named Sergeant 1st Class Sam Spangler. Spangler is a troop leader for the 91st Engineering Battalion out of Fort Campbell, Kentucky. A fifteen-year army veteran, Sparger's easy-going style and slight drawl are belied by the intensity in his eyes.

On the evening of January 29, we were standing outside near the vehicles and I was looking forward to going out on Sam's patrol. The 91st had been having success at decreasing the quantity and effectiveness of Improvised Explosive Device (IED) attacks in their West Baghdad area of operations (AO). So I would ride along as part of a roadside bomb task force to observe the related tactics, techniques and procedures (TTP) employed by the unit. The 91st has not only served a full tour in Iraq, but was extended in order to help out with the elections. Their experience in country and success against IEDs mean that there are a lot of lessons learned that could be gained from them and passed on to the troops that are just arriving in theater.

The soldiers strained to listen to Spangler's pre-mission brief, but the same noise seemed to come from every direction. Several nearby generators powered the floodlights that kept us out of the dark, while our Humvees warmed up for the mission. The closest comparison might be to go to the sound test room of·a giant stereo store, crank up the loudest system, and shout to the salesman, "Do you have this in diesel?"

We stood in ankle-high mud in a yet-to-be-paved part of Camp Victory as Sam described the mission ahead, referencing the likely insurgent plans to attack polling sites.

"We will mostly be floating around the AO, ready to support the IPs if they make contact—and they probably will."

Within five minutes of going outside the gate, a radio call proved him right. A reported firefight was taking place at a nearby polling station. One IP was already wounded. Our two groups of four armored Humvees rolled toward the site. While en route to the elementary school that had been transformed into a polling site over the last several days, we looked at imagery of the area and assessed the residential terrain. Spangler assigned different elements to secure various points and intersections around the school.

As we got closer, I noticed that the anticipation of contact with the enemy was making me feel thirsty and my heart seemed to beat faster. That nervousness converted to energy, though, when it was time to dismount. Moving into a hot area and preparing to stop resulted in competing questions dueling in my mind: "Why would anyone get out of a perfectly good, armored vehicle?" "At the same time, how 'perfectly good' is that same vehicle when an RPG hits?" It is a soldier's secret that the rocket-propelled grenade represents a powerful motivator for troops to move from their stopped vehicles.

About twenty soldiers moved out to take assigned positions. One troop and I moved to cover a residential intersection about 150 meters from the school. SFC Spangler walked toward the school to find the wounded policeman, while we stood at the intersection facing out, weapons ready, scanning the streets through night-vision goggles. After a few minutes, I caught my breath as my pulse started to slow. Fear shrank to curiosity.

Nothing was moving. Things were quiet.

Perhaps the enemy was regrouping. Or not.

Over the course of an hour or so of continued quiet, trying to figure out what was actually going on became too much for the troops. At one point, a young, male voice with a gentle Midwestern accent summed up the evening perfectly when he keyed his mike and said, "Pretty quiet for a firefight."

Yes, indeed. Actually, an Iraqi policeman had shot himself in the foot. There had been no firefight.

At that point, though, Spangler knew that, but those of us pulling security outside still did not. What turned out to be the entertainment of the evening was listening to his radio calls as he attempted to tell us the situation, so we could assume a more relaxed posture. His challenge, though, was to describe an accidental, self-inflicted gunshot wound without embarrassing the Iraqis, who had an English-speaking translator with the wounded IP.

"Well," rang Sam's voice into my earpiece, "the entry wound is just *above* the right ankle."

My colleague across the street and I exchanged big grins. With that, everyone basically realized what must have happened, since we have become accustomed to seeing Iraqis holding their AK-47 rifles, fully loaded, safety off, finger on trigger, with the barrel hanging toward their feet. Any one of these guys could be the poster boy for a "What Not to Do" weapons safety campaign.

Sam continued, "And, uhhh, the exit wound is, well, just *below* the right ankle . . . So, you guys copy? Ok, I think what happened is that his platoon was taking fire, he was in the prone position, and took a round from a shooter at an elevated position from about three o'clock. Maybe the shooter was on top of that three-story building over there." Moments later, he repeated the assessment, with a tone of "That's my story and I'm sticking to it."

A few minutes later, it was reported that an Iraqi ambulance was on its way. We returned to our vehicles and moved out, returning to base soon thereafter.

While SFC Spangler did not get a chance to lead his troops in combat that night, he performed well in another way: as a diplomatic communicator. While his report on the cause of the IP's gunshot wound may have surpassed the chuckle threshold for the troops, it kept things on good terms with the Iraqis. He managed to combine respect and creativity, even going so far as to create his own "Magic Bullet" theory, to avoid embarrassing the Iraqi Police, who on Election Day ended up losing some of their own while bravely protecting thousands of polling sites— and the millions of Iraqis who voted yesterday.

To Sammy Spangler, though, it was all in a day's work. Actually, it was his last workday in Iraq. He just sent me an e-mail saying that he will try to stop by to share a few more lessons learned before he departs the AO tomorrow. Nice going last night, Sam. Yours is a job well done by a man who is a gentleman, a soldier and, who knows, perhaps one day—a diplomat.

,　　,　　,

Influencing events to make sure that you are where you want to be can be tougher than you'd think. First Lieutenant Neil Prakash of *Armor Geddon* decided against medical school and opted for a military career. Prakash, a tank platoon leader in Iraq, had a large role in the Battle of Baquba. He writes of returning to Iraq from his two-week R&R in the States to find that he might not make it back in time to lead his platoon during the Battle of Fallujah:

,　　,　　,

I left Syracuse at 06:00 on November 2, 2004—Election Day for the United States. An auspicious day to begin a journey. I arrived in Kuwait on November 3 and had to spend the night there. It was frustrating. I asked if there was any way of getting to Iraq right now, maybe catch a bird on its way out delivering parts. There wasn't a man or woman anywhere in the world who wanted to get to Iraq as bad as I did right then and there . . . except for maybe a jihadist—and if that was the case, I had something for him. I was among the same group of people who had left Iraq to go on R&R at the same time I did. There were lieutenants that I was friends with and we were sharing R&R stories. But for me it was just a distraction. I couldn't stop thinking about hurrying this up. I wanted to grab them and say "I AM GOING TO FALLUJAH." The thought of it kicked so much ass. There were very few people who were going to be a part of this operation, but I was going to be one of them, hopefully. I did notice that 1LT Meier wasn't among the group. CPT Fowler had sent both of us on R&R so we would be back to command our platoons. He also sent 2nd Platoon's platoon sergeant. I didn't see either of them. Did they manage to get back early? How did they do it? *Dammit, I asked for CPT Fowler to get me back early.*

On November 4, our R&R group picked up our IBA body armor and kevlar helmets from a giant warehouse where we had turned them in before going home. We boarded our ship and flew on a C-130 cargo plane back into Iraq as scheduled. We had flown into Balad Air Base, or what the Army calls Logistical Support Area Anaconda. I had to spend the night there in tents and the anticipation grew. I was now among a few soldiers from Avenger Company who were sent on R&R just like me. Just a few sergeants and a PFC medic and a PFC tanker—PFC Kupitz. The few of us talked on and on about Fallujah and fed off of each other's energy. We wondered if we were going to make it in time. I decided to call 2-63 Battalion Headquarters at FOB Scunion using a DSN [Defense Switched Network, the military telephone system] phone. "2-63 Armor Battalion TOC, SGT Erwin speaking. Can I help you Sir or Ma'am?"

"SGT Erwin! It's 1LT Prakash. Listen man, I'm at Anaconda with a few other Avenger guys and some BRT [brigade reconnaissance troop] soldiers. Can you guys come get us? We're supposed to go to Fallujah with the company."

"Hey Sir! They already took off for Fallujah. They left from Warhorse yesterday. And the LOGPAC [logistics package] already left Anaconda and is headed back here."

"Ah shit! You gotta be kidding me?" I said, brokenhearted. Almost every day, Support Platoon took cargo HEMMTs, 5-ton trucks, and humvees back and forth from Scunion to Anaconda. It was the logistics package (LOGPAC) they carried. They hauled food, parts, and soldiers who were going to and coming from R&R. But it looked like that train already left the station.

"But listen Sir, the Colonel guaranteed that he would get you down to Fallujah. Avenger left a few guys behind that they weren't going to take. I think SGT Theiss, one of the engineers, is in charge. He's got the plan to square you guys away and get you guys down there."

"Awesome, thanks SGT Erwin, out."

I felt entirely satisfied. The task force just left yesterday for Fallujah. They would have to set up camp first, which would take a day or two. Then they would have to go over the plan, maybe do an "eyes on" reconnaissance of the city and then do rehearsals of the plan after that. I was looking at a good two or three days minimum before they would assault Fallujah. I wondered why the assault had gotten bumped up to begin with, though. I thought they were going to wait for Ramadan to end. Right now, Ramadan had just kicked off a few days ago.

The next day at 1300—November 5—Support platoon showed up with empty 5-ton trucks. In the back of the 5-ton was a wooden trunk filled with M9 pistols—our pistols we had left behind before taking leave. Before leaving FOB Scunion to go on R&R, we had turned our M4 and M16 rifles in to the company arms room. Then when we arrived at Anaconda, we gave our M9 pistols to the soldiers of our battalion who were dropping us off. Now they were returning them to us. I grabbed my pistol and holster and strapped it on. I noticed that someone stole one of my three magazines full of rounds. *Ah well,* like I've always joked—if it comes to the point where my tank and rifle are expended, then I'm already doomed.

We reached Scunion by 1500. I dropped my small assault backpack that I had taken with me on R&R in my room, and bumped into SGT Theiss in the hallway. He was disappointed that he wasn't able to go to Fallujah, but there just wasn't room for everyone in all of the vehicles. And furthermore, the company had to leave a detachment back here at FOB Scunion to take care of soldiers like me while the main body was gone.

"Sir, you need to link up with the guys in the TOC. They have some stuff for you. Here's the packing list for what they took to Fallujah. I think SFC Kennedy left some maps for you in your room. Let me know whatever you need. You guys will be flying out of Warhorse by bird to Fallujah."

"Thanks, SGT Theiss." I turned to the soldiers in my company who had come back with me from R&R. It was 6 of us—a couple of tankers, 2 sergeants and a medic. Since we were a gaggle of random soldiers in the company, I grabbed the senior sergeant of the two.

"SGT Scott, don't let any of these guys go anywhere. Priority number one, get all this shit packed. Then eat chow. And if there is time—shower. Eat as a group and make sure you know where everyone is. I don't know how much time we have before we get off this FOB." And with that, I sprinted to the battalion Tactical Operations Center.

The NCO in charge told me we had to catch a helicopter around midnight tonight and explained that I should try to catch a ride with someone who was going across the street to FOB Warhorse. The problem was that with Avenger Company gone, the other two companies were stretched thin. They had to pick up the slack left behind by our absence.

FOB Warhorse was only a literal stone's throw away from FOB Scunion, but we still had to take a minimum of two vehicles and four personnel to drive and command the trucks. Since we weren't coming back, we needed to find four guys who would volunteer to drive us over there and come back. With the operational tempo kicked up, it wasn't easy at all. Finally I ran into some mechanics who were ground-guiding a 5-ton truck.

"Yeah we're going to Warhorse to pick up some parts. We can give you a ride, Sir. We're gonna SP [start point] around 1800."

SHIT. That's two hours from now. "Sounds good, thanks a lot guys. We'll be standing by right outside Alpha Company barracks."

I sprinted back to the barracks to brief SGT Scott. "The bad news is that we have to be packed and downstairs ready to go in two hours. But the good news is that we will be going to Warhorse in time for dinner. Get the guys moving."

"They're already finished packing, Sir."

"Fucking sweet. Then if they want to shower, let them. But that's about it. Tell them they will all get a chance to call home when we get to Warhorse. They got better phones over there anyways. I don't care if they don't talk to their parents. They will tell *someone* that they are here."

We had less than two hours to empty my R&R gear and pack what we needed for Fallujah. A duffel bag with shirts, socks, PT gear, 2 boots, sleeping bag, 2 extra DCUs, and snivel gear for the cold. I gathered all of my sensitive items like my rifle and night vision goggles, which SGT Theiss had kept locked up. In my room, my platoon sergeant left a note for me on the white board that we always used for tasks and mission planning. It was wiped clean except for in big letters: "Pack your shit, check under your pillow, and get your ass to Fallujah."

Under my pillow, he left me all the maps, friendly graphics, and enemy graphics, and some intelligence reports. I was getting psyched. By 1800, the six of us were on a humvee to go across the street to FOB Warhorse. I walked into the Brigade TOC and met up with CPT Jon Boggiano. He explained that a CH-47 Chinook, the parts bird, was supposed to fly in from Anaconda carrying tank parts, pick us up, and take us to Fallujah at 2300.

We grabbed a delicious dinner at the dining facility. Warhorse was a brigade FOB so it was huge and had all of the important people. There were all kinds of brass here. And there were also Special Forces guys here, Air Force personnel, and tons of civilian contractors. There were also various Army units. Over at FOB Scunion, it was just our tank battalion, 2-63 AR. Such a big FOB like Warhorse was of course catered by KBR. They had fantastic meals and incredible variety. To me, it seemed just short of restaurant quality.

After dinner, we went over to the MWR trailer on FOB Warhorse which had the voice-over-internet protocol phones, internet, and a nice-looking living room set up with couches and lamps. A few soldiers were in there watching *Monsters Inc.* In another room, there were maybe eight TVs set up; four with XBOX, four with Playstation 2. A bunch of soldiers were in here going at it against each other in some combat video game. As I looked at all of these Warhorse soldiers who were assigned to this FOB, I would glance back at the faces of the soldiers who were with me. Even though some of them were just kids no older than 19 or 20 years of age, these Avenger soldiers seemed so much more significant to the cause than anyone else in that trailer, regardless of rank. All six of us signed in to use the phones and waited the 30 minutes or more that it took for a phone to free up. There was a little voice inside my head that wanted to butt into one of these Warhorse-based soldiers' conversations on the phone and say: *Excuse me, can you get off the phone? I've got real soldiers here who would like to use that phone. We're on our way to Fallujah and we're just passing through.* That voice was my ego, and with the work that we had done this far into the deployment and with the mission set before us, it was hard to keep those thoughts from just blazing through my mind. Yeah I know it's arrogant and conceited. But find me one Combat Arms soldier who doesn't think the army exists to support him in his mission—to close with and destroy the enemy.

After we all made our calls to our families, we regrouped outside of the Brigade TOC and stood by our duffel bags. All of our stuff was in a giant pile in a corner and we sat or lay down on top of the bags rather than sleep on the golf ball–size rocks on the ground. It was almost 2200 and we were expecting the parts bird in the next hour or so.

As I sat there in the dark with those soldiers, I gave away my excitement just from how restless my limbs were. Some of the soldiers were quiet, and that's when it dawned on me. Was it possible that some of these guys were scared? Was it possible that they didn't even want to go to Fallujah and that they feared the reality that they might die? It didn't even occur to me that someone wouldn't want to be a part of this. I decided to find the chaplain. I wasn't much on saying prayers or asking for God to help us out on this one. *If it's your time, it's your time,* SSG Terry said at least once a week. I had seen the chaplain earlier in the Brigade TOC and after tracking him down, I approached him.

"Hey Chaplain, how's it going? I gotta ask you for a favor. You know we're heading to Fallujah in just a little bit. I was wondering if maybe you could say a little prayer or give us a blessing. It might make the guys feel a little better," I asked. He obliged immediately.

It's a funny thing about chaplains. They are the most non-threatening soldiers in the Army. *Yeah, obviously, they're chaplains, stupid.* But that's not what I mean. Everyone knows that chaplains typically don't carry arms. What seems to make a chaplain great is that in my feeble two and a half year career in the army, every chaplain I've ever met has always been approachable. Chaplains always ask, "How you are doing, my son" and if everything is ok. That last part is very comforting. Nobody in the army calls you *my son*. Asshole, idiot, booger-eating moron, schlomo, knucklehead—those are more commonly thrown around. A chaplain is never going to chew you out. Even though we salute our chaplains, we're never expected to stand at attention when we talk to them. They are just simply comforting to have around. The only downside is that even though they never condemn us for it or even mention anything about it, I always feel bad when I say "god-dammit," "Jesus Christ," "shit," "fuck," and "hell" around a chaplain.

The chaplain stepped out of a tent flap with me and I gathered the soldiers around to hear his prayer. He didn't start off with a prayer but instead talking about something or other. The reason I have no recollection of what he said is because it seemed like complete rambling to me. I was completely expecting to hear something about "strength to carry these fine soldiers into battle" and "look after their families if it is this soldier's time" and so on and so forth. I guess that's the cool dramatic sequence found only in Hollywood. Instead he started talking to us about God knows what. Everyone did as I did and stared intently at the chaplain to hear his words. And although to this day I can't recall if he ever even said an actual prayer, for twenty minutes out of the past 96 hours, this small group of soldiers was liberated from the burden and anxiety that was building up while waiting for the parts bird. For a small slice of time, the chaplain put our minds at ease in that pitch-dark night with his calm voice.

A master sergeant from inside the TOC stepped out of the flap and almost stepped right on top of us.

"Gotta give those eyes time to adjust, Sergeant," I said.

"The parts bird isn't flying tonight," he replied. "They're saying it's too windy and it's causing too much haze with the sand and all. They'll pick you up tomorrow."

I swear something was trying to keep me out of Fallujah. "Dammit!" I cursed. "That fucking sucks." *Whoops, the chaplain.* "All right guys, I'm going inside to talk to a captain friend of mine. I'll be out shortly. Do you guys want to find a place to sleep or are you guys good here?" I asked.

PFC Hamilton, the medic, was already unrolling his sleeping bag and getting comfortable on the rocks and sand. "We're good here, Sir."

Everyone echoed Hamilton. "All right guys. Hardcore. Good shit. Then we'll just crash here," I said.

I walked inside the TOC and found CPT Boggiano. My only concern was: "What if I miss the LD [line of departure]? Once they cross into the city of Fallujah, how are they going to get me into the fight?" Right now, the whole Task Force was living on USMC Camp Fallujah prepping for the battle and we were stuck here. To take my mind off of that and to focus on what was important for me as a leader, I showed him my graphics that SFC Kennedy had given me. I wanted to be familiar with my ground. He had the same graphics, only larger, on butcher paper. We looked at the map and he pointed out how the city was divided into sectors. Some for the Marines, some for the 1st Cav, some more for the Marines, "and look what they gave to 2-2," he said. He showed me the east side of the city with little boxes at the top north edge of the city— they were little symbols for scouts, tankers, and mechanized infantry.

"Yeah, so?" I said.

"Let me show you the enemy SITEMP." He flipped the page. It was the same image as the map on the last page, only this time there were no little boxes at the top edge of the page. Instead, the entire page was covered in little red and yellow dots. At some locations, the dots over- lapped so badly that it looked like someone just splotched the page with red ink. It was the enemy situational template. Based on suspected and actual intelligence and confirmed reports, the S-2 (the intelligence shop) created an enemy SITEMP to give us an idea of what we were up against. "All these little dots are confirmed POOs (points of origin) of small arms and RPG attacks. These dots here are IEDs that have gone off historically. These are suspected IED and VBIED (vehicle-borne or car bomb) factories. These are bunkers that the enemy has dug. They plan to hide in these underground bunkers and tunnels, wait for the tanks and Brads to pass, and hit them in the rear." He also showed me fight- ing positions the enemy had created out of the barriers that the Marines had emplaced but abandoned months ago. There were enemy strong- holds in certain houses and kill zones created out of open spaces that we knew we would have to cross and probably occupy. "The Marines gave 2-2 the most dangerous sector in Fallujah."

That was fine with me. We were an armored task force, we had Bradleys. And we had tanks. We had the M1A1 Abrams Main Battle Tank with 120mm smoothbore cannon. We were going to be all right. I also doubted the enemy's ability to be patient enough to let us roll on by and shoot us in the ass. And this was coming from my personal experience in Baqubah on June 24th. Usually they just go crazy with jihad power, and in a suicidal mad dash for their 72 virgins, they come running at us or stand right in front of my tank as I wash them down with 7.62mm at 900 rounds per minute.

"Check out this video," he said. "This was just two days ago. And in the sector you guys are going to be in." We watched a black-and-white digital video on his laptop of a five-block section of the city clearly taken from a fighter jet. Suddenly there was a huge explosion. "That's the JDAM." I didn't even see it drop but I didn't miss the giant fireball and continued to watch. Suddenly, up and down the city block, smaller explosions went off to the left and right. The explosions continued to work their way around the dense row of buildings that was two or three blocks in length.

"Goddamn! Those are IEDs?!?" I was shocked at the sheer number. The entire city seemed to be rigged to blow. Immediately, an image of the movie *Black Hawk Down* came to mind. I pictured dismounts on either side of that neighborhood walking in the streets, just like when the Rangers were moving parallel with the enemy. "That would have wiped out an entire company!"

"Yeah, that JDAM was dropped because they were targeting that house as a stronghold. But when it hit, it set off all of the IEDs. Nobody was expecting that."

Damn, can you do that to the whole city, before we go in there? I wasn't really worried, though. I had already seen plenty of IEDs go off on my tank and I was no worse off.

"Pray for rain," he said to me as a final piece of advice. "The insurgents use cheap det[onation] cord and when it gets wet, the IEDs usually don't set off." The whole city was littered with more IEDs than probably anywhere else in Iraq. I wasn't surprised. The insurgents had gone 6 months unmolested within the city limits. Pray for rain. I should have asked the chaplain for that prayer. Because I was born in Bangalore, India, there was no doubt in my mind that, if my friend Chris was here, he would have just asked me to do an Indian rain dance.

When I finished talking with CPT Boggiano, I went back outside. Most of the men were lying on their duffel bags, some were curled up in their sleeping bags. A few were still awake and just as restless as me. I started to unroll my sleeping bag when some officer came outside.

"You guys need to find a tent to sleep in. You shouldn't sleep here."

"I don't know, Sir. Everyone seems pretty comfortable. And we should be leaving early tomorrow morning," I replied.

"No, you guys can't sleep here. There are scorpions on the ground. Go find some tents."

It was 03:00. I was pretty pissed. I wasn't in the mood to do the Duffel Bag Drag in the pitch black all over this giant FOB looking for a place to sleep. I wasn't too excited about waking up these soldiers either.

I gathered the group up and we searched around for a half hour until we found an empty tent with some cots folded up. We prepared our sleeping areas and everyone immediately hit the sack. Who knew when we were going to sleep again?

The next morning we caught a bird and I got us to Camp Fallujah just one day before the assault on the city.

,   ,   ,

First Lieutenant Jason Van Steenwyk of *CounterColumn* was a Florida National Guard infantry platoon leader in Iraq. He writes of the choices you have to make—to kill or not to kill—in "The Anatomy of a Decision." Sometimes, it's more difficult to *not* pull the trigger:

,   ,   ,

This morning I hopped on a convoy going out on a short run to pick up bottled water and MREs [meals ready to eat] and to drop off and pick up soldiers at the brigade medical clinic. I wanted to go along myself because I wanted to visit the soldier that got wounded last night, and talk to the public affairs office. I used to lead most of those convoys myself, in the early days here, but as we've gotten settled we've handed off the routine functioning of the unit to the Non-Commissioned Officers—the Sergeants—which is as it should be. Good units are commanded by Officers, but they are run by NCOs!

So the NCO in charge of the logpacs got his missions from me and the battalion S4 [logistics staff officer] the evening before, and took

care of everything—lining up the vehicles, trip tickets, vehicle mani-
fests—everything that needed to be done. The security escort came
from Bravo company and was led by a very strong Sergeant First Class.
The Mess Sergeant was all over the water and MRE resupply mission,
assisted by a couple of the unit Supply Sergeants. The ambulance
knew exactly what to do and where to go with the medical transfers.
And the security escort of gun trucks knew how to get us there and
back safely, and was well drilled in the case of enemy contact. Radio
and equipment checks were done right on time. So all I had to do was
get the latest intel update from the Tactical Operations Center and go
along for the ride.

I was very pleased.

So I hopped in the passenger seat of a Humvee that just happened
to be going along for the ride. The chaplain was driving. (He usually
drives himself, since he doesn't carry a weapon. That leaves someone
else who DOES carry a weapon free to shoot it.)

Although several vehicles in the convoy had radios, the Humvee I
was riding in did not, and so I was incommunicado if anything happened en route.

But all was well, and we left the gate to the kachunkering sound of
chambering rounds.

I don't know if I can describe how it feels to hear a vehicle full of
people all locking and loading simultaneously. I don't know if I'd call it a
ritual in the religious sense—it's a purely practical gesture. But it definitely has a way of preparing the spirit.

Along the way we passed an intersection on the banks of the
Euphrates River, with several fruit and vegetable stands underneath an
overpass. As my vehicle, towards the end of the convoy, approached
the turn, I saw a man turn and walk away back toward the crowd,
behind one of the stalls. He was wearing a coat, a red scarf around his
head (in the Palestinian style), and most significantly, carrying a stock-
less AK-47 across his shoulder as if he were Opie from *The Andy Grif-
fith Show* carrying a fishing pole.

There was nothing about him identifying him as a policeman or
security guard, authorized to carry a military style weapon. I hadn't

seen policemen wearing head wraps before, either. He was moving away from us. His back was turned, and he was not, himself, an immediate threat.

My first instinct was to jump from the vehicle and capture him, yelling "Kiff!!!" ("Halt!!!"). But that's problematic in a vehicle with no communications. If I jumped out, the two vehicles behind me would stop, but the rest of the convoy would keep rolling, and I'd be left with me, one gun truck by itself, an ambulance crew, and a chaplain. Hardly the force I want to gather if I'm going to be out picking a fight.

I was also worried about getting hit from the flank by an unseen buddy of his. If he's an "Ali Baba," the Iraqi designation for insurgent, he's not working alone.

My second instinct was to drop him on the spot, center of mass.

No, that would be a stupid idea. I didn't have a clear shot. I would have had to fire left-handed. I was in a moving vehicle. He was standing right next to a market. There were kids around, and if I fired, everyone else might have fired wildly in the same direction and we'd have a Fallujah-like moment on our hands.

So I stayed put, kept an eye on him, got the soldier behind me to keep an eye on him—probably too excitedly, in retrospect, and scanned for his buddies.

A few seconds later, I realized that although he could easily have done so, he was making no effort to conceal his weapon. I lowered my rifle, scanned the overpass and anywhere else he might have buddies hiding, but we let the man go. We took no action.

The time elapsed between the spotting and the decision to move on was about five seconds or less.

When we got to brigade, I went into their ops center and gave a report to the intel officer, so they could send a patrol to investigate.

It was nagging at me for a couple of hours. Did I make the right call? Would another convoy run into a deliberate ambush because I let this guy go? Would WE run into it on the way back?

I mentioned it later to the NCO who was behind me and said, "I don't know . . . maybe I should have shot him on the spot." I'm not sure myself how serious I was about that statement. But the sergeant said,

"No. We're not kids. That's something a dumbass kid would do, and you would have caused a massacre, because everybody would have shot in the same direction."

He was right.

I found out later that it was an Iraqi security guard who works at that intersection all the time. He wears an armband, but apparently had put his overcoat on, concealing the armband.

The decision to live and let live, in this case, turned out to be the right one.

This time.

,　　,　　,

Corporal Michael Bautista of *Ma Deuce Gunner* is a cavalry scout in the Idaho National Guard out on an escort mission in Iraq when he finds himself regarded by one Iraqi family as a neighbor instead of a soldier:

,　　,　　,

At night in Iraq, many people spend the evenings outside in the yard or out in the street. Whole families sit around and interact. It is neat to see 3 or 4 generations of a family enjoying each other's company. We all know about how some families in the US are, who rarely eat together at a table, and if they do, they retreat from each other to watch TV, go to the mall, go out with their friends . . . so on and so forth.

Last night, we were out in the city, on an escort mission. We stopped and got out while at one of our objectives, and we happened to be next to this family. The patriarch of the clan immediately stood up and came to me, offering his chair and a cigarette. I declined the chair, accepted the cigarette, and continued to "pull" security. The children immediately surrounded me, saying whatever phrase they knew in English, which is normally "Mistah." A lot of the time, kids beg for candy or soccerballs, but these kids just wanted to know my name and where I was from. I dug into my cargo pocket and found some peppermint candies, the soft kind, which are just plain confectioners sugar and peppermint oil, and hand them to the kids.

The patriarch then stood again and walked to me with his hands in front of him, making a stirring motion. We have learned that this is the Iraqi hand signal for tea. "Chai? Chai?" he said. I shot a glance to my squad leader, who smiled and said, "Go ahead, we have plenty of security."

To the patriarch I turned, and said "*Naam, Shukran,*" which is Arabic for "Yes, thank you." A flash of a flowery dress is all I see, as an older teenage girl disappears behind the gate, destined for the kitchen. I nod and smile at everything they say, and they all giggle at the faces I make, as they try to communicate with hand signals and few English words.

Before I know it, the young woman appears at the gate, holding an immaculately polished silver tray with eight steaming cups of chai. Pre-poured into small glasses with gold rims and ornate flowers carved into the glass, and matching saucers, and miniature brass spoons jutting out the top of the glass. Sugar is already in the tea, in ridiculous quantites. Iraqi tea is served VERY HOT, and the sugar dissolves with a few swishes of the diminutive spoon.

I have learned, over the past 11 months, that you DO NOT attempt to sip from the cup, or your lips and tongue will pay the price. You stir for a while, both to dissolve the sugar and attempt to dissipate some of the heat. When you are ready for a sip, you pour a little into the saucer, which is an art all unto itself, because I always end up with some tea running down the side of the glass. You then sip from the saucer, because the tea cools rapidly to a comfortable drinking temperature.

We all stand there sipping in the dark, lightning flashing in the distance, illuminating the southwestern sky. Now it is time to go. The element we were escorting is ready to move to the next site. I take a final sip of tea, replace it on the waiting tray, now held by someone who looks like the patriarch's son. I turn to the old man, and again thank him, shake his hand and then momentarily place my hand on my chest, an Arabic gesture of gratitude. Instantaneously, right hands surround me, for everyone wants to shake mine. Even the women, who sometimes shy away from us, smile and shake our hands here. Smiles abound.

As we mount the vehicle, the family stands on the curb, waving and smiling. I reach into my pocket and feel some more soft peppermints, which I toss to the kids, and they smile even bigger, if it was possible to seem any happier. "Win their hearts and minds," they say. In this little microcosm of Iraq, a curb in a neighborhood under the desert stars, "Mission Accomplished."

I shall never forget the 10 minutes I spent with this family. No conversations of substance transpired, no earth-shattering foreign policy formed. Simply hospitality and gratitude; just smiles, body language and handshakes. For a while, there was no fighting, no explosions, no terrorist possibly lurking around the corner. Even though I was in full combat gear, sharp steel sheathed, ammunition and explosives strapped to my chest, rifle slung at my front, for a moment, I was just a guy enjoying a hot beverage and some candy with the neighbors.

᠃　᠃　᠃

First Lieutenant Scott Langlands of *Medicine Soldier—A View from Iraq* is an Army Reserve officer in Iraq. The title of his blog is a play on his civilian career and education as a biomedical engineer and on his being Native American. In Iraq, his role is that of executive officer, the second in command of an Army company. He writes about a very long day during a raid on suspected terrorists:

᠃　᠃　᠃

I woke up yesterday at about 5:30 in the morning, after an explosion or report of some roadside bomb in the area. I am getting used to hearing explosions around our camp, often followed by some gunfire. It is often conversation while we are brushing our teeth in the shower trailer. In any event, we sent out a patrol to assess the situation. I could not fall back to sleep so I started some of my morning chores and went to the normal meetings. The afternoon was more exciting because we spent the afternoon packing a shipping container with all our non-essential gear. Everything had to be clean, inspected, and sealed for shipping. Hopefully the container will meet us home. After that was done, I ran around camp helping the platoons get ready for a night mission. I did not really get a chance to eat lunch or dinner; I managed to squeeze in some peanut butter and jelly sandwiches.

We ended up conducting a raid in the wee hours of the morning. It was a little fireworks to kick off Ramadan, but the mission justified our reason for being here. There were reports of suspected terrorists visiting somewhere near our camp. As I have been busy trying to organize our movement back home, I was not sure what part I would play in the raid, but I ended up running the paddy wagon. It is kind of amazing, after trying to visualize the missions through the rehearsals, to actually see it come together in a good way. It actually went how *Black Hawk Down* should have gone. We only had a piece of the mission, but everyone did their part and it went well. After sneaking and waiting for hours, I hit the ground out of my truck to hear the early morning prayers broadcasting over megaphones. I approached the raid teams crunching through the sand and trash on the ground. Blindfolded and startled, our captives waited while we negotiated them one by one into the truck. I never really thought myself much of a police officer, and I thought about how dehumanizing it must be to stand almost naked amongst armored strangers yelling words they don't understand. Still, I am sure I gave them more consideration than they for their would-be victims.

After processing them into our "county lockup," I wandered back to our company area to make sure all the lights were off in the vehicles and make sure they were locked. Then I went to the operations center and convinced them to let me turn in my reports early so I could get some sleep. Now it is over 24 hours later and I am ready for a nap. At least it has been cooler here; the lows have been in the 70s and a high of only 95.

⸱ ⸱ ⸱

First Sergeant James Thomson is the top enlisted soldier in an aviation unit in Afghanistan. He writes about his role as the right arm of the commander and his own project, Operation Shoefly, to bring shoes to the many barefoot kids of Afghanistan. Here, First Sergeant Thomson writes on his blog, *Sergeant Hook*, about keeping one of his soldiers motivated during the long deployment in Afghanistan:

⸱ ⸱ ⸱

Sitting in my hooch [living area] watching the 13" television set atop a plywood bookshelf, I felt tired. It had been a long day. I flew on one of those missions that I can't tell you about, but suffice to say I'm damn glad to be wearing the stars and bars on my right sleeve. Sleep well America, because you can.

It was a good kind of tired, though, an honest day's work. David Letterman was on, he's funny. I remember watching him every weeknight in the day room of our dormitory at Syracuse University in my younger days. We've both aged, but I still find him funny.

"First Sergeant?" came the dreaded question from outside my door.

"Come on in," I replied, knowing that I'd regret it.

In walked my headquarters platoon sergeant, a seasoned, tough, and reliable sergeant first class with his platoon leader, a young, wet-behind-the-ears lieutenant, in tow. They launched into a story about Specialist Willis, outlining their displeasure with the Soldier's attitude and performance. It seemed that young Willis had a bit of a breakdown moments earlier and lost her composure, demanding through teary eyes to be reassigned to another unit. When I asked why she would say such a thing I got shrugs and "I don't know" for replies. The platoon sergeant said that he didn't care if she was reassigned, that she didn't do much for the team anyway. He added that he informed the Soldier that he would make an appointment for her with the Chaplain in the morning.

"Where is the Soldier now?" I asked.

After my two visitors left, I sat back down to think this one over. A knot had formed in my gut and wasn't sitting well with me at all. SPC Willis is a twenty-one-year-old young woman who joined the Army off the streets of Los Angeles just about three years ago. She signed on to work in a very specific MOS [military occupational specialty], and, unfortunately for her, I'm only authorized one soldier: Willis. Unfortunately, her expertise is not really required in this theater of operations, at least not yet, so we've assigned SPC Willis to work in our Command Post. She pulls the swing shift from 2000 hours to 0600 hours each night. The "CP" was in fact the answer to my earlier inquiry into her location.

"What's going on, Willis?" I asked, sitting down on a stool adjacent to the crying Soldier.

"Nothing, First Sergeant," came the expected reply.

"Oh, so you normally sit up here all night crying?" I asked.

She looked at me. It was obvious she had been crying for a while and was very upset. "Look, Willis, if you're upset about something, and it's obvious that you are, I can't fix it unless you tell me what 'it' is," I explained to her.

Taking a deep breath, she went on to tell me that she feels very unwelcome and useless to the unit because she's stashed away every night listening to the radios and waiting for the phone that never rings to ring. It became pretty clear to me that she needed to feel more productive. I explained to her that I could find her a reassignment if she wanted, but that wasn't what I wanted and that I didn't think it would help as her MOS just isn't critical in this environment. "I could, however, move you out of the CP working alongside other Soldiers within the unit in a job that produces more visible results," I offered.

Her eyes brightened ever so slightly as she looked at me as if I had horns growing from my head.

"Willis, you want out of this lonely, boring, radio-watch job or not?" I asked the tough kid from LA.

"Yes, First Sergeant, that would be much better," she answered.

I asked her to give me two days to work out a replacement for her in the CP, and to give me 100% during those two days, and I'd get her out of there. She agreed and then asked apprehensively, "First Sergeant, do I have to see the Chaplain in the morning?"

"Do you want to see the Chaplain in the morning, Willis?" I asked.

"No, First Sergeant, I ain't really religious."

"Hell no, you don't have to see the Chaplain," I said. She smiled.

SPC Willis is now working with a smile on her face and dirt on her hands and only complains about being tired at the end of the day. I think that she might even reenlist.

＇　＇　＇

Mark Partridge Miner is a Florida National Guardsman who volunteered to go to Iraq with the Louisiana National Guard's 256th Brigade Combat Team. Mark's blog, *Boots in Baghdad,* reflects on his year in

Iraq, patrolling the streets of the capital looking for information, terrorists, weapons caches, and even goodwill, among other things. One
day, instead of finding trouble, Mark found "Courage":

It was a really good week. We had a lot of fun, made some good con-
tacts and gathered some solid information. We went out several times
doing daylight dismounted patrols. Our mission was pretty basic. We
were to make our presence known, interact with the locals, find out if
they needed anything and try to gather some intelligence. I love day-
time foot patrols. It's almost a form of therapy for me. On foot your
observational abilities are substantially increased. Your interaction with
people is on a much more personal level. An armored humvee sitting
behind you can be pretty intimidating. On foot, it's just you and the
people. It is a lot easier to read people . . . to pick up on their vibes.

I got an M203 (grenade launcher) added to my M-4 (rifle). Carrying
the extra ammo along with the dismounted element's radio can get
heavy. I like carrying the radio, though. Relaying traffic between whoever is in charge, whether the Squad Leader, Platoon Sergeant or Company Commander, means I always know exactly what's going on and
where.

We went out yesterday afternoon. It was a hot yet beautiful day. The
skies were crystal clear. We got dropped off and patrolled for a little
over an hour, stopping to talk with some of the locals and give candy to
the kids along the way. We then stopped on the side of a berm to rest.
Two little Iraqi boys had followed us and hung out with us for a while.
They spoke broken English but we were able to communicate pretty
well with them. After we got to know them we asked them where Ali
Baba (bad guys) were. They looked around and one of them said,
"Mista, guns there." He quickly pointed and then pretended to be wiping his face.

We thanked him and began moving in the direction he pointed.
There was a large warehouse surrounded by some small shacks. We
were careful not to head straight in that direction. We didn't want it to
be obvious to anyone watching from a distance that the kids had just

told us something. I called the mounted patrol, gave them our grid and told them we had some information on possible weapons in the area. They had a hard time seeing us because we were between a wall and a wheat field. I got to use my M203 (grenade launcher) to shoot a green smoke canister. They came right to us.

We moved to the warehouse with the humvees pulling outer security around its perimeter. The warehouse was locked so I climbed a home-made ladder that was lying near the fence to look in one of the windows. The warehouse was full of neatly stacked boxes. We went to some of the surrounding shacks to find the owner of the warehouse. A teenage boy came and unlocked the door. After a thorough search of the warehouse and the surrounding shacks all we found were building supplies.

A hundred meters or so from the warehouse we continued our foot patrol down a fairly busy road. As we were walking I noticed an Iraqi woman standing just inside a gate. I made eye contact with her and something told me to approach her. I crossed the street and she disappeared behind the wall. A second later, she peeked out the gate and motioned for me to go over there. I realized she was hiding from the passing cars. I grabbed SGT H who was already on that side of the road to go over to her with me. Another few cars passed. We waited until the road was relatively clear and went up to the gate. The woman put her hand on my shoulder and guided me inside the wall with SGT H right behind me. She quickly closed the gate behind us. Behind the wall there was another woman, quite a bit older, I presume either her mother or mother-in-law.

The younger woman began to speak frantically in Arabic, her hands trembling with nervousness. Her eyes were deep. She was extremely concerned about being seen talking to us. I radioed the mounted element and informed them of the situation. SSG P, the NCOIC [NCO in charge] of the mounted element, snuck behind the wall with us. We removed our Kevlar helmets and eye protection, a gesture of trust, and did our best to figure out what she was trying to tell us.

She continuously grabbed her wedding ring and said, "Insurgents, Ali Baba." At first I thought maybe her husband had been arrested and was being held in a prison by coalition forces. This was the only day this week we didn't have a translator with us. SSG P radioed battalion requesting a translator. Another unit a few miles away had one available. SSG P had me and SGT H stay with the women while he took two of the five humvees that made up the mounted element to go and get the translator. The rest of the dismounted element was about a hundred meters down the road pulling security on our location with the three humvees that stayed. They did a great job of being discreet and not revealing there were any of us behind the wall.

SGT H and I continued to communicate with the women while we were waiting on the translator. We did our best to calm them down and establish trust. It is amazing how well you can communicate with just your eyes and body language. In a matter of minutes I felt like I had known these women my entire life. It was apparent they were getting the same feeling from us. I could see the pain and the fear in their eyes. Buried beneath the layers of desperation was some of the purest sincerity I have come across in my nearly twenty-two years of existence. I now knew, without a doubt, whatever she had to tell us was substantial, substantial enough to get her killed for telling us.

About ten minutes passed before SSG P and the translator returned. The women requested not to be photographed or videotaped, so we only recorded the audio from their conversation. The information the woman gave us was colossal. It was detailed, in-depth firsthand intelligence we were able to verify through her specific and calculated accounts of recent events. I wish I could go into it. Due to operational security and concern for her personal safety, I'll have to save the details for another day. I will say, however, she informed us of where insurgents had been going to launch rockets. Literally seconds after she told us this we heard the screeching roar of a rocket ripping through the air.

Within five minutes the beautiful rumbling thuds of Apaches coming in low and fast was right on us. They were circling the entire area looking for whoever launched the rocket. Since SSG P was on my radio updating Battalion of the situation on the ground with both the women and the rockets, we didn't have direct communication with the rest of the dismounted element and the humvees. SSG P had me run out and tell three of the humvees to go to the proximity grid where the rockets were fired from.

I waited for the road to clear of passing cars and ran out the gate, sprinting to the closest humvee. I relayed the order, gave them the grid and told them we'd be back on internal net in about five minutes. The humvees moved out to work with the Apaches in a sweep of the area.

The dismounted element was then called in to assist in the sweep. SSG P stayed with the translator and two of the humvees to continue questioning the women. The dismounted element started moving out at a fast pace toward the grid we were given. I was monitoring the radio net traffic between the mounted element and the Apaches. The Apaches had eyes on three men on the edge of a canal between two berms . . . but the humvees were unable to get across the canal.

We didn't have a visual of the humvees yet but we could see the Apaches circling the area and hovering in some spots. We were running though a field when we hit the canal and saw a trail of dust flying toward us. It was the mounted element. They blew past us on the road running parallel to the canal. About five hundred meters down the road they stopped and started getting out. We couldn't see over the berm on the other side of the canal, but the three men were right across from the humvees. I jumped in the canal but couldn't make it up the other side, its banks were too steep. The black water was about thigh high. I started to just slosh through the disgusting muck down the canal toward the humvees when SPC P and CPL N came up to the edge and screamed, "Are you crazy, that's human shit in there." I grabbed the barrel of my rifle and reached out to CPL N who grabbed the butt stock. SPC P was holding CPL N's arm and together they pulled me out. It was one of those times I wished I didn't have the radio on my back. We continued running down the road toward the humvees. The mounted guys threw a wire across the canal so they could pull themselves up the other side. Once we got to the wire I jumped back in the canal, used the wire to pull myself up and ran up the berm. They already had the three guys coming up the other side and were bringing them to the edge of the canal.

We searched the area where they had been. It turns out all they had been doing was fishing. We had them sit with us for a few minutes until SSG P and the interpreter arrived so we could question them. They denied seeing anything but admitted to having been fishing for several hours. The rocket definitely came from that area. They had to have seen something but adamantly denied even hearing the rocket. We reminded them that one of these days one of those rockets could easily hit their house or their kids, and the only way to stop that from happening is to let us know what they see and hear. The sun was setting. Our day was done. We let the three fishermen go, packed up and headed back to the base. At least I wouldn't be the only one smelling terrible on the ride home.

What amazes me is the courage that the previously mentioned woman showed. The information she gave us has since been verified by the proper authorities within Battalion and Brigade. The risk she is subjecting herself to is a brutal and miserable death. Her entire life has consisted of totalitarianism, fear, death and brutality. Without ever having experienced the pleasures of freedom, without a tangible example of common decency . . . a gauge to base right and wrong on, she has somehow managed to overcome her incomprehensible fears and pressures and do what is right. She grew up under Saddam Hussein who brainwashed and manipulated these people. He controlled all aspects of their life. For the past few years she has experienced terrorism and war, hell all around her. For her to have the intestinal fortitude to come forward just amazes me. One thing is for sure: the ability to know what is right and the courage to act on it is instilled somewhere in us all. I know that I will never forget this woman and the example she set for me. For the rest of my life, when I think I have it rough or am put in a situation where doing the right thing seems difficult, I'll think back to yesterday afternoon and the humble Iraqi woman who showed me what courage was first hand.

While writing the last paragraph I was just notified by my team leader that one of the locations the woman gave us was searched by another element of our Company. They found tunnels buried in a field that were full of 155mm artillery rounds (used in roadside bombs), rocket-propelled grenades, rocket launchers, mortars and numerous other weapons and explosives. That find right there just saved a lot of lives.

Seldom is the average American subjected to decisions of right and wrong where consequences result in death. That's a good thing . . . don't get me wrong. I just wish more Americans realized how lucky they have it and how minuscule most problems we stress out about are compared to the rest of the world. I guess, in closing, next time you're stressing out about something . . . ask yourself, "Is this going to kill me, is this going to get my family killed?" Sometimes putting things in perspective can help you realize how great your life really is.

,　　,　　,

Sergeant Michael, an infantry team leader in the 3rd Infantry Division, records a chance encounter on his blog *A Day in Iraq*—a meeting that meant a lot for a little Iraqi boy and for Sergeant Michael:

,　　,　　,

A boy walked into my life for a brief moment this past Easter Sunday, and I am better because of it. Thomas and I were pulling guard on top of a tank that stands at the entrance to our FOB. We were tired, bored, and busy complaining about the endless hours we spend guarding something.

Didn't we come over here to fight bad guys?

It's as if we came over here for the sole reason to guard ourselves.

Why can't we go on more wild rides on the Iraqi highways, letting adrenaline and chaos fuel our souls?

At least the time would go by quicker.

We were sitting there on top of the tank, watching the Iraqi world pass us by and feeling sorry for ourselves. Since it was Easter, there weren't many convoys coming in or out of the gate, making the four hours seem endless. I tried hard not to glance at my watch again, knowing that I would be disappointed with what it had to tell me. Thomas and I had run out of things to talk about and were both in a daze of exhaustion.

I was behind the M240, and he was behind the .50 cal. Both of us were secretly wishing for a reason to make these guns talk. The guns sat lifeless, inanimate tools of death, begging to be brought to life.

Do I really want someone to ride by and shoot at us?

In the back of my mind I was grateful not to have bullets whizzing past my head. I know what that's like, and as soon as you're in that situation, you begin to imagine a million other places you would rather be. I was beginning to think that a firefight would be a welcome intrusion into my otherwise peaceful, boring day.

I must have been busy with these thoughts because seemingly out of nowhere, like angels sent from heaven, two young boys appeared at the gates, beckoning us with their voices.

Where the hell had they come from?

Thomas looked up and wondered the same thing.

What did they want?

One of them waved a piece of paper in his hand as if he was a messenger, anxious to deliver his message.

"I'll go see what they want," Thomas said. "Hopefully they won't blow me up."

As I held up my hand to signal for them to wait there, I realized that his comment didn't hold the sarcasm that it might have a couple of weeks ago, before a boy their age blew himself up outside our FOB, killing four Iraqi soldiers in the process.

Thomas got off the tank and began walking toward the boys, holding up his hand at one point when they began to duck under the gate. They got the message and stood there waiting, leaning against the long arm stretching from one side of the gate to the other.

As Thomas got close to the gate, the boy with the message held out the paper for him to take. The boys both smiled and looked at each other with relief, as if their mission had finally been accomplished in handing this young American soldier this piece of paper. I could see Thomas shake his head a little as he read the piece of paper. With the boys still smiling, Thomas walked back to the tank with a bleak look on his face.

"What does it say?"

While he read it to me, I couldn't help but look back at the boy with sadness. He looked right back at me with a smile still on his face, oblivious to the message he had carried with him. It was a note from a doctor at another FOB in the area asking if someone would evaluate the boy and give him any treatment they could. He was a 14-year-old boy, named Ahmed, with signs of possible liver failure/cirrhosis in his lower extremities.

Dammit. Why couldn't it be someone other than this boy? Why couldn't it be an old man who had lived a full life?

"What do you want to do?" he asked.

"Let me see the paper."

He handed it up to me and I read it for myself. He's not even supposed to be at this FOB. It's for a doctor at the med station of another FOB close by. They better take a look at him anyway, or I'm going to walk him down there myself. I picked up the radio, called battalion, and let them know the situation. Thankfully the guy on the other end had a heart. He told us to search him and call an escort to escort him to the aid station. I called back and asked if it was okay if he brought his friend along too. He said it was fine, and we waved the two boys to the tank.

While they are walking up, Thomas and I decide that if what this paper says is true, this boy may not live past his youth.

"He doesn't even know, does he?" he asked.

"No, I doubt he does."

"Man, this sucks."

"Yeah, but hopefully they can do something for him." I said this knowing full well that Iraq probably doesn't have some kind of donor program, and that this kid will never receive a donor or transplant in this country.

As the boys got closer, I noticed the one that was holding the paper walked with a pronounced limp. They got up to the tank and looked up at it with awe. Both of them said hello and waved to me again. I could tell they didn't understand English and confirmed it by asking them. I could tell Thomas didn't want to subject them to a search but did anyway, joking around with them as he waved the magic metal detecting wand over them. They didn't mind the search, even seemed to think that it was neat. I called an escort over the radio and told him to come to our location to pick up two boys that needed to go to the aid station. I knew it would be a few minutes before he arrived, so I got down off the tank to talk to them.

Ahmed's friend's name was Mohamed. They were both wearing long-sleeve t-shirts with sweat pants that were dirty from the knee down. Ahmed and Mohamed, good ol' pals, were having the time of their life just getting to walk into the Americans' camp and talk with some soldiers.

"Look at his foot," Thomas said. "It looks pretty bad."

His right foot was twice the size of his left, so that it wouldn't fit into his sandal. Ahmed saw me look at his foot, and I tried to hide the surprised look on my face. With the hand signals that became our way of communicating, he asked me if I wanted to see it.

"Yeah, let me take a look at it."

He slid his pants leg up and pulled his sock down, revealing a hugely swollen foot with a bandage around it that had been stained by blood and pus.

At least they can clean it up and put on a new bandage, I thought, as I tried to hide the disgusted look on my face at the sight of his wound.

"What happened to your foot?" I asked.

Mohamed somehow understood and began moving his arms in an upward motion around his body.

"Was it fire, did he get burned?"

Mohamed understood the word fire and said yes, it was fire. Ahmed, still smiling, showed me another burn scar on his hand. This poor kid got burned and now it won't heal.

Letting my fingers do the walking, I asked them if they had walked all the way over here from the other FOB. They didn't understand until I asked them if they had ridden in a sierra over here. Sierra is Arabic for car, and with that word they understood. I wouldn't have been surprised if Ahmed had limped all the way over here with his bad foot.

Where were Ahmed's parents? Why hadn't they come with him?

They only answer that I could come up with was that they too knew nothing of the severity of his wound.

I wanted to give this kid something, anything that would maybe make him happy. I wish I could've given him a ride in the tank. I wish I had the power to get him a ride on a helicopter. I wish I could've put him on a plane to the U.S. with the best doctor in the world waiting to greet him as he arrived. I wish they could've saved the liver of one of the Iraqi soldiers that had been killed by another boy Ahmed's age and given it to him.

All I had with me was what I'd brought with me to my guard shift. I jumped up on the tank and got a few pieces of bubble gum, two packs of Trident, a Dr. Pepper, Mountain Dew, and a small bag of Life Savers. Unfortunately it would take a lot more than candy to save this boy's life.

Their eyes lit up with joy at the sight of these treats. They put the drinks in their pocket for later and started piling gum into their mouth. They looked at each other and laughed as they struggled to chew the big wad of gum. I tried to tell them that the bubble gum and peppermint Trident mixture might not be that good, but they didn't understand and didn't seem to care.

We showed them our guns and tried to explain all the trinkets that were attached to our vests. I wanted to give them all of it and let them play American Soldier for a while.

As they continued to point at different things with curiosity, the escort showed up to lead them away. This escort was some young punk, who made a show of slapping a magazine into his weapon as he approached. I wanted to take him around the other side of the tank and punch him in the mouth.

"Have you already searched them?" he asked.

"Yeah, *Rambo*, we already searched them, but be careful, these kids may try to take over the FOB," Thomas replied as he rolled his eyes.

I wanted a damn General to drive up in his armored Suburban and personally give them a ride. I wanted him to be treated like a King.

The boys gathered up their gum and candy and started to follow behind Rambo. Both of them looked excited about the prospect of entering this world of wonder.

As Ahmed began limping away, smile still stretched across his face, he looked back at me right in the eyes, gave me a thumbs up and said *thank you*.

I waved back and said thank you to him, wishing I could do more. He turned, caught up with his friend, and walked out of my life. His message had been delivered. Ahmed reminded me that I should be eternally grateful for all that has been given to me.

At this point, guard duty didn't seem like that bad a deal.

CHAPTER FIVE

THE WARRIORS

It doesn't take a hero to order men into battle. It takes a hero to be one of those men who goes into battle.

—GENERAL H. NORMAN SCHWARZKOPF, _IT DOESN'T TAKE A HERO_ (1992)

For those who have never heard a shot fired in anger, one of the most sought-after items in the military blog arena is the story of a battle. People want to know "What was it like?" Many want to know what it feels like to open up with a squad automatic weapon; others want to know what it's like to have fear course through your veins as you contemplate entering a known terrorist safe house or patrol the streets of Baghdad.

Military bloggers bring you closer to understanding what it is like to fight in combat.

Corporal Michael Bautista, a cavalry scout team leader in the Idaho National Guard, writes about coming back to Iraq from his R&R in the States and gearing up for a patrol on his blog, _Ma Deuce Gunner:_

It's time to Ride.

0300. It is dark. The moon is high and bright, but filtered through the camo netting, it provides an eerie white glow on the warriors who are preparing for a mission.

The smell of diesel exhaust wafts through the motor pool. Radios beep, crackle and hiss . . . "Animal Base, this is Renegade 3B, radio check, over." "Roger, out" comes the reply.

Clink. Clank. Piink. The sound of .50cal headspace and timing gauges being tested in machine guns. Orange-red cherries from the tips of cigarettes dot the motor pool. Light-hearted banter between the men fills the air, recounting humorous movie lines, laughing about funny occurrences on previous missions. Feet shuffle and scrape through the round rocks in the parking lot, as the almost ceremonial pre-mission wrestling match breaks out. Someone has blindsided his buddy and has him in a headlock, and they twist and push and pull, much to the amusement of bystanders. Questions from superiors to subordinates regarding loadplans, gear, and provisions pierce the laughter from time to time.

Red-lensed flashlights surround HMMWV hoods, illuminating maps and imagery, schedules and charts. Questions are asked, roles in the upcoming mission confirmed and reconfirmed. Every once in a while, someone calls out, "Hey . . . Where did you put that . . . ??" or "Anyone seen my . . . ???"

Then it happens. "Mount UP!!!!!" cries the Lieutentant, and circles of men scatter, striding quickly to their modern-day up-armored chariots. The riiiiiiiip of Velcro can be heard, from body armor being adjusted and re-adjusted and thin, sturdy tactical gloves donned, the snap of plastic buckles being connected, and gunners clambering onto the roofs of their gunships. "Good to go!!!" can be heard throughout the motor pool, over slamming doors and idling engines, as final crew checks are done.

"RedCon 1" comes over the radio, as the truck commanders check in with the Platoon leader. All is ready. Armor is on, ammo ready to be loaded into clean weapons, radios constantly chattering.

"Renegades, this is Renegade 6, follow my move." The truck lurches forward as we pull out of our spot and into line. The dust fills my nostrils as we move; I grip the handles of Mama Deuce for stability . . . I am back, and it is time to ride.

I love this stuff.

⸱ ⸱ ⸱

Army Sergeant Robert Florkowski is a highly trained sniper team leader and a two-time Armed Forces Europe boxing champion. He fought in northern Iraq and took part in many major combat operations, including the offensive in Samarra. He captures the intensity of his mission as he writes about one of his sniper team's engagements on his blog, *Sniper Eye:*

,   ,   ,

Brian, Walter, and I were two days into the major offensive of Samarra. We were attached to an infantry platoon that had occupied a house with a platoon of Iraqi soldiers that was directly on the phase line their platoon was responsible for securing.

At around 1700, we were inside the house taking a quick break from our hide site on the roof, which I thought wasn't needed since this platoon already had 3 soldiers on roof guard, when all of a sudden we heard several shots. We simultaneously grabbed our vests and rifles and headed for the roof.

"What's going on?" I yelled to the roof guard.

"It looks like that convoy up there just took shots from somewhere over there," the roof guard yelled as he pointed west to a convoy of 5 tan up-armored Humvees stopped at an intersection over 600 meters away.

We could see several people running around there, but it was hard to distinguish what was going on. One of the convoy's gunners began to fire like crazy. Then a spray of AK47 fire came from behind a building near the Humvees. By this time the entire platoon was on the roof, and, after those AK shots were fired, an area that we could clearly engage became apparent.

The platoon's M240 gunner set his gun on the roof's ledge, and he, as well as 10 other soldiers with their M16s, began to let rounds fly. Since our house soared above all the other houses in the area, our engagements did not put the houses below us into too much danger. Furthermore, the majority of the city had already evacuated prior to the offensive.

"Let's go to the other roof top," I said to Brian and Walter since our roof top was too crowded, and it looked as if we would have a better viewpoint from there anyways.

I climbed over our roof's wall, and held on to the wall while swinging my legs over the 2-foot gap that separated the 2 roofs from each other. I landed on the thin ledge of the next roof top, and then immediately grabbed the M24 from Walter's outreached hand, so that he could climb over.

All of a sudden, out of a tree right next to the convoy under attack, an RPG back blast ripped through the leaves and branches.

Luckily, the RPG missed the convoy. But, I couldn't believe it; they were attacking from the fuckin' trees! I couldn't engage with my M16 from there, so I said, "Hurry up, we got to get set up!"

Brian was right behind Walter, waiting to climb over, and yelled out anxiously excited, "Did you see that? They're in the trees! Ahhhhh yeah, let's get these fuckers!"

We made it over to the next roof top with all our gear and began to search for a place to shoot from; I had the binos, Walter had the M24, and Brian had the radio. Walter found a suitable firing position at the edge of the roof's west wall, and I positioned myself next to him in order to spot. Brian got on the radio and began to call in support by fire.

Since the insurgents were taking too much fire from the platoon on the roof and the convoy they were attacking, they made their way up to the roof top of an abandoned factory inside an industrial compound to gain higher ground. Seeing that this factory was directly in front of our position, Walter, Brian, and I looked at each other and gave a smile.

Now the insurgents were relentlessly attacking the convoy from behind a row of offices on the roof of the old building. So, in order to get a shot, we had to wait for them to run across one of the 4 office windows. I set Walter on a specific section on one of the 4 windows and told him to "send one" so I could confirm his rifle's wind and elevation adjustments. "Ah yeah, did you see that?" Walter said after he fired. With a big grin on my sweaty face I replied, "Yeah—you're dead on!"

"Hey, there're shots coming from over there too," shouted a soldier from the other roof as he pointed to a building's roof top in the south about 250 meters away. I got up and moved to where I could get a better shot while Walter sat there waiting for that fucker to pop up on the other building. I looked through the scope on my rifle and didn't see anybody. So I fired some rounds where I thought they could be hiding.

I went back to my spot with Walter. I asked Brian, "What's taking so long with the air support?" Brian explained that his message gets relayed through at least 2 other people before it gets to the birds.

"Fuckin' great," I replied.

All of a sudden, an insurgent ran across the office windows without ducking; Walter quickly fired 2 rounds, but the insurgent was too fast.

"Fuck!" Walter and I both yelled.

"Don't worry, we'll get him," I said.

The M240 and the other soldiers' M16s were still lighting up the area while we waited for the insurgent to cross back behind the office's windows. Then, without warning, he popped up. He began to run the other direction when Walter fired a shot with a slight lead to compensate for his running, and, just like that, he was gone. It was if the Earth opened up beneath him, and swallowed him whole.

"Whewww, did you see that?" Walter said with excitement.

I congratulated him, and told him that it was a hard shot—shit, a moving target 600-something meters away through a small window! But there were still some more of them out there.

I was fed up with the delay on the air support and grabbed the radio, and continually repeated the grid and a detailed description of the building that the insurgents were playing hide-and-go-seek in.

Finally, 40 minutes after this whole thing began, 2 Apache helicopters could be seen coming from the north, slicing through the clear blue sky. When they reached the compound, the 2 Apaches hovered over the adjoining building the insurgents were playing on. Even though I thought they could see them, since they were hovering so close, I continued to describe the old factory building. I thought maybe the rest of them took cover inside one of the offices, which would be somewhat of a smart move, since they couldn't leave the building with the convoy waiting for them on the ground.

After several minutes of closely hovering over the compound, bright orange flames shot out from the back of a Hellfire missile and descended . . . into the wrong damn building!

The adjoining building was hit. A mass of flames, sparks, and clouds of thick gray smoke shot out of its windows as the building's foundation crumbled and caved in.

I quickly yelled over the radio, "That was the wrong damn building!"

The Lieutenant on the other end said, "Ok, I'll see if I can get them to send another one, but, if there is no more contact and they can't see them, they won't fire another one."

The sun was now setting as the Apaches continued to hover closely over the compound. All insurgent movement and attacks came to an end after the Hellfire missile was fired, so the 2 Apaches turned around and flew off into the sunset.

And the unlucky convoy drove off. It looked as if this fight was finished, so we climbed back over to the other house and went inside.

A Specialist, who insisted on taking part in the battle of Samarra even though he wasn't needed to go, was sitting on the floor with the medic and a bloody brown t shirt with a hole in it. I looked at his shoulder, which had an ugly bruise and a lump in the trapezoid.

"You got shot?" I asked him, sort of puzzled since his wound looked so clean.

"Yeah, I was with the 240 gunner on the roof when a fuckin' Haji came out of the side streets next to our house, and started popping off his 9 mil at us," he said while the medic taped his shoulder up.

"Did you get him?" I asked.

"No, he came out of nowhere, and took off too quick," he said with regret.

The brave volunteer was taken to the casualty evacuation site, where he was flown out of Samarra and treated.

The next day a fire team went into the old factory compound and found 4 dead insurgents—one with a gunshot wound in the neck.

,　　,　　,

Captain Charles Ziegenfuss of *From My Position . . . On the Way!*, a tank company commander in the 1st Infantry Division invested with the task of hunting down and destroying terrorists, writes about the first man he killed:

The first man that I killed disturbed me. Not so much for the loss of human life, or the whole killing-is-wrong concept. Not because I wasn't well within my right to do so (self-defense) or because (as any 5-year-old will tell you), "He started it."

The first man that I killed I looked in the eye when I shot him. Right dead in the eye. It was actually my aiming point, but that's beside the point. I did not see the fire of Martyrdom. I did not see rage. I saw neither honor nor vengeance. I saw a look, an emotion that can only be summed up as "Oh Shit!"

This man brought a gun to a gunfight. I brought thirty. He brought about ninety rounds. I brought over three thousand. He had a fully automatic rifle. I had pistols, rifles, machine guns, and grenade launchers. And I had something he didn't, sixteen of my brothers.

I pulled the trigger that released the hammer that hit the firing pin that ignited the primer and powder that propelled the bullet that sent him to see his 72 Virgins. I watched him shudder; and fall. I watched him flop and flail. And then I ran into his burning house and dragged his body out in case he survived and went back in to find his family and get them out.

What really disturbed me after all this (during the event I wasn't doing any real thinking, just acting and reacting) was that I felt nothing. Not a tear, a sigh, or even a melancholy. I also took no joy in it. The utter lack of feeling or emotion bugged the shit out of me.

Well, I actually shared these feelings (or lack thereof) with people. Okay. I shared it with TWO people. The Mrs. (who I figure really doesn't need to hear any more of these stories) and a fellow Patriot. They both gave good advice. It boiled down to this:

> You were defending yourself and your men.
> You followed the rules of engagement.
> You had no other choice. (Except not to fight. If you even thought
> that for a second, put your Birkenstocks and socks back on, stuff
> your granola up your ass, and get out, hippie.)

All true statements. I came to this conclusion:

It wasn't personal, just business.

You see, the Army is my job. It's my 9–5 (or, rather, my 0400–2359). If you ask me who I am, I'll tell you about my family, my beliefs, and somewhere in there, I may mention that I am in the Army. Way back when I was a youngster, my mom wondered aloud to Dad if I would do well in the Army (this was after I graduated from Basic Training). She was worried because I was still the same goofy kid at home. Dad told her, "Yeah, he'll be fine. What you don't see is that when he goes around the corner, he's not your little boy anymore. He's now a Soldier, and a damn good one." (Thanks, Dad.)

Killing is my business.

Uphold, Defend, Bear True Faith, Allegiance, Obey. These are the Pledges in my Oath. They sum up nicely as "Do what my President says, and follow the constitution or I WILL KILL YOU. We don't train to shoot to wound. We don't have to fire a warning shot. We follow the rules, we fight by the rules, and we die either because we follow them or because others don't. War is brutal. War is hell. War is what I have hardened my heart to bring on the heads of my enemies. Dissension is intellectual cowardice."

And business is good.

Sometimes we find bombs. Sometimes we don't. Some days you see the elephant, and on other days you're the stuff between his toes. My men have been shot at, nearly blown up—one of my platoon leaders had a mortar round land five feet from where he stood, and it failed to explode. I've rolled right over a fifteen pound PE-4 (Russian C4 explosive) charge that didn't explode because I actually squashed the trigger device. We've been blown up by IEDs, Car Bombed, and had Mohammed's Revenge—which is like Montezuma's Revenge, but caused by Iraqi food and water. Don't insult the locals when they offer you food by refusing to eat it. You'd better eat hearty in the name of good manners and national policy.

Atkins can eat my heart out. There's nothing better for weight loss than 110 degree temps, 40 pounds of gear, 20 pounds of body armor, and a case of the screaming shits to drop a quick 2 inches off the waist-line. (See, I told you no topic was too sacred.) We keep finding their bombs and caches, we root them out of their hides, we kill them and kill them. They recently said that it was okay to kill fellow Muslims when attacking us—basically, that it was okay to kill Iraqi Army and Police to get at us.

Outstanding.

That means that we're winning, people. They see their grip fading on the people that they held so tightly. Kamikazes didn't work for the Japanese. It seems supply does equal demand.

Goodnight, sleep well.

Rough men stand ready to do violence on your behalf.

⸱   ⸱   ⸱

Unfortunately, our soldiers aren't always the ones on the offensive. Lance Corporal Eric S. Freeman kept a journal of his second tour in Iraq. Eric graduated from high school at age 16 and completed almost two years of college before joining the Marines. His entry, posted on *Blackfive,* recounts the day he and his brother Marines were wounded:

⸱   ⸱   ⸱

I feel myself jerked backward against the outward-facing bench seat in the back of the 7-ton. A high-pitch ring fills my ears and the world has become dust. I can feel my face being peppered with sand and debris. It finally happened . . . the debris continues to rain down, the left side of my face is on fire and I can see the drops of blood fall onto my SAW [squad automatic weapon] which is between my legs. I spit solid, bright red blood.

Holloway yelling, "Riddler's down!" I'm a combat aidsman. Just then I notice he's slumped across my lap. My gun somehow flies out of the truck, it's on the ground. I need that gun; we could get ambushed.

"Holloway, I got Rit, get my gun!" I turn Rit over and he's bleeding all over his face.

"Tell me where it hurts Rit!" I yell at the top of my smoke- and dust-filled lungs.

"My face, it burns, my face," he says shakily. His hands are up near his face and he's violently shaking all over, shock, he's in shock. Surreally, I'm somehow on the ground now, out of the truck, and the dust has cleared. People are yelling for the corpsman (Medic). I pull out my first-aid kit and start wiping the blood from Rit's face so I can see the wounds. They aren't bad, so why is he in so much pain? He's groaning and shaking while I check him all over for any other wounds. But it's just his face that's wounded.

My face is fucked up too. I'm afraid to touch it or ask or look for myself. I know the left half of my face looks like raw ground beef. I think about how my glasses must've saved my eyes and realize that I can't even see through them cause of the blast residue. I blearily realize that I've been looking out from below them the whole time. I take them off.

Rit is gone now with the corpsman and Cpl. Lipe is being led from the cab. His face looks like mine feels and his right eye is gone, just a bloody pinkish mess between his cheek and his eyebrow. The doc's got him. I run to everyone, one at a time to make sure they aren't bleeding out and don't know it because of shock. Everyone is bloodied in the face mostly, except Brooks, who says he's fine, walks with a limp and refuses to let me help him, and Sgt. Ramos, who took a piece of frag to his right flank. His flack vest stopped it from causing too much damage.

The truck is totaled, it leaks antifreeze in huge green puddles that collect around the enormous, flat tire. The engine casing is dotted with huge shrapnel holes and the entire windshield is out. I look at my face in the rearview mirror. I'm peppered with small bits of rock and shrapnel and my lip is cut open and caked with blood. Somehow, it really isn't very bad, despite how it feels. I'm pretty sure it'll heal with almost no scars.

I was one of the luckiest.

Sergeant Michael's writing about his experiences in Iraq has produced a popular blog, *A Day In Iraq*. Michael has completed one tour in Iraq and is near completing his second year-long tour. Here is one of his missions during the invasion of Iraq on April 3, 2003, where he recalls fighting in the streets of the suburbs of Baghdad:

Today was more intense than our last day of fighting. We woke up early and moved into our objective before 0700. The Bradleys, ours included, had many engagements, destroying vehicles and dismounts. There's no better drama than listening to the radio chatter during these chaotic moments. Our crew trying to identify targets, identifying them, and then the thump-thump-thump of the 25mm or the familiar sound of the coaxial machine gun.

With the Bradley still firing, the ramp suddenly unlocks and begins to go down. We're forced out of our protective shell, emerging onto the mean streets of Baghdad's suburbs. Once we're out, we find ourselves next to a brick wall that's blocking an entrance to a house. Amid the confusion of suddenly being in the middle of a firefight, our Bradley still engaging enemy down the street, I notice the edge in everyone's voice. To dismount in this environment is scary but exhilarating, not knowing where enemy fire is coming from and being disoriented from being in the back of the Bradley. I've never felt so alive in my life. Explosions going off all around, fireballs rising into the sky, quickly replaced by black smoke, the already familiar smell of charred bodies, the Brad's guns exploding in your ears, TOW missiles whooshing through the air, not knowing where the enemy is and frantically trying to find him.

We're up against the wall when we receive fire from the second story of a building on the opposite corner of the street. We couldn't see the shooter, making us even more pissed about being shot at. Sgt. W unloads three rounds of HE (high explosive) with his 203, hitting the second story with perfection and impressing me in the process. One block down to my left, I can see the other Bradley in our section engaging down their street. The guys in the back have already dismounted and are pulling rear security for the Bradley. I start looking around for something to shoot at, feeling guilty for wanting to shoot at anything, wondering if someone is on the other side of the wall I'm against, patiently waiting to lob a grenade over.

As soon as I was getting my bearings, we mounted back up in our time machine. A minute later we were getting out again, this time at the corner, one block down from the other Bradley. Like the other dismounts, we tried to find some cover and pulled rear security on our Bradley. I was facing towards the street, with a woodline on the other side. Our Bradley was now situated on the road perpendicular to the one I was over-watching. I had decent cover to the left of a small mud mound that was supporting a telephone pole. Sgt. W was to my right, while the rest of the squad was at my nine and ten o'clock.

About 100 meters down to my left, a truck carrying three guys with AKs pulled out of the woodline parallel to the road. Other elements, farther down the road, open up on it with small arms fire, killing the three guys as the truck slowly comes to a stop. An instant later, small arms fire erupted from the woodline at my 11 o'clock, the rounds whistling over my head. Until this moment I didn't realize how little cover I actually had, especially from that angle. Pissed off at being shot at again, with little or no cover, I strained to see someone. All I could see was smoke and the rustling of leaves from their fire. Hopelessly looking for better cover with none to be found, Sgt. W and I have a quick laugh before responding. Nobody else seemed to know where the fire was coming from, so I fired in that same area, to try and suppress if nothing else. Once I started, everyone else started firing in the same direction. Sgt. W fired two 203 rounds, one starting a small fire in the woods. The firing from the woodline ceased shortly thereafter. I have no idea if I hit or came close to hitting anyone.

With a lull in the action, I roll on to my right side, unbutton my fly, and commence to taking a much needed piss, all the while joking and laughing with Sgt. W. Adrenaline pumping, feeling comfortable behind my M16, almost hoping for someone else to fire on us so we could fire back. Another Bradley was busy shooting up a weapons cache nearby, causing some kind of rockets to randomly fire off into every direction, at one point sounding like one was going to land on top of us. We finally secured that area, with other elements still fighting in the city.

Later I heard that a sergeant from another squad panicked during a firefight their squad got into one block down from us. He left his men to fend for themselves, he panicked, started banging on the Brad to let him back in, and with his hand over the 203, it goes off, hurting his hand. His men were mad as hell that he left them, but like me, weren't surprised by his reaction. He's now back in the rear where he should be. I also later found out that a Brad from another platoon got hit by an RPG, giving one guy a concussion.

Having secured the area, a huge convoy comes lumbering through, guys waving at us as they pass. Later that night we went to our AO, which was between a main highway and a canal. The place was by no means secure. While we were sleeping and on guard, we would hear small arms fire cracking in the distance, their tracers sometimes getting close. The crazy thing is, it really didn't bother us. We just tried to stay low to the ground. While lying on the ground to sleep and sitting on guard, I didn't even move when hearing these shots.

I guess I'm getting used to it.

, , ,

One of the most memorable photographs of the invasion of Iraq was of U.S. Marine Corps Gunnery Sergeant Nicholas Popaditch. The picture was of Gunny Popaditch smoking a celebratory cigar with the statue of Saddam Hussein being pulled down in the background. From that day forward, Gunny Popaditch was known as "the Cee-gar Marine." Gunny Popaditch didn't see the end of combat after that day. His account about his "Fallujah Fight" was published on *Blackfive*:

, , ,

I was the Tank Commander of Charlie 1-4, and the Platoon Sergeant of Charlie Company's 1st Platoon. We had just relieved the Army in Fallujah. My Platoon had been operating with relatively little rest in support of the 1st Marine Regiment, although the contact had been pretty light. We had been operating on the east side of the town and the enemy insurgents there had little desire to tangle with Marine Tanks.

My Platoon had just come in from 3 days' duty out at a coalition strongpoint out in town. Regiment had nothing planned for Tanks that day so it appeared my Marines would get some overdue rest and a chance to turn a few wrenches on the Tanks. We had only been back about an hour when bad news arrived. We were eating breakfast in the firm base chow hall when word arrived about some Americans killed out in town. Worse still, their bodies were being desecrated in the streets. Very shortly after that, I received the word to ready the Platoon to move out again.

I informed the Marines of 1st Platoon about the morning's events. I told them, "Nobody does that to Americans," and to mount up and prepare to move out! The looks in their eyes and on their faces told me that the insurgents had made a grievous error in picking a fight with the United States Marine Corps.

By the time we departed the firm base, more details had arrived. The enemy insurgents (I only use this term to describe them for lack of a better one as there really is no good term for such a dishonorable excuse for a human being) had hung the corpses from a train trestle and were vowing to turn Fallujah into a graveyard for Americans.

The first couple of days of the Fallujah offensive were mostly uneventful. We did a lot of reconnaissance of the enemy and they occasionally probed us. After a couple of days of this, the Marines were itching for a fight. We would get one soon.

I received orders to take my Tank section (two Tanks—mine and my wingman) to support Fox Company, who had been in contact with enemy probes the night before. I arrived at Fox's AO (area of operations) on the northwest corner of Fallujah, and located their CO. After a brief meeting we agreed the best place for my Tank was at the center of their company's defensive line, with my wingman protecting my flank. My position was good. I was about 200 meters from the first row of buildings, I had a good berm in front of my Tank to protect from RPGs, a train trestle overhead for mortars, and a lot of Grunts in elevated positions. Life was good except that we weren't here to defend, we were anxious to attack!

About mid-day, Fox conducted a security patrol to prevent the enemy from working in close for a mortar or RPG shot. We were unaware of how close the enemy had already come. About ten minutes into their patrol, the infantry squad was ambushed. I couldn't see it, but I heard the insurgents open up with RPGs, AK-47s, and RPK machine guns. This was a little more committed than the enemy usually engaged.

The infantry squad took a casualty, set up a base of fire, and called for support. I asked the CO if he needed the Tanks. He agreed, "Roll Tanks!" At last, we were on the offensive.

I took the lead with my wingman behind me. As I passed through the infantry squad, I saw a Corpsman rendering first aid to a Marine who had been shot in the face. I was to later learn that this Marine not only survived but returned to his unit to finish the deployment. SEMPER FI!

My Tank crew and I were like sharks with blood in the water, and the enemy insurgents were eager enough to fight with Tanks. There was no coordination or reason to their attacks. They would pop out of buildings or doorways and take a shot at my Tank. Usually their RPG shot wouldn't hit, but almost always my Tank's machine guns or main gun would. In a short while, I had taken a couple of RPG hits (resulting in no damage) and had inflicted over a dozen kills on the enemy. By now, Fox Co. 2nd Platoon had worked their way into the city alongside of my Tank. Fallujah was going to be a graveyard all right, but not for Americans.

We began to work our way into the city. I would lead with my Tank. My wingman would trail about a block back, covering my flanks and rear. The infantry would work building to building, covering my move from the rooftops. This technique was very successful as enemy insurgents would attempt to shoot and then flee into buildings, not knowing our infantry were over the top directing the Tank's main gun onto target of whatever room in whatever building the enemy thought he was safe.

We used this tactic to take block after block. Soon we had a pretty good tally of enemy kills and the remaining enemy were getting less eager to tangle with a Marine Tank. The next tactic we employed was, after a period of more than ten minutes without a contact, I would start to back up the Tank as if I were leaving. The enemy would come out for one last shot. I would then order the Tank back forward again and continue to kill the enemy. I was amazed at how often this would work.

My Tank crew and I fed off each other's motivation and intensity. My gunner, Corporal Chambers, surgically removed enemy from the face of the Earth with the Tank's main gun and coaxial machine gun. My loader, Lance Corporal Hernandez, courageously manned his machine gun and put down many insurgents. My driver, Lance Corporal Frias, flawlessly maneuvered the Tank down tight city streets. We took block after block. The infantry rallied behind the carnage the Tank was dispensing. The only problem was that we were expending a lot of ammunition.

Late that afternoon, I began to run low on ammunition. Because I was in the lead, I had expended much more ammunition than my wingman, Staff Sergeant Escamilla. His Tank still had a relatively full combat load. I backed up closer to his Tank and the infantry put down some good suppressive fire. Our two crews quickly transferred ammunition from his Tank to mine. The problem was solved, at least temporarily.

Back into the lead and back into the attack I went. I was only monitoring my Platoon's radio frequency and that of Fox Company, so my situational awareness of what was going on with the rest of the Task Force was limited. The CO informed me that we were the furthest penetration into the city, which was very motivating. This also was good news because with no friendly units to the left or right or ahead, there was no need to deconflict fires before I shot. The enemy fights very asymmetrically in Fallujah, and the ability to engage more quickly resulted in fewer insurgents getting away. A Tank in a city is like a bull in a china shop. With all the friendlies well behind us, this was a very good thing and very bad for the enemy! The attack was going well, but the enemy had prepared to make a stand against us up ahead.

About two blocks to our front was a courtyard. Blocking the entrance were two telephone poles with power lines strung between them like a fishing net. Generally all obstacles are covered by fire and it was obvious that the courtyard was the killsack for this ambush. As I closed on this obstacle, I observed many sandbagged fighting positions in the courtyard. I didn't know if the power lines were electrified and I really didn't want to find out the hard way. The one thing that the enemy didn't count on was that about a half block short of the obstacle, I could see almost the entire courtyard. I stopped there and showed the insurgents that a few sandbag bunkers against a 68-ton Main Battle Tank was a poor choice and a quick end to your life. We killed about ten enemy and only a few were quick enough to escape. The power line obstacle had brought our advance to a halt, however.

I called up higher on the radio and asked if we had any engineering assets available. I don't think anybody thought that a Bangalore torpedo or line charge would be an overly useful item in an urban fight. We had none. I looked for a bypass. There was an alley unblocked to the right. About ten meters down that alley was a fuel tanker truck trailer parked. Obviously this was the route the enemy wanted me to take. I was sure it was full and wired to blow. I began to plan other options. I couldn't stand the fact that our attack had been halted and I began to grow impatient.

Luckily, during this time there was a building in the courtyard that must have been a stockpile point for weapons for them. About every ten minutes, an insurgent would attempt to make it across the courtyard and enter it. Sometimes they would actually make it only to get killed taking an RPG shot at us on the way out. This kept my gunner busy while I plotted.

I figured that the power lines would get tangled in my track and possibly halt my Tank in the courtyard. In addition to this, I still didn't know if they were electrified. I eliminated the bypass as an option, due to the fuel trailer. I didn't have any main gun ammunition to spare to attempt knocking the telephone poles down which supported the power lines. That would be a difficult shot and I figured it would take too many rounds before I hit it. Also, there still was a small portion of the courtyard that I hadn't been able to see up to now.

The success we had caused me to grow more impatient with this halt in our attack. I had a plan. I wasn't overly thrilled with it, but even more, I couldn't stand the thought that the enemy insurgents had stopped me. I informed my wingman and the infantry platoon that I intended to ram the obstacle at an angle where I would hopefully hit mostly telephone pole and entangle as little power line as possible in my track. If I sealed my hatches shut, I figured that the distance from the fuel trailer was enough that it would do no damage other than spray burning fuel on the outside of the Tank. I was mostly concerned about the fire I would inevitably take when I entered the courtyard. I knew that between the power lines and the certain RPG shots, there was a good possibility that I would be immobilized in the courtyard so I needed Staff Sergeant Escamilla's Tank and the infantry platoon to be prepared to enter the courtyard close behind me and take the lead if my Tank was immobilized. As I said I wasn't thrilled with this plan, but it was the best I had. Luckily, just prior to executing it, the CO called on the radio and presented another option.

I was informed that a C-130 Gunship would be on station.

The first impacts from the aircraft were most impressive. The burst of the first salvo went all the way to my Tank, very impressive! The Gunship continued to pound the target. The resulting fuel explosion confirmed my suspicion that the tanker was full of fuel. Soon the air strike ended and it was time to assess the damage.

I drove my Tank up and reported the following, "The obstacle has been reduced." The IED (tanker truck trailer) had been destroyed. Half of a city block had been destroyed (to include the previously mentioned stockpile point). I could sense the motivation amongst the Marines at the overwhelming success of the air strike. What next? Night had fallen and the CO of Fox had asked for a SITREP (situation report). I told him that the road was open and I wanted to continue to press the attack! The enemy had surely been decimated and demoralized by the Gunship's strike. We definitely had the initiative and as a bonus, the Gunship was going to remain on station for a while more. The CO gave the go-ahead to continue to push deeper into the city.

I used the Gunship's overwatch to search for enemy out ahead. With this and the Tank's thermal sights, I really had the advantage at night. I chose to violently take the fight to the enemy. The insurgents had very poor night vision and could easily be caught in the open at night. Due to the rotor wash of the Gunship, they often didn't hear the Tank coming until the first burst of my machine guns. The speed that my Tank section and the Gunship could take the fight to the enemy meant that the infantry were going to be left out of the night's festivities.

We moved fast and shot accurately. We pushed deeper and deeper into the city and left a trail of dead insurgents. Hunting was good that night. I really think we caught them off guard being so deep into Fallujah. Their communications weren't good and so few escaped my fires that, combined with the speed we moved at, we consistently had the initiative and what seemed like complete surprise on the enemy. I was so caught up in the attack that I had lost track of my ammunition situation.

At approximately 0400, my gunner, Corporal Chambers, informed me, "Gunny, I'm down to my last 200 rounds!" I informed the CO that I was black on ammo and could no longer continue the attack. He ordered my Tank section to return to where we had left the infantry, go firm and await resupply.

I ordered Staff Sergeant Escamilla to turn around and go back exactly the same way we had cut our way through the city. I would be the last one out. Due to the casualties we had inflicted on the enemy going in, we encountered no contact on the way back. In about a half an hour we were back alongside our infantry, still about 1,000 meters deeper in the city than any other Coalition forces. We turned around again and hunkered down for the next 2 hours until daybreak and, hopefully, resupply.

My Tank crew and I alternated standing watch so that we all could get at least a little rest. I shut the Tank's engine down and we became a big metal bunker in the middle of that Fallujah city street for the next 2 hours. After the previous 16 hours' worth of firing and destruction, everything seemed amazingly peaceful now. It was strangely quiet. The enemy was going to take one last attempt at my Tank before dawn, however.

I was standing watch, while the rest of my crew slept in their crew positions. They had earned the rest even though they weren't going to get much. Out of the pre-dawn quiet came the CRACK CRACK CRACK of an assault rifle. It was not an AK-47 but it was very close. About a second later, just as I was figuring out that the shots were from an M-16, came a short burst from a SAW. It was the infantry in the buildings next to me who were firing and they were shooting close! The firing then stopped as suddenly as it had started and it was eerily silent. Shortly after that, I heard the Marine infantry who had shot start to laugh a little. Marines are amazing in our ability to find humor in just about anything.

"What's going on up there?" I called to them.

"Three of them were trying to infiltrate you, Gunny. You'll see them when the sun comes up," they replied from the rooftop.

Soon the dawn broke on Fallujah. I must admit that I was surprised to see that the dead enemy insurgents were only about ten meters from the rear fender of my Tank. About as quickly as thoughts of what could have happened were it not for the infantry came into my head I put them back out and focused on the task ahead. I then had a great sense of satisfaction. I thought of how the enemy had vowed to make Fallujah a graveyard for Americans. Today, they would awaken and see two Marine Tanks and a platoon of infantry defiantly set up in the middle of their city. Many of the dead enemy combatants still littered the streets around us. I figured this would serve as a warning to any other insurgents as to the consequences of tangling with us.

Soon civilians began to slowly appear in the streets. I knew some of them were certainly insurgents with weapons hidden nearby. I was sure they were looking for an opportunity and I didn't plan on giving them one. We stood poised for a fight but due to our ammunition situation could not continue to push forward into the city again.

I called on the radio and inquired about the resupply. I also informed them that my Tanks were running low on fuel and that by tonight that would be an issue also. I was informed that we were pretty far into the city and moving ammunition to where we were at would be difficult and to get fuel to me would be impossible. I couldn't stand the thought of giving any of the ground we had taken back to the enemy, so I figured we would deal with the fuel issue later. While I waited for more ammo, I watched Iraqi civilians picking up all the expended brass from my machine guns off the streets.

The resupply arrived about an hour after daybreak. It came on foot! Resupplying a Main Battle Tank is not a small task and is usually done with large trucks. The high volume of RPG fire in this area of Fallujah meant that no trucks were coming in here, certainly not a fuel truck! I looked behind me and saw a column of running Marines. They were in pairs, with ammo crates slung between them. The Marine Corps commitment to mission accomplishment is amazing and the Fox Co. Marines were going to get ammunition to me if they had to carry it by hand, which they did!

The infantry platoon surged out of their buildings and pushed forward ahead of my Tank to provide an overwatch while my section uploaded. The civilians saw the infantry moving and due to the life the insurgents have forced them into, know how to anticipate when a firefight is going to break out in their streets. They disappeared.

In the Iraqi Theater of operations, whenever the civilians are not present at all, it indicates an impending insurgent attack. They know who the enemy is and protect themselves from their violence.

The infantry's surge forward must have caught them off-guard. No attack came and we were resupplied with machine gun ammunition. Main gun ammo was again transferred from Staff Sergeant Escamilla's Tank to mine, but again this was only a temporary fix as both of our Tanks were extremely low on them. My crew and I linked up 2,600 rounds of 7.62 mm and loaded it into the ready bin of the Tank.

I called the Fox CO and informed him that the resupply was complete and we were prepared to continue the attack. I reminded him of my low fuel situation and that I was very low on main gun ammunition. He was going to resupply the other two Tanks in my platoon (the Platoon Commander's Tank and his wingman) since they were still not into the city yet. They would then relieve my Tank section and we would go upload fuel and main gun ammo outside the city since those trucks couldn't come in.

The infantry moved back into the two buildings that they had been occupying and I moved back into the lead. We were ready to take the fight to the enemy again. The CO told us to hold. We were much further into the city than anyone else at this point and combined with our fuel and ammo that wasn't the best scenario for an attack. Much to our disappointment, we stayed defensive and held the attack.

The enemy has the ability in Fallujah to move around unarmed as a civilian and conduct reconnaissance on us for their attacks. All you can do is present as tough a target to them as possible: be hard to kill. We must have done this well because it took about an hour and a half before the first attack came. The urban environment allows the enemy the ability to get very close to you before he has to commit. The first enemy RPG shot was a good one, taken from very close. It passed right between Lance Corporal Hernandez's head and my head. It was so close that I felt the heat of its rocket propulsion on my face. The shooter was gone as quick as he shot. Not many got away from my Tank, but this one did. He must have inspired the lesser trained insurgents to fight.

Just like the previous day, they came out to attack my Tank. Again there was no coordination to their attacks. The result was the same. A few hits on my Tank, producing no damage, and many dead insurgents. The only thing different about today was that we were stuck sitting on the defensive and the enemy had the initiative. The attacks were coming from a lot closer. I was getting anxious to get back on the offensive. I wanted to take the fight to the enemy, not the other way around.

This continued through the morning, netting us ten enemy kills. I was then informed that the Platoon Commander's Tank had thrown a track outside of the city and had still not conducted its resupply yet either. It appeared our next attack would not be for a while. I would be wrong.

One of the infantrymen on the rooftops spotted a dozen insurgents gathering three blocks ahead. I called the CO and requested to go back into the attack before they could get away. "Go get 'em!" was his reply. That was the best news I heard all day. I commanded, "Red 3, this is Red 4. Follow my move. Driver, move out!" We were back on the attack and I was happy.

The speed that we were going to move with again meant that the infantry would stay behind. My Tank charged ahead a couple blocks. We had caught them in the open on a city street. They were assembled outside of a mosque. All were males of what we referred to as "military age" and most had weapons, AK-47s. Half tried to flee into the mosque; none made it. The other half of them ran around the corner down a narrow street. It appeared to me that the mosque was a staging area and almost certainly a stockpiling point for insurgent weapons. I could stay and secure the mosque or pursue the fleeing insurgents. I decided to stay on the attack and take the fight to the enemy. I commanded my Tank and wingman to move out around the corner and down that narrow street.

Once I entered the street, I observed that the fleeing insurgents had taken cover. My gunner, Corporal Chambers, searched with the Tank's high-powered optics while Lance Corporal Hernandez and I scanned from our hatches for enemy. The insurgents quickly darted from doorway to doorway. Some we got, some got away. They were definitely attempting to get down this street away from my Tank. I didn't want to give them a chance to dig in and defend so I kept up the pursuit.

The street got narrower as we went further down it. Soon, I could no longer traverse my Tank's turret. I still had the two machine guns on top to fight with so I continued. I couldn't stand the thought of giving back any of the ground we had taken. I passed a small crossroad about 8 feet wide. As I entered this intersection, I scanned to my right for enemy. I spotted one about 50 feet away just as he fired an RPG at my Tank.

I dropped into my hatch to swing my machine gun over and kill him. His rocket hit the side of my turret, doing no damage. As I was swinging my fifty calibre over, I didn't see the second insurgent firing from the rooftop of a 3-story building next to me.

I heard a hiss about a split second before it hit me. The Rocket-Propelled Grenade hit right inside my hatch striking me on the head. I saw a bright flash of light and then nothing but blackness. I had been blinded in both eyes. It felt as though I had been hit in the head with a sledgehammer and it knocked me down onto the turret floor. I was still conscious so I stood back up. I couldn't hear anything except a dull static-like humming in my ears.

I knew at the time that it was an RPG that had hit me. I couldn't see anything so I reached up and felt my face. It was wet and gooey feeling.

My first concern was to get the Tank moving out of what was obviously a bad place for it to be. Since I could not see to direct the Tank, I grabbed Corporal Chambers by his flak jacket and said to him, "Chambers, you've got to get the Tank moving. You've got to start working on a medevac for me."

I could feel Chambers moving but he was not answering me. I repeated my commands to Corporal Chambers. Again I received no response. I was to figure out later that he had been answering me but I couldn't hear it. Corporal Chambers had been wounded himself yet he unhesitatingly moved out of his gunner's position and into the Tank Commander's hatch, the same hatch I had just been blown out of. I felt the Tank begin to move forward and I felt good about that.

The RPG had hit me on the head inside the Commander's hatch. The majority of shrapnel ended up in my Flak jacket, helmet, and head. Shrapnel struck Lance Corporal Hernandez in the left hand and Corporal Chambers in the left tricep. I wonder what the insurgent who fired the rocket must have thought after seeing it score a direct hit inside the hatch and then see all the crewmen of the Tank still on their feet, including the one he had hit with the rocket. He must have thought, *What do I have to do to kill these Americans!*

The gunner on a Main Battle Tank has the most restricted field of view and perception of the world outside of the Tank, although he is the second in command. Corporal Chambers got the Tank moving, but he didn't know exactly where we were at. We were deep into the city at this time. Lance Corporal Hernandez, because of his position up top manning a machine gun, knew the way back. He directed Chambers which way to go. Hernandez's hand was bleeding profusely and he had to drop down to apply a pressure dressing. At this point the driver, Lance Corporal Frias, took over the direction of the Tank. There would be no medevac to where we were at, so my Tank had to return to the Fox Co. defensive line and Frias knew the way.

I must wonder again what the enemy must have thought after hitting this American Tank with everything it had only to see it drive right through their ambush and continue on its way. I was truly lucky to be in command of what I believe to be the best Tank crew in the Marine

Corps. Pressure brings out the best in some people and I am alive today because of their actions under fire.

During the trip back to the Fox defensive line, I began to try to figure out how bad I had been hit. I couldn't see and I couldn't hear and that wasn't good. I could feel that I was bleeding badly from my head and neck, which also wasn't good. I was still conscious and I was still standing up. This was very good. I was in little pain; my whole head felt somewhat numb. I felt both nauseous and sleepy, very sleepy, as if, if I just lay down on the turret floor and went to sleep I would feel better. I knew that was bad and I focused on staying awake. I grabbed onto the Tank's turret to help me stay on my feet.

The next thing I remember was feeling the Tank pitch back and then slam forward forcefully. I knew this could only be one place. We had just crossed the same berm I was set up behind two days ago in the Fox Co. defensive line. I knew the medevac was soon. I felt good about things at this point and knew that everything was going to be all right. The Tank stopped and I climbed to the top of the turret and waited for someone to come and get me.

Soon Marines and Corpsmen came and pulled me down from the Tank and began to render first aid. During this, mortar rounds began to impact near us. The Corpsmen who were treating me took off their own body armor and piled it on top of me to protect my wounded body. The dedication and skill displayed by these men was truly extraordinary.

Next I was placed on a Humvee and transported to a surgical unit. While I was there, I could hear (I was starting to get a little hearing back in my left ear) a commotion going on near my stretcher. I asked who was there. The response was, "General Hagee." Although the Commandant of the Marine Corps is not a doctor, there is something about his presence in the hospital that makes you feel that everything is going to be all right. Marines take care of their own!

I was then sedated for the removal of what remained of my right eye. I awoke and felt as though I was moving. I asked into the darkness, "Where am I?"

"You're on a plane to Germany, dude," was the response.

,   ,   ,

Staff Sergeant CJ Grisham is a Military Intelligence analyst assigned to a combat brigade of the 3rd Infantry Division during the invasion of Iraq. On his blog, *A Soldier's Perspective,* Sergeant Grisham recounts the day he entered battle:

,   ,   ,

Two days ago, we got attached to 4/64 Armor for a mission to seize some bridges in a small town between Karbala and Hillah. The purpose of the operation was to feint an attack on that town and proceed about 20 kilometers east towards Al Hillah in an attempt to force units from that town or Karbala to expose themselves and try to reinforce the town in which we were fighting.

Initially, we were supposed to be the second company to go through. We broke our team up into two small teams so that we could augment two separate companies instead of just one. Mr. Young and Vince went with Attack Company and Nate and I stayed with Assassin Company. Attack's mission was to go into the town first and seize the first bridge over the Euphrates River. Then Assassins would come in, cross the bridge, and continue on to seize the next bridge crossing a canal further east. Beast Company was supposed to go and block a route to the north so that we could do this. What ended up happening was that Assassin Company did the blocking mission, which meant we went in first. Nate and I were in the back of a 577 Armored Personnel Carrier so we couldn't see anything. We came into contact as expected when we got to our position. We could hear the bullets and mortars landing all around us. A few bullets hit our track and the First Sergeant had to duck a few times. After a very long hour of fighting, things calmed down a little and the company took some EPWs.

We were also beginning to see a bunch of civilians "surrendering" to us. One group of civilians lived in a house located right next to where we were. One of the guys threw an incendiary grenade toward the house to burn down the bushes so that we could see through them. They created a huge dead space. After he threw the grenade, the people started crying that there was another family member in there. We let one of the civilians go in there and get him. He ended up being a 70-

year-old-looking man. He was walking with a cane and could barely really move. We pretty much told them to get walking. The family consisted of about 6 women, 2 little girls about 9 years old, 3 men and a baby that was breastfeeding off one of the women. It's amazing how the baby didn't cry throughout the whole thing. It was probably about 3 months old, I'd say. There are guns being fired, tank rounds going off, and mortars landing and that baby just kept sucking. A bit of humanity in a world of chaos. We sent them on their way to where they said a family member lived. It was away from danger, so we let them go.

We took a few EPWs as well. One guy came up and was all shot up in the leg and part of his left foot was missing. It looked like his big toe and the one next to it were gone, all mangled. We got some information from him and treated his wounds. Other guys were shot in different places in varying degrees of pain and difficulty in treating. Nothing really gross or disgusting. I think we're getting used to seeing these type of things so it's probably relative. Most people would probably puke looking at this stuff.

There came a point when it was clear to get out and look around the town on foot. The first target was the building that this family came from. We went down to the house and looked in the truck that was in their front yard. The house was a decent-size thing about the size of my house. It was made of brick and mud like most houses we've come across. Inside the back of the truck was a bunch of RPGs, a couple of launchers, some mortars, a few chains of PKM [light machine gun] ammunition, a bunch of AK-47 ammunition, and an AK-47 behind the seat in the cab. There were also a couple of bags that we went through. The bags contained mostly clothes but each one had an AK magazine in it. One of the bags also had bundles of money. We checked inside the house but didn't find anything. We think that the house was probably a company CP for the Republican Guard that we got into a fight with. They were good at forcing civilians to let them use their homes and just taking whatever they wanted.

A little bit later we started walking around the sector and collecting ammunition and weapons to gather up and destroy. While they were out doing that, Nate and I walked around to search the dead soldiers for documents and other things we needed. We've been taking the money off of the dead soldiers as well. They don't need it anymore and we can use it to pay off informants for information. I think we've amassed over 200,000 dinars, which really isn't a lot of money. The exchange rate is about 3,000 dinars to the dollar. So, you're looking at just under $70 there. The money will go right back to the Iraqi people who help us find the bad guys.

While we were out searching the bodies we heard gunshots. As I turned around I saw one of our soldiers shooting into a ditch and diving for cover. More gunshots came from the ditch. It sounded like automatic fire, an AK-47. We all found cover quickly behind trees. The shooting continued for a few minutes and we exchanged gunfire. There were probably 7 people shooting at us from that ditch at least. The commander was with us as well as a reporter from the *Boston Herald*. The commander told one of the guys to shoot a grenade from his M203 and bound forward. The guy shot his round and I ran forward a couple of trees. When I looked over, no one had bounded with me, except Nate behind me. I told the engineer, the guy with the M203, to fire another round and that as soon as it goes off to rush forward towards the trench. He fired another round and as soon as it exploded I took off towards the trench, but noticed that no one was running with me on either side. I didn't pay attention to who was behind me. I stopped just short of the trench behind a tree located about 7 feet away from the guy that was shooting trying to dodge bullets and stay alive. Every time I stopped running I'd yell in Arabic for the guy to surrender: "Esteslem! Esteslem!" There were actually 5 guys left in there, but the other ones had either been shot or killed already and kept their heads down. So, here I was about 7 feet from the guy and he's still firing at me, not knowing there were still 2 more guys injured but alive in the same trench. The tree that I'm taking cover behind is throwing bark all around me from the rounds hitting it right where my head was. If the tree wasn't there, neither would my head. I wouldn't be standing up if the tree weren't there. It was just big enough for me to stand sideways behind, so I couldn't kneel or go prone or I'd be exposed. I told one of the guys to my left to throw me a grenade. I took the grenade and pulled the pin on it. I popped the spoon and let the grenade cook off for a second before throwing it into the ditch. I saw the guy's head pop up and threw the grenade right where his head was. About 2–3 seconds later it exploded and I charged in with my 9mm. I had already shot 10 rounds at the guy from behind my tree. Again, I charged the ditch alone thinking that these guys were gonna run up with me. I shot a few more rounds at the guy and hit him right in the tailbone and killing another beside him. He started whining in pain and I dragged him out of the ditch and began searching him. The other guys had finally come up to help clear the ditch. There was a dead guy near where I had thrown the grenade that may have died as a result of it. I stripped the guy I shot of his weapons and forcefully searched him for documents and identification. Of the five guys shooting at us, two died, two were wounded, and one surrendered. There were a few more shots going off as the other soldiers with me cleared the rest of the ditch. I asked the guy how many more people were in the ditch. He said that there was one more soldier in the ditch to the east. I saw some grass moving as if someone was low crawling through the ditch in that area. I borrowed an M16 from one of the soldiers and shot about ten rounds where I saw the grass moving. Then, I had the engineer shoot another grenade down there just to make sure. The whole time we were fighting I was yelling for them to surrender in Arabic. "EstesLEM! EstesLEM!" Obviously, no one wanted to surrender. I took the guy's AK-47 that was firing at me as a reminder and hopefully to use to fire back at future Iraqis. After the encounter, we left the area. I guess we had accomplished our mission. Why do I always get in these situations when I don't have my rifle with me? An M9 pistol versus an AK and I came out on top. Weird!

I never in my life thought that I'd end up in a man-on-man firefight. That's the kind of stuff that the infantry do. You've seen it in WWII movies. You'd never think that MI soldiers would be required to perform that kind of task. And to think that I was the only one sane enough to charge the trench too. I should have made the Iraqi soldiers feel like idiots by telling them they were just overtaken by an MI soldier. I guess all that soldier training pays off. I can't complain anymore that I'll never need that stuff. But, to be completely honest, I'm not sure I'd have done the same thing if I had known I was alone charging that thing. Some things you just do to stay alive. I'm just glad I still get to go home when this is all over.

,   ,   ,

In March 2005, a coalition convoy traveling in Iraq was protected by a team of Military Police, call-sign "Raven 42," and was ambushed. The insurgents were so confident of a victory that they videotaped their attack. The MPs from the Kentucky National Guard fought back tenaciously, recorded on tape and recollected in an after-action review (AAR) of the ambush. Many blogs posted the AAR, and retired Major John Donovan reviewed the engagement on his blog *Argghhh!*:

,   ,   ,

This fight certainly shows that at least in this kind of fight, properly trained, motivated, and led (not to mention doing the leading themselves), they can hold their own. I will allow that the issue of women in the infantry is a different issue. But the issue of women in combat . . . well, my position all along has been: if they are in the Army, then they can take their chances, too. And I don't wanna hear any Regulars (Active Duty) talking down the Reserve Component (the Army National Guard and the US Army Reserve) unless they are being specific about people and places. Don't hand me any generic crap. Talk to the hand. And yes, I'm a Regular.

On to the AAR:

Everyone,

Over the next few days you will see on the television news shows, and in the print news media the story of a Military Police Squad who are heroes. Through those outlets, I doubt that their story will get out in a truly descriptive manner. I can't express to you the pride, awe, and respect I feel for the soldiers of callsign Raven 42.

On Sunday afternoon, in a very bad section of scrub-land called Salman Pak, on the southeastern outskirts of Baghdad, 40 to 50

heavily armed Iraqi insurgents attacked a convoy of 30 civilian tractor trailer trucks that were moving supplies for the coalition forces,
along an Alternate Supply Route [ASR]. These tractor trailers, driven
by third-country nationals (primarily Turkish), were escorted by 3
armored Hummers from the COSCOM [Corps Supply Command].
When the insurgents attacked, one of the Hummers was in their kill
zone and the three soldiers aboard were immediately wounded, and
the platform taken under heavy machine gun and RPG fire. Along
with them, three of the truck drivers were killed, 6 were wounded in
the tractor trailer trucks. The enemy attacked from a farmer's bar-
ren field next to the road, with a tree line perpendicular to the ASR,
two dry irrigation ditches forming a rough L-shaped trenchline, and
a house standing off the dirt road. After three minutes of sustained
fire, a squad of enemy moved forward toward the disabled and sup-
pressed trucks. Each of the enemy had handcuffs and were looking
to take hostages for ransom or worse, to take those three wounded
US soldiers for more internet beheadings.

About this time, three armored Hummers that formed the MP
Squad under callsign Raven 42, 617th MP Company, Kentucky
National Guard, assigned to the 503rd MP Battalion, 18th MP
Brigade, arrived on the scene like the cavalry. The squad had been
shadowing the convoy from a distance behind the last vehicle, and
when the convoy trucks stopped and became backed up from the initial attack, the squad sped up, paralleled the convoy up the shoulder
of the road, and moved to the sound of gunfire. They arrived on the
scene just as a squad of about ten enemy had moved forward across
the farmer's field and were about 20 meters from the road. The MP
squad opened fire with .50 cal machine guns and Mk19 grenade
launchers and drove across the front of the enemy's kill zone,
between the enemy and the trucks, drawing fire off of the tractor
trailers. The MPs crossed the kill zone and then turned up an access
road at a right angle to the ASR and next to the field full of enemy
fighters. The three vehicles, carrying nine MPs and one medic,
stopped in a line on the dirt access road and flanked the enemy positions with plunging fire from the .50 cal and the SAW machine gun

(Squad Automatic Weapon). In front of them was a line of seven sedans, with all their doors and trunk lids open, the getaway cars and the lone two-story house off on their left.

Discipline, training, leadership. Attacking into a "near" ambush is the correct response. It's also hard, and takes great confidence in yourself, your buddies, your leaders, and your gear—especially when, by definition, an ambush is a surprise. Reacting, and reacting correctly, is the purpose of training and drill—however sometimes repetitive it might seem.

Immediately the middle vehicle was hit by an RPG knocking the gunner unconscious from his turret and down into the vehicle. The Vehicle Commander (the TC), the squad's leader, thought the gunner was dead, but tried to treat him from inside the vehicle. Simultaneously, the rear vehicle's driver and TC, section leader two, open their doors and dismount to fight, while their gunner continued firing from his position in the gun platform on top of the Hummer. Immediately, all three fall under heavy return machine gun fire, wounded. The driver of the middle vehicle saw them fall out the rearview mirror, dismounts and sprints to get into the third vehicle and take up the SAW on top the vehicle. The Squad's medic dismounts from that third vehicle, and joined by the first vehicle's driver (CLS trained) who sprinted back to join him, begins combat lifesaving techniques to treat the three wounded MPs. The gunner on the floor of the second vehicle is revived by his TC, the squad leader, and he climbs back into the .50 cal and opens fire. The Squad leader dismounted with his M4 carbine and 2 hand grenades, grabbed the section leader out of the first vehicle who had rendered radio reports of their first contact. The two of them, squad leader Staff Sergeant and team leader Sergeant with her M4 and M203 grenade launcher, rush the nearest ditch about 20 meters away to start clearing the natural trenchline. The enemy has gone into the ditches and is hiding behind several small trees in the back of the lot. The .50 cal and SAW flanking fire tears apart the ten in the lead trenchline.

Recognize what you are seeing here. The "good guys" are getting hit. But cohesion remains. People do their jobs. They help each other— but never lose sight of the mission. "Duty First, People Always" is a hackneyed phrase to many people . . . but what do you think about it now? The casualties they are taking could well have justified a with- drawal. But they didn't. Why? I can't answer definitively without inter- viewing the troops—but I'll offer these hypotheses.

1. Body armor. People are hit, and wounded, but not taken completely out of the fight.
2. Combat Lifesaver training. People know how to treat the wounded, and do so. That gives *everybody* confidence and a willingness to stick it out. It also returns troops to the fight . . . which isn't happen- ing on the other side. Though CLS training in our military is not as universal as you'd think, as is mentioned at the end. The bad guys are just getting ground down (their dead-to-wounded ratio supports that point)—and ground down by a smaller group than they are who just won't quit fighting . . . and the squads doing this fighting are *not* enjoying the traditional advantages of the defender. At best, this is a meeting engagement. At worst, it is an in-stride assault on a defended position by an inferior force. It doesn't get any harder than that, guys.
3. Training. From training comes confidence. You'll see that mentioned later, too.
4. Leadership. Cool, and calm under fire. Leadership that directs. Con- trols. Leads. And we're not talking senior leaders. We're talking Staff Sergeant and Sergeant. The crucial link in any Army.
5. Trust & Confidence. Confidence that they can handle this fight—and trust that other people are busting their ass to get there and help out.
6. Discipline, discipline, discipline. Those of you who were in the Army during long periods of no-combat peace—remember how people bitched about load plans, and uniformity? Read on.

Meanwhile, the two treating the three wounded on the ground at the rear vehicle come under sniper fire from the lone house. Each of them, remember one is a medic, pull out AT-4 rocket launchers from the HMMWV and nearly simultaneously fire the rockets into the house to neutralize the shooter. The two sergeants work their way up the trenchline, throwing grenades, firing grenades from the launcher, and firing their M4s. The sergeant runs low on ammo and runs back to a vehicle to reload. She moves to her squad leader's vehicle, and because this squad is led so well, she knows exactly where to reach her arm blindly into a different vehicle to find ammo—because each vehicle is packed exactly the same, with discipline. As she turns to move back to the trenchline, Gunner in two sees an AIF [anti-Iraqi forces insurgent] jump from behind one of the cars and start firing on the Sergeant. He pulls his 9mm, because the .50 cal is pointed in the other direction, and shoots five rounds, wounding him. The sergeant moves back to the trenchline under fire from the back of the field, with fresh mags, two more grenades, and three more M203 rounds. The Mk19 gunner suppresses the rear of the field. Now, rejoined with the squad leader, the two sergeants continue clearing the enemy from the trenchline, until they see no more movement. A lone man with an RPG launcher on his shoulder steps from behind a tree and prepares to fire on the three Hummers and is killed with a single aimed SAW shot thru the head by the previously knocked out gunner on platform two, who now has a SAW out to supplement the .50 cal in the mount. The team leader sergeant, she claims four killed by aimed M4 shots. The Squad Leader, he threw four grenades taking out at least two baddies, and attributes one other to her aimed M203 fire.

The gunner on platform two, previously knocked out from a hit by the RPG, has now swung his .50 cal around and, realizing that the line of vehicles represents a hazard and possible getaway for the bad guys, starts shooting the .50cal into the engine blocks until his field of fire is limited. He realizes that his vehicle is still running despite the RPG hit, and drops down from his weapon, into the driver's seat, and moves the vehicle forward on two flat tires about 100 meters into a better firing position. Just then, the vehicle dies, oil spraying everywhere. He remounts his .50 cal and continues *shooting the remaining of the seven cars lined up and ready for a getaway that wasn't to happen. The fire dies down about then, and a second squad arrives on the scene, dismounts and helps the two giving first aid to the wounded at platform three. Two minutes later three other squads from the 617th arrive, along with the CO, and the field is secured, consolidation begins.*

That's just simply Audie Murphy stuff. Wounded, stunned from the RPG blast—but still thinking, not just of reaction and survival—but thinking ahead, past the immediate end game. Taking away the ability of the enemy to escape. Hoo-ah! This is why the Armies of the western democracies are so lethal. Not just the weapons—but the inherent flexibility of the soldiers. US Sergeants have more authority and initiative than many Colonels in some second-tier armies. And it shows.

Those seven Americans (with the three wounded) killed in total 24 heavily armed enemy, wounded 6 (two later died), and captured one unwounded, who feigned injury to escape the fight. They seized 22 AK-47s, 6x RPG launchers w/ 16 rockets, 13x RPK machine guns, 3x PKM machine guns, 40 hand grenades, 123 fully loaded 30-rd AK magazines, 52 empty mags, and 10 belts of 2,500 rds of PK ammo.

The three wounded MPs have been evacuated to Landstuhl. One lost a kidney and will be paralyzed. The other two will most likely recover, though one will forever have a bullet lodged between second and third ribs below his heart. No word on the three COSCOM soldiers wounded in the initial volleys.

Of the 7 members of Raven 42 who walked away, two are Caucasian Women, the rest men—one is Mexican American, the medic is African American, and the other three are Caucasian: the great American melting pot. They believed even before this fight that their NCOs were the best in the Army, and that they have the best squad in the Army. The Medic who fired the AT-4 said he remembered how from the week before when his squad leader forced him to train on it, though he didn't think as a medic he would ever use one. He said he chose to use it in that moment to protect the three wounded on the ground in front of him, once they came under fire from the building. The day before this mission, they took the new bandoliers that were recently issued and experimented with mounting them in their vehicles. Once they figured out how, they pre-loaded a second basic load of ammo into magazines, put them into the bandoliers, and mounted them in their vehicles—the same exact way in every vehicle—load plans enforced and checked by leaders! Leadership under fire—once those three leaders (NCOs) stepped out of their vehicles, the squad was committed to the fight.

Their only complaints in the AAR were: the lack of stopping power in the 9mm; the .50 cal incendiary rounds they are issued in lieu of ball ammo (shortage of ball in the inventory) didn't have the penetrating power needed to pierce the walls of the building; and that everyone in the squad was not CLS trained.

Yesterday, Monday, was spent with the chaplain and the chain of command conducting AARs. Today, every news media in theater wanted them. Good Morning America, *NBC, CBS, Fox, ABC,* Stars and Stripes, *and many radio stations from Kentucky all were lined up today. The female E5 Sergeant who fought thru the trenchline will become the anti-Jessica Lynch media poster child. She and her squad leader deserve every bit of recognition they will get, and more. They all do.*

I participated in their AAR as the BDE S2, and am helping in putting together an action report to justify future valor awards. Let's not talk about women in combat. Let's not talk about the new Close Combat Badge not including MPs.

,   ,   ,

U.S. Army First Lieutenant Neil Prakash found his way back to his unit after a few weeks of R&R in the States. He was reacquainted with his tank platoon just before the assault on Fallujah. On his blog, *Armor Geddon,* Lieutenant Prakash—call-sign Avenger RedSix—describes the use of tanks, infantry, and artillery in the battle for Fallujah:

,   ,   ,

ZZZip. P-e-e-e-w-w-w-w

*Crack . . . Crack*CRACK

"Oh SHIT!"

"Hey! How does it go in that movie? 'If it's a whiz, it's close, if it's a crack, it's hitting you,' or something like that?" I hollered at the humvees next to me.

That wasn't the exact quote. But I think it was from *Black Hawk Down*, I'm not sure. I was standing ball-defilade in my hatch. That means, from my crotch up, I was exposed. Dawn was rising in the east and we were all situated on the overpass bridge now. The tanks were in the center of the bridge, hull facing south, gun tubes facing west. This gave anybody on the ground behind the tanks the maximum friendly cover from the sniper fire. Either way, whoever was shooting at us, wasn't far off.

CRACK . . . CRACK.

The bullets were just snapping as they hit the metal all around me.

"Good lord. Where the hell is it coming from?"

It was funny as hell as we all looked around bewildered. It's a funny thing about getting sniped. You're probably waiting for me to elaborate, but I can't. That's it. It's just funny. Ok . . . so some guy has you in his sights and he's trying to kill you. And he hasn't yet. But the bullets are coming damn close. And you don't know where he is. So that's funny. And for some reason, any time you come real close to death, but live . . . that's just absurdly funny. Maybe it's also funny because somebody is shooting little bullets at this huge tank. A tank that withstood more than ten rocket-propelled grenade strikes in Baqubah in a single day and never stopped rolling. But here we are standing ball-defilade because that's where the best view is.

I licked my teeth. My mouth started feeling like a Chia Pet and I had a beard now. All of us needed to get out of the tanks. Our legs and backs were killing us. We climbed out of the hatches. As we did, more bullets started snapping all around us. "Oh SHIT!"

We scrambled to get off the turret and onto the ground behind the hull. Once we were safely there, we just laughed some more about getting sniped.

"Oh man. I gotta brush my teeth." But the only thing accessible was a case of 20oz. Riptide Rush Gatorades in the bustle rack for rinsing my mouth. I took a few breaths and laughed as I scrambled back up on the turret. Bullets cracked on the turret as I dove onto the blow-out panels on the back of the turret. I had some cover from the lid of my tank commander's hatch, which was open. I reached down into the bustle rack, grabbed a bottle, and scrambled back onto the ground. I brushed my teeth and rinsed out with Gatorade. It was pretty gross-tasting but I felt like a million bucks afterwards. I grabbed my electric shaver and buzzed my face. My face was filthy and covered with dust, but it didn't matter. I felt just a smidgen cleaner now.

The BRT commander wanted to push west into the top or north side of the industrial zone so we could take our objectives. We had spent the early morning clearing the houses immediately to our west but they were scattered and had random shooters in them. We moved along the bridge and took the off-ramp that led us into the city. The tanks led, the Bradleys followed, and the scouts were right behind us. We pushed forward until my tanks sat on the objective. From behind us, the scouts started taking some decent sniper fire. Windows and windshields started filling with bullet holes. Tires on the humvees started blowing out. Phantom 6 sent his scout platoons back up onto the bridge.

"Red 6, Phantom 6. Come to my location. My humvee is in the middle of the road behind you. I'll show you where the sniper is."

I turned our tank section around and kept the Brads up front. I raced back where I saw a green humvee in the middle of the road all by itself. Phantom 6 was standing by the shotgun seat with his radio's handmike up to his head. There were a few bullet holes in his windshield.

"Do you see that building all by itself way out there in those palm trees?"

"Roger," I replied.

Hit that fucking thing. He didn't say it on the net. He shouted it at me. I couldn't hear him with my CVC [combat vehicle crewman's helmet] on and the turbine running, but I didn't have to be deaf to read lips. It was clear.

"Damn, SGT P. He's pissed as fuck. Let's blow some shit up for him."

I grabbed the override and laid him onto a rundown gray brick shack tucked into the trees.

"On the way." BOOM.

Gray smoke and debris blasted out from all sides. I turned to Phantom 6. He still looked pissed but he gave me a thumbs-up. He loved having the tanks. They were like big huge toys to him. And it gave him a power he never played with before . . .

"Red 6, Outlaw 1. My LRAS [Long-Range Advanced Scout surveillance system] guy is going to lay you on a building with bad guys. There're two guys with weapons on the rooftop. Can you take out the building with main gun?"

"Yeah, just tell me where to go."

He guided us forward, describing things we should be seeing in the road. Landmarks. Suddenly, we saw what he was looking at.

"Jesus. Look at the size of that thing," I said.

"I don't think he realizes we can't take down that whole thing," SGT P said.

In the distance, a huge hotel building loomed. It looked about 6 or 7 stories high.

"Hey, there are some guys crossing the road," SGT P called out.

I looked down and saw three guys race across the road from north to south into the hotel. They were too far out of range to engage with the coax machine gun.

Damn.

"Let's hit it, 8." SSG Terry and I began to pound the building with HEAT rounds. Even if we couldn't bring it down, anybody inside was definitely getting a mouth full of 120mm.

Suddenly five guys came out of nowhere from the left, sprinted in front of the hotel, and then crossed the road.

I sent a sitrep to Phantom 5, the XO, telling him what I saw.

"Roger. Send a grid and continue to observe," he said.

Hmmm. Ok. They seemed to be running towards a central location up ahead. It looked like they were running into a mosque. So I looked at my map. I had a grid to where I was.

"SGT P. Give me a range to where you saw those guys."

SGT P fired his laser range finder and called out, "2490 meters." I subtracted 2,490 meters from the 10-digit grid I had and called up the grid I calculated.

"Shit, there goes some more!" SGT P said. Five more guys scurried across the road from the left to right. They had AK-47s slung and a few had RPGs.

"What the fuck?" I wondered what the hell was going on.

For the next 20 minutes, we kept seeing guys in groups of 3 to 5 sprint across the road and into a building in front of a minaret. I couldn't see what they were doing once they crossed the road. I didn't even know if they were still there or if they had moved north, but at least 40 or 50 guys had crossed the road so far.

A guy came running back into the middle of the road from the north and threw something. It landed in the road and exploded into flames.

"Molotov cocktails!" I hollered. A few more guys came out into the road and started throwing more bottles into the street. The fire got bigger. One dude started pouring something all over the flames. It grew into a huge curtain of fire pumping out black smoke. These dumbasses were trying to make a smoke screen. I guessed that the fuel was probably diesel, judging by the way it burned and the black smoke.

I called up what we were seeing.

"Roger, Red 6. Continue to observe."

Jesus. Can't we do something about this?

"Hey, this is Red 6. Can we get some indirect dropped on these guys? It looks like these guys are going into a building by a mosque."

I made it clear on the net exactly what we were seeing. Phantom 5 started explaining the trickiness of this fire mission, since it was so close to a mosque. "We need to be absolutely sure of this grid. You're definitely seeing guys with weapons running into a mosque?"

Suddenly, I became filled with doubt and fear. I knew that they were running into a building. And I wasn't sure if it was at the mosque or real close to it. At 2,500 meters, you lose precise depth perception, looking through a monocle sight.

"Sir, I don't know if this is such a good idea," SGT P said. "Remember what a stink they made about Baqubah." My gunner was doing his job of looking out for his lieutenant.

I was getting frustrated. I started worrying about getting in trouble and being solely responsible for destroying a mosque for no good reason.

"Dammit, but we saw those dudes just running across the road with AKs."

"Sir, I know what you're seeing. I see it too. I just don't want to see you fry, that's all." He felt my frustration. He had a good point. If I did nothing, then there was no way I could get in trouble. But if I called for indirect, I could either kill some bad guys, or destroy a mosque for some bad press.

Inside of me, I felt like this was a bad idea now. I started thinking that I was going to hang. But there was a part of me that didn't want to buckle on my own convictions. I couldn't back down now. Maybe it was pride. That's a bad reason to ever make a decision, but I felt like it was worth frying. I knew what I saw.

The BRT was still back on the bridge at the cloverleaf more than a kilometer behind me. They pulled the truck with the LRAS mounted into a position on the bridge where it could see what I was seeing. They were going to help me out by getting a second set of eyes on the scene. Chris Boggiano radioed a grid based on what his operator was looking at.

I copied the grid and looked down at my map. "No, that's not right. The grid you gave is too close to me. This mosque is about two and a half clicks away." Here was the problem. The whole damn road had mosques all along it.

He sent me another grid and it was much closer to what I had calculated. He also sent me an azimuth of 265 degrees. Once we were both looking at the same thing, he called up to higher to confirm everything that I had seen. The bad guys, the fire, everything.

I thought about Chris's grid. He got it from lasing the minaret. His LRAS provided a grid number, where my laser just provided a distance in meters. But we had lased a tiny building in front of the minaret. "Hey SGT P. Lase the minaret that 1LT Boggiano is talking about, and tell me how far away it is from the building where all those guys went." 300 meters. I added 300 meters to the grid Chris sent me. It was right on the grid that I had originally calculated. Chris had gotten a grid to the minaret, which was 300 meters behind the building that I had calculated a grid for.

"Red 6, Outlaw 1. Get on the Fires net and talk to Ramrod 18 directly. And if they ask for a 10-digit grid, just add a zero at the end of both numbers I gave you. Don't worry about it, it's fine. Also, if they offer you close air support, accept it." Chris had been the champion of indirect and close air support so far. He was killing plenty of bad guys. And just like the rest of us, he liked blowing shit up.

"You know what? Fuck it. 1LT Boggiano is backing us up. So is Phantom 5. Let's do this shit." SGT P was fired up now.

I was talking with the captain who was in charge of the artillery.

"Red 6, this is Ramrod 18. You need to be absolutely sure of this grid."

"Roger." I sent him the grid. "I've got troops in the open. Distance, 2490 meters. Direction, 265 degrees. One round, adjust fire, over."

"Roger, send that direction in mils."

Shit. Well, I knew there were 6,400 mils in a circle. And due west was 4,800 mils or 270 degrees. And the direction was 265 degrees . . . so . . . um . . . "4,700 mils." Sounded right.

"Roger. Shot over." The one round to make adjustments just left the gun back at camp.

"Shot out," I replied. I was ready to observe.

"Splash over." It was about to impact.

"Splash out." Any second now.

K-k-r-r-BOOM. An explosion went off right where they had all been gathering. It was dead center of where the guys had disappeared.

"Ramrod 18, Red 6. That shit was right on. Fire for effect. Fire for effect!"

"Roger. 20 rounds. Observe effects."

"Holy shit. 20 rounds? That's gonna be bigger than the barrage."

K-k-r-r-BOOM. K-k-r-r-BOOM. K-k-r-r-BOOM.

"Oh SHIT! Look at that! No WAY that just happened." I was in shock.

Explosions went up 5 to 10 stories. Huge gray clouds shot upwards. It looked like volcanoes were erupting. But that wasn't what shocked me. On top of the explosions, bodies were thrown straight up into the sky. It wasn't like the movies at all, where the explosion goes off and the guy is airborne, flailing his arms and legs. It looked like a child threw some action figures straight up in the sky. They didn't flail at all. They just went straight up end over end and bloomed outwards like the petals of a flower blooming in fast-forward on the Discovery Channel. It was unreal. Each explosion sent 3, 4, or 5 terrorists up into the sky.

K-k-r-r-BOOM. K-k-r-r-BOOM. K-k-r-r-BOOM. It was the funniest thing we had ever seen. It was also unreal. You never expect to see bodies do that. So when you see it, it feels surreal.

"Red 6. Ramrod 18. How was that?"

"That shit was dead on. It was perfect."

"Hey, if there's anything left, call for a repeat mission."

Good Lord. We hammered the shit out of them. Maybe there were some more bad guys around. Ah what the hell.

"Roger. This is Red 6. Repeat 10 rounds. I say again, repeat 10 rounds." And the rounds came in.

Three bad guys came stumbling out of the smoke. One was clutching his belly with one arm and holding onto the sling of his AK with the other. K-k-r-r-BOOM. They disappeared.

"Daaaaammmn!" SGT P laughed. "I shit you not. I swear that round landed directly on his head."

A round impacted on a huge hotel-looking building off to our left.

"Oh shit!" said SGT P. "There was a guy on the roof." When that round hit the building, it looked like God himself came down and pimp-slapped him off the building. He just flew sideways like he was cata-pulted into orbit. And this other dude got slammed down from the roof. He hit the ground and then bounced off the pavement for another 60 meters. SGT P told us everything he saw as I kept the artillery guys informed of what was happening.

"Red 6, Ramrod 18. Send me a BDA (battle damage assessment) if you can."

"Roger. That shit was dead on. I saw groups of about 5 guys blow straight up into the sky with each round that was impacting. About 3 guys survived the first attack. They came out of the smoke doubled over and grabbing their stomachs. The repeat mission hit those guys right on the head and finished them off. I'd say about 20 guys were killed."

"Red 6, Ramrod 18, roger. What about that building?"

"Roger. That building that the guys ran into is obscured from the debris but it looks gone. The minaret is still standing. The mosque looks fine."

"Hey, good job on the guns, guys. Red 6 said he saw guys blowing up."

Ramrod 18 was now talking to the guys on the gun line. We were all on the same net. Me being the forward observer, he being the guy back at camp keeping track of friendly locations and where the bad guys are, and the guys loading and firing the 155s. He relayed to them everything I saw, letting them know their work was appreciated and well employed.

Later that afternoon, we pulled off of the objective and let the rest of the BRT occupy the ground. When we reached the logistics resupply point, some guy, Toby Harnden, and some lady from CNN were looking for me. I was told they wanted to interview me but I had no idea why. Then Phantom 5 and 1LT Chris told me about the buzz.

The reporters found me on the ground and started asking me a few questions. Major Johnson was serving as the First Infantry Division historian. He seemed to be operating in some sort of public affairs role, so I felt good with him there. I was extremely skeptical about talking to the media. For one thing, I didn't want to say anything that would get me in trouble. Second, I didn't trust them to portray things how they really happened. And worst of all, I didn't want them to convey how excited we all were about killing bad guys. I didn't want to come off looking like a blood-lusting warmonger.

I described the situation as it unfolded without a problem. I tried not to show any excitement. I stuck with the facts. I avoided talking about how I felt . . . until he asked me what I saw. I knew that I loved what I saw. And I knew nobody at home would understand that.

"Hey Sir," I stepped away and beckoned for MAJ Johnson. "Can I tell them what I saw? I saw bodies flying in the air and all kinds of crazy shit. I don't know what I can say or not."

"Yeah, it's fine. Tell them what you saw. This was a huge success."

I felt a lot better now. "Man, when those rounds hit, bodies went flying up. It was fucking awesome, because I was so frustrated that we couldn't kill all these bad guys who were right in front of me . . ." I went on.

I finished up the interview and I asked Major Johnson what the big deal was.

"You haven't heard? They think they got Omar Hadid with that fire mission. The military intelligence and psychological operations guys went through there and think maybe 50 to 70 bad guys were killed in that indirect attack. And from the looks of the intelligence, it looks like there were a lot of key leaders in there."

Now I was really pumped. I thought about all of the key players on this mission. If Chris hadn't backed me up, I'm not sure if I would have gone through with the mission. I felt like the entire Brigade had my back on this one.

CHAPTER SIX

HEROES OF THE HOMEFRONT

Separations from loved ones can be anywhere from seven to eighteen months. Having a loved one in harm's way is a very stressful and trying experience. Lucky families get help from friends, relatives, and neighbors. Many others, especially those on bases or in neighborhoods where everyone is deployed, can find themselves struggling alone.

Last January, I traveled to Kansas City to help out at Chief Steve Arsenault's home while he was in Iraq. His wife, Sue, had just given birth to their son, Benjamin, and was taking care of the house and their three other children, Madalyn, Danielle, and Nicholas. I spent the extended weekend hooking up their computer system so the family could videoconference with Steve in Iraq, fixing broken drawers and floor strips, and doing other things to help out while Sue took care of Ben. But, mostly, I played with the kids—the kind of roughhouse play only dads know how to do. Me against the three of them. I never had a chance . . .

When I finally left to go home, Sue told me that the girls cried a bit because I reminded them of Steve. Of all things, that made me feel satisfied that in some small way I measured up somewhat to their father. And I felt sad that I made them miss him more. In time, the girls will learn how to adapt to missing someone. They'll learn how to build fences to protect themselves.

With friends and loved ones in harm's way, we all maintain ways to keep ourselves from letting our fears get the better of us. Retired Army Lieutenant Colonel Tim Fitzgerald of *CPT Patti—The Sweetest Woman on the Planet Goes to Baghdad* writes about his way of dealing with fear that something might happen to his wife, Captain Patti Fitzgerald, while she is in Iraq with the 1st Armored Division:

,   ,   ,

Fences.

I don't know what else to call them . . . the analogy is apt in my mind.

They are the intellectual construct by which I deal with the barrage of bad news from Baghdad. They work for me . . . I'm not sure how others do it . . . and I'll be honest: in the end, my fences are very, very selfish.

The fences come into play when I hear or read a news report that says "Another soldier killed today."

I listen carefully. If the report says the tragedy took place somewhere other than Baghdad I am relieved . . . and all my fences are intact.

But if that report is from Baghdad . . . the bad news just breached the first of my fences.

And so I listen some more . . . I search the internet. I look for any clue. Sometimes the report will indicate the Soldier belonged to the 4th Infantry Division or the 82d Airborne Division. If so . . . my second fence remains solid.

But if the report says 1st Armored Division, my second fence has been breached, my fences . . . my defenses . . . are weakening.

I have other fences. Unlike most, I have the "female soldier" fence. I've noticed the press is likely to make special note if a casualty is female . . . or perhaps the story will refer to the soldier as "he."

If I can be reasonably sure it isn't a woman, the third fence has protected me.

Inside the 1st Armored Division I have the 1st Brigade, 2d Brigade, and 3d Brigade fences. Inside the 1st Brigade I have five battalion fences.

Not quite as useful, but handy occasionally, are the Officer/NCO/Enlisted fence, the Quartermaster versus Infantry fence, and the east-or-west-of-the-Tigris fence.

But the ugly little secret that we don't really talk about is that in the end, I have about 120,000 fences . . . in the end the fences are about protecting *my* Soldier.

I don't want any Soldier to die. But there are varying degrees of that—and they work in the inverse sequence of the fences.

First and foremost I'm concerned for my wife. Next, is for her soldiers . . . because she *really is* the sweetest woman on the planet. I know how devastating it would be for her to lose one of hers. Beyond that, I pray for the 1st Brigade . . . because somehow I believe that every time that 1st Brigade fence is breached, it becomes just a bit weaker and doesn't protect quite as well.

These are my fences . . . I don't have to ensure they are rational.

I don't really like to look at my fences too closely. I like to pretend they are real and solid and offer true protection. But some days when I'm weak, if I look at them carefully, my fences look like the slot dividers on a huge roulette wheel. There may be thousands of slots on that wheel . . . but if they spin that little white ball it must come to rest somewhere.

I wonder sometimes about those who don't need fences . . . because they have no personal stake in this war. And I wonder how that feels.

I can't remember how that feels.

I was a child during the Vietnam era. As I learned to pray in the Southern Baptist church I learned that every prayer must include the phrase "and Lord, please bless our Soldiers in Vietnam." I suppose I had no personal stake in that one, although I was very aware when my big brother got his draft number—and it wasn't a particularly good one. But the example set in my church led me to feel as if I had a duty to pray for those Soldiers . . . as if somehow God had a huge scale and the weight of the prayers had to tip the balance in the Soldiers' favor.

On the eve of Desert Storm I took my little brother to the airport. Ostensibly he was heading for a new unit in Germany but we had it figured out . . . soon after his arrival in Germany that unit would be shipping out for Iraq by way of Kuwait in a serious shooting war. I fought that war at "maximum standoff range." I was in Atlanta. He has sand in his boots, a Bronze Star medal on the wall, and demons that sometimes still call in the night.

I learned a couple of days ago that my neighbor, the guy whose front door is ten feet from my own, the guy with whom I had a beer and barbecue only a few weeks ago—he was wounded on Friday. He's been airlifted from Iraq to Germany and they are talking about flying him to the US. He has severe burns and needs skin grafts.

And my wife is in Baghdad. And many of my friends.

A dear friend of mine whose husband just concluded his R&R leave told me that while preparing breakfast this weekend she popped the seal on a can of Poppin' Fresh biscuits. He flinched. As she told the story I got the feeling that the flinch was almost more disturbing than if he had reacted in a greater way. As if all the evil and heartache and fear symbolized by a sudden, quick sharp noise has insidiously taken up an unshakable residence deep inside his soul.

So I don't know—indeed I'm not sure I ever knew how it feels not to have a personal stake in a very dangerous endeavor.

Without that stake, is all this just something happening "over there"? If one has no personal stake . . . is that what allows some politicians to use this all as their political football, posturing for the pithy sound bites and the provocative headlines . . . and votes?

I don't know. I don't know how it feels. Perhaps it is an exhilaration that one needs no fences of one's own. Or perhaps it feels like liberty . . . the sweetness of which can only be tasted in its absence.

Or is it sweet? I don't know.

History is being made and we are on the right side of it. Of that I am not in doubt. And I have a personal stake in that. Virtually every one of us living here in Giessen and Friedberg, in too small apartments shopping at too small commissaries and tiny little PXs . . . getting together for frank discussions of our fears over lunch . . . opening our hearts to our neighbors to fulfill the palpable need for human contact and understanding . . . virtually every one of us has a personal stake in the liberty of 25 million Iraqis . . . and possibly the peaceful future of the world's most troublesome region.

I have a stake. I own a piece of that. And I am proud that I do. I am proud of my wife for her sense of duty to her country and to her Soldiers. I don't mean some jingoistic sort of arrogance sort of proud. I mean being a part of something that is greater than oneself. I mean having a speaking part in a role that is noble.

And I wonder what it feels like to have never held the fickle hand of a noble calling. Do the concepts of duty, honor and sacrifice hold any meaning for those? I don't know. Does knowing that one will bear no cost balance with one's lack of investment?

For I don't know . . . until the bill is delivered . . . the price that will be required of me for my personal stake in history. None of the stake-holders do.

And so I build my fences. I build as many as I can . . . as strong as I can. I bolster them with prayers and scripture and bravado and probability and sometimes too many glasses of wine.

I vent my anger to strangers on the Internet and my hopes to that tiny inner circle of the truest of friends.

I build my fences and polish them with optimism. I hiss loudly at trespassers who would cheapen the value of my investment.

Stay away from my stake! Don't stain it with your fingerprints . . . I don't know what it cost me yet!

My fences keep me sane.

Britt from *CaliValleyGirl* is dating an Army Chinook helicopter pilot who is now in Afghanistan. After learning of a Chinook crash in the mountains, she writes about waiting to find out if her boyfriend was flying the doomed copter and mourning the others when she finds out:

Yesterday when I heard the news that my boyfriend was all right, I was okay. I slept like a log and woke up rested this morning. I came to work chipper, but when I was sitting in front of my lunch tray in the cafeteria I realized I had no appetite. I forced myself to eat something, but after a few minutes I realized I was fighting against tears, against being sick.

Usually I nag my boyfriend to call and email me more, but now I am just happy with the knowledge that he is all right. He could go a month without calling me now, and I would be okay with that. My heart goes out to him right now. I wish I could hold him, and tell him how much he means to me. And I wish I could be there for him. The whole unit must be under considerable shock.

I think everyone is in mourning right now. Mourning those lost and mourning the days we had of blissful ignorance of the possible dangers. The unit made it through a deployment in Iraq with no casualties, so Afghanistan seemed like a piece of cake. I did realize that the biggest danger they would be facing would be weather. Also they are flying over a lot of mountains at pretty high altitudes and I knew that would also be an issue. But somehow, I always thought, "Well, they are experienced." And somehow that was translated into my mind as "They are invincible."

I think the worst thing about this experience was the hours of not knowing. The hours of emotional limbo. Part of me just wanted to know . . . but another part of me kept on saying "Not knowing still holds hope."

I cursed the news for telling us about the accident, telling us just enough, so we knew for sure that it was our unit, but then leaving us hanging when it came to what we wanted to know most. The emotional turmoil caused by letting thousands of people know that someone they love is possibly dead is an incredible power. The news struck fear into everyone I knew. I am thankful for The Information Age, but I curse the fact that the news is faster in reporting on deaths than the military is in notifying families about casualties.

I am very thankful for my friends. I was supposed to have coffee with my friend who lost her husband in Iraq and another close friend. They both came over at 4PM and another friend joined later. They didn't leave until 1:30AM and one of them spent the night. I can't thank them enough. They allowed me to worry, but didn't allow me go into an abyss of worry.

Although I am grateful for everyone's comforting (cyber included), I am especially grateful for my widowed friend. It was obviously something she would have rather avoided. She even admitted later that she cursed when she heard the news, and was asking why this couldn't have happened when she wasn't here. But somehow being with someone who had gone through casualty notification with the worst-case scenario as a result comforted me.

At about 8PM I finally decided that their suggestion of having a drink might be a good idea. So we opened a bottle of red wine and we toasted my boyfriend. And we opened a bag of chips. (This is going to sound morbid, but I was conscious of eating chips that I didn't really like that much, and thought that was a good thing, because it would be terribly tragic if I were eating salt and vinegar chips when I got the news of my boyfriend's death, and then would have a lifelong aversion to my favorite chips . . . yes, your mind does crazy things when under stress, as if in an attempt to keep some sort of control over a situation where one is just helpless.) Actually, most of the evening resembled a girls' night, except the fear that ripped through our hearts every time the phone rang. It was a kind of surreal evening.

I got an email from my friend yesterday afternoon:

It is very difficult to go through a deployment, even if it is an "easy" one. When they are so far away it makes everything harder and with yesterday as an example the media always reports the bad news. If you ever want to vent about the military, or say good things, or freak out because the news reported something bad, please feel free to always contact me if it helps. I'm not always the first one people want to talk to since my situation ended the way it did, but I do understand the waiting, the unknowing and the frustration in general of a deployment and of dating a military boy.

It was nice to hang out yesterday even if there was a gray cloud over the evening.

It was definitely an evening I will never forget, and the best evening I could have had under the circumstances. It was a celebration of friendship and life. And I am relieved that I can look back on it as such, and not as a schism between my life up to then, and the life that would have come after losing my boyfriend. And I feel terrible about those families who are living that schism right now.

While the fear of getting a phone call didn't materialize for Britt, many others have received the dreaded ring announcing that loved ones have been wounded. Carla Meyer Lois blogs as *Some Soldier's Mom* and writes about her life as a military wife and mother. She recounts how she learned that one of her sons, Army Specialist Noah Pincusof, was wounded in Iraq:

✦ ✦ ✦

So here's how the tale begins:

My husband and I were just about to sit down to dinner . . . and the phone rang . . . caller ID said the name of the Fort where my son is stationed when he's not in Iraq. (Note to self: If the caller ID says "Fort Benning," ***do not answer phone*—IT'S BAD NEWS.**) Of course, I didn't have that thought . . . and the Rear Detachment (they're the guys that stay behind and make sure things are going good back home) and I have the following conversation (as best I remember, but forever seared in my brain):

Rear Detatchment: Hello is this ——?

Me: Yes . . . (tentative)

RD: This is Sgt. F with the Rear Detachment.

Me: Yes . . . (still tentative)

RD: I'm calling about your son, Noah . . .

Me: Yes . . . (quiver in voice)

RD: Your son has been injured in Iraq.

Me: Yes (sob) (grabbing kitchen counter)

RD: He was injured by an IED . . .

Me: (gasp, sob, sob) (lying across counter)

RD: He has a serious spine injury . . .

Me: Oh no, no. (gasp, sob, sob)

RD: and he's in surgery.

Me: OK . . . (fighting pure hysteria) Where is he? Germany?

RD: No, he's in Iraq.

Me: OK, so my son has been injured by an IED, he has a serious spinal injury and he's in surgery in Iraq.

Husband: Oh, Noah!

RD: Yes, ma'am.

[I think it was in here I asked if I should make arrangements to go to Germany and he advised that it would be premature to make those plans, something about the Army discouraging family members from going to Germany before all the details are worked out . . . and I think my response might have been a guttural "Uh huh" and the RD saying something about when they called back they would discuss those arrangements . . . but I was really reeling at this point and fighting desperately to maintain some semblance of control . . .]

RD: I'm very sorry to have to call you to tell you this.

Me: When will you know something more? (gulp, gulp, whimper, sob, gasp, sob)

RD: I don't know ma'am, but I'll call you as soon as we know anything.

Me: Yes (gulp), please call (sob) me as soon as you (sob, gulp) know anything.

RD: Again, I'm very sorry to have to call you with this news.

Me: Yes, thank you. Please call me.

At some point, my husband thought I was about to "go down" and he stepped close and put his arm around my shoulders, and I quickly flip around and dissolve into gasping sobs, all punctuated with "No! No! No! No!"

Every Parent's Nightmare was upon us!

Almost immediately, I knew that there were *things* we needed to do, but couldn't get my brain to stop screaming long enough to know what they were. I knew that we needed to call Noah's two brothers and sister . . . we had to call his aunts and uncle . . . We made those calls . . . with healthy periods of wailing (on my part) during and between these calls. Our dogs were beside themselves because I was crying and they began barking and had to be put in the garage so that we can hear ourselves think (but we're really not doing much thinking . . . more like a mental game of bumper pool—lurching from task to task and bouncing from thought to thought).

I pull out a suitcase and begin packing clothes. I know we'll have to travel somewhere . . . but where? When? We talk about whether both my husband and I should go to Germany at the same time or should I go and based on what's happening there, have my husband come later? We decide that this will all depend on what the Army tells us when next they call. Who makes the travel arrangements? Do we do that? Does the Army do that? Questions not asked in the confusion that engulfed me during that call.

We answer calls on our cell phones from family and friends as word spreads and people offer their prayers and ask what can they do?? We don't know what to say because we don't know what *we're* supposed to be doing ourselves! My twin sister calls to say her bags are packed and passport is ready and she's going wherever I'm going no ifs, ands, or buts (none from this sis).

I pull out our passports . . . I ask my husband whether he thinks I'll need the power of attorney I have from our son. I get it out, too. I ponder for a moment whether I think I'll need the official Army record/file that Noah gave me before he deployed. I decide I'd rather not lose the file somewhere and if I need it, it can be overnighted. Although this seems like a logical string of actions, in reality they are herky-jerky tasks strung together by time and episodes of gasping sobs and crying . . . and praying to God to *please, please* let our son be OK. I'm not really praying, I'm *begging* God to please spare my son. I'm bartering . . . I'm badgering . . . At some point, I decide that I have to let dear friends know and ask for their prayers, so I draft the 21-word email that became my last post and send it to the "Noah Network" of friends and family that have been devoted and loving since he left for Basic Training almost 2 years ago. I decide I have to call his closest friends, Mike and James and Nick and Mish and Veronika . . . they have all been friends, since second grade . . . Inseparable whenever Noah is around and when he isn't—well, he's mostly who they talk about—especially since he went to Iraq.

Mike—who was just here with Noah when he was home on R&R—just about falls apart but promises to call the "kids" and let them know . . . none of the others answer their phones, but Mike knows how to find out where they are and locates them all . . . who then, in turn, call us on our cell phones wailing and crying . . . some conversations taken over midway by weeping parents . . . This does not help me get control of my crying at all. I am wishing we hadn't retired and moved away from them all because these wonderful creatures are my physical link to my now injured son—a link to the son who ran, played football, crewed (rowed), danced, bounded through the house . . . and now had "a serious spinal injury." I told God it didn't matter to me—just bring him back to me, we'd deal with everything later.

I was overcome on more than one occasion throughout the night by thoughts of my beautiful son being in pain and wondering if someone was there to comfort him and tell him it will be ok (which sends me into spasms of weeping). I know that there are nurses (angels in scrubs) and am truly comforted knowing that these angels will do whatever it takes to give our son comfort and care like no others. Oh, and did I mention that every 15 minutes or so after every episode of crying—either collapsed in my husband's arms, talking on the phone, seeing Noah's R&R suitcase still packed on the closet floor—great waves of nausea would overtake me and I'd throw up? (Sorry for the visual.)

At some point (a detailed timeline is mental mush today) I decide that my Military Mom friends and Military Wife friends would want to know and I email them . . . They get to work and put out the call for prayers . . . they go all out soliciting God's love and mercy for my son. I putter on my desk . . . Michael's Mom Stacey calls and she and I cry a little and she offers me love and encouragement . . . I unpack the suit-case . . . I repack the suitcase . . . I look at pictures of my son . . . I cry some more. I try to eat some toast (nope). My head is all stuffed up from crying, my eyes burn and my head is splitting . . . I figure more prayers can't hurt and the people I know that can mobilize the military "family" (those in it, near it or grateful for it) for prayers and good thoughts are *Blackfive* and *The Mudville Gazette,* so I email them with the same 21-word email as it's all I can manage before I dissolve back in tears. In the meantime, I'm answering instant messages from Noah's friends but have nothing more to tell them. I stare with looks that could kill trying to *will* the telephone to ring with news.

I speak with Patti Bader (a true Saint on Earth!) from *Soldiers' Angels* who gave me more information and comfort in the span of a 10-minute telephone conversation than I have ever experienced. She has mobi-lized (along with *Blackfive*) the *Soldiers' Angels* worldwide network and tells me things that will happen, things to do, what the Army will do and what we (they) will do to help . . . that a Soldiers' Angel will be in Germany to meet our son, comfort him, bring him necessities and a message of love from his mom . . . and another Angel will be waiting if he comes to Walter Reed Army Medical . . . they'll do whatever they have to in order to bring comfort and aid to our soldier—to ALL our sol-diers—their motto is "May No Soldier Go Unloved." I tell you honestly that I could not have made it through last night without the assurance and calm of the Angels.

As you can imagine, I was an ugly blubbering momma for a good part of last night . . . Many people urged us to try and get some sleep because it was unlikely we would hear anything for a number of hours. We would need to have all our wits about us and our strength for Noah. So about 11:00PM (yes, all this activity happened in 5 hours!) I swal-lowed a few sleep aids and lay down, but sleep was elusive.

I slept off and on but tossed and turned a lot. About 3:50AM, my cell phone rang . . . once. I try to redial the number and a voice announces that it was a prepaid service and could not be reached that way. Noah! It must be Noah! Now I'm actually talking out loud, "Please call back . . . please call back." 4:00AM. "Hey, Ma!" and voila! Sunshine where before there was darkness. No two more beautiful words than "Hey, Ma!" Except that he told me the details of the incident in which he was injured, the results of our conversation are in the update to my last post.

We believe he left Iraq about 3:00PM Pacific time (which is 1:00AM Iraq time) but are still waiting for someone to tell us officially that he has left (maybe there is no "official" in these cases?), when he'll arrive, the nature of his injuries, how long he'll be there and whether he'll be moved someplace else or returned to duty. We will now have to wait to see what the doctors in Germany think . . . he could be sent to Washington, DC, if they think he has an injury that requires treating OR they could hold him there in Germany and see if the swelling and tingling in his extemities (from being thrown into a wall by the force of the explosion) subsides on its own (and then go back to Iraq) OR who knows? That's the phone call we're waiting on . . .

We hate that he may go back . . . All of us with loved ones deployed can't help but occasionally think about getting the call . . . it's unavoidable especially when we see and hear and read about others who got the call and such thoughts evoke repulsion and sadness . . . but imagining last night's phone call can not begin to approach the actual horror of it—and now that I have experienced that, I'd prefer to not experience it again (been there, done that!). I know the nightmares generated by that call will be a part of me for all of my days.

We are otherwise hanging in there . . . suitcase and passport at the ready to travel wherever they are sending or keeping him. Waiting, waiting . . .

, , ,

Waiting seems to be the bane of military families, but in many cases it is an opportunity for the family to show strength and support. Wendy Marr writes at *Biting Their Little Heads Off* about what she's learned over the past eighteen months while her husband has been deployed to Afghanistan with the Iowa National Guard. She writes this as she prepares for her husband's imminent return:

, , ,

The year and a half that felt like it would never end is finally drawing to a close.

My brain has ceased all functions. The only thing that my eyes can focus on are the hands of the clock, and they are moving much too slowly.

In about 12 hours, I'll be standing in an armory, my heart in my throat, waiting for a glimpse of the love of my life.

I can't pretend to speak for other military spouses, as we are all individuals. I can only tell you what this deployment has been like for me . . . just a woman in the middle of nowhere, waiting for the man I love.

He was the last thing I thought of every night before I fell asleep, and the first thing I thought of every morning when I woke up. The thoughts never stopped during the day, I couldn't lose myself in anything no matter how hard I tried. The thoughts of him were always there.

This year has been the worst, and it's been the best. It seems like it's been forever since he left, but it also seems like yesterday.

I've been so fortunate in life. A wonderful husband, two great kids, lifelong friends. But now I've added more, another family so to speak. A group of wives and children that I can't imagine me surviving this last year without.

I've learned a lot this year.

I've learned what longing is. I've learned that there really is an empty spot in your heart when someone you love is gone for a long period of time. It's not just a figure of speech.

I've learned where dark humor comes from. I've learned to laugh at situations that would make most people shake their heads. But I've also learned that dark humor can help to save your sanity.

I've learned that even when you think you know what you are dealing with, that you can't kick your own butt out of depression.

I've learned about fear. I learned how scared I could be while sitting safely in my own home on those days when I didn't know . . . and we sat waiting for a phone call or a knock on the door. I learned that hours can be an eternity.

I've learned about guilt and self-hatred, being relieved when it wasn't my Soldier and then hating myself for that relief when someone that I know and care about was living my worst nightmare.

I can't say that I've learned what sadness is, as I already knew the pain of losing someone you love way too early in their young lives, but I have also learned that it can hurt almost as much to see another parent live through it.

But I've also learned that my worst day, worst fear, worst guilt . . . doesn't even scratch the surface of what many of our Soldiers live on a daily basis.

I can't even begin to imagine what it must be like to walk in their boots.

I've also said this year has been the best, and it has.

I've learned that I cry at the drop of a hat . . . but that those tears are more often tears of pride or thanks, than tears of sadness or anger.

In many ways I've had my faith restored. I've been reminded what it's like when a community pulls together.

I've learned that the kindness of a stranger can make an amazing impact. Lynne? I can never thank you enough.

I've learned that someone reaching out to say "Hey, I'm here and I care" can give you strength.

I've learned that "If there is anything I can do" isn't a throw-away phrase uttered by people when they don't know what else to say. I've also learned that sometimes people just do it without ever saying a word.

I've learned that I am a complete sucker when it comes to that man of mine. I also know that he's worth it.

I've learned to be so very thankful for what I have.

I've learned to be in awe of what we as a country have. I pray I never again take it for granted . . . because I have.

I can only say I'm very proud of my husband. When he left he promised me he'd "do it right" and he did . . . they did, all of them. They are all now a part of history. They've risked themselves for me and for you. They've made a difference in a struggling country. No matter how the media portrays them, they know what they've accomplished. So do I. And I'm proud of them.

So now my year of extremes is almost over . . . but for others it's only beginning. Please keep them in your thoughts and prayers.

,   ,   ,

Retired Army Major Donald Sensing is in the midst of his second career as a minister in Tennessee. His blog, *One Hand Clapping*, covers a lot of topics, including the military. Reverend Sensing's son is a Marine in Iraq:

,   ,   ,

It is early on November 10, 2005. I am surfing the internet to find a photograph related to the 230th anniversary of the founding of the U.S. Marine Corps. My son is a Marine serving in Iraq, so I try the Marines' main web site to find the commandant's message commemorating the day is there.

No luck. I can't find a link to the message so I decide to take a look at the photo gallery, featuring dozens of photographs taken by Marine photojournalists around the world. About six pages along my heart almost stops. There, in the middle of the page, my eye falls on this caption:

> CAMP FALLUJAH, Iraq—LCpl. Stephen Sensing, left, from Nashville, Tenn., and Sgt. Matthew Starr, Richmond, Minn., from 1st Platoon, 2nd Amphibious Assault Vehicle Company, 2nd Marine Division kick back prior to departing on an evening patrol Nov. 5.

Beside the caption is a small photo of the two Marines reading magazines. One is *Popular Mechanics*, the other's cover is not visible.

My wife later told me a moan escaped my lips before I cried, "It's Stephen!," causing her and Stephen's younger brother to come running, thinking I had called in despair. But their faces lit up when they saw the picture. My wife noted the web address so she could email it to her friends. On the Marine Corps' birthday they gave us a wonderful present.

Iraq. My son is there as I write these words. He managed to get access to a satellite phone to call yesterday, Dec. 15, the day millions of Iraqis went to the polls to elect a permanent parliament. It was 9 p.m. in Fallujah when he called. I was just about to be seated for lunch with a Catholic deacon, a close friend who was also a field-grade military police officer in the Tennessee Army Guard and a veteran of Afghanistan.

"How'd election day go in your area?" I asked him.

Stephen replied, "Not much happened here. The Iraqi army did the security for the voting. It was quiet as far as I could tell."

I try to imagine what it was like for him and his brother Marines, members of 2d Assault Amphibian Battalion, to deploy to Iraq in September 2005. My family and I went to Camp Lejeune, N.C., to see him off. Some of the NCOs in his chain of command had been to Iraq twice already and had seen heavy fighting in the invasion of 2003. But most of the unit consisted of young men like Stephen, 18–20 years old, inexperienced and not really comprehending what they were about to do. Even so, I knew they were as well trained for the months ahead as they could be.

I discovered it was so much harder to watch my son go than it was for me to go, almost 30 years before. I posted some photos on my blog of our farewell, including one my wife took of me embracing my son before he was called to formation to depart. I captioned it:

There were many "last" embraces, but there was one that you make count and you give it before you know it's time to watch him run to final roll call. It's so hard to let go; you want to make time stand still. You barely breathe and try to feel his heartbeat in your own breast because his heart will always beat in yours.

Not long afterward, he and his comrades boarded buses for Cherry Point Air Station and they were off.

Iraq. Car bombs and suicide attacks. Abu Musab al-Zarqawi and "al Qaeda in Iraq." The daily news reports hammer the losses. Thankfully, in the four years since 9/11 the news media seem to have learned the "Marines" and "Soldiers" may not be used interchangeably, so my wife, other two children and I don't clutch when we hear a report of "soldiers killed," but we pray for the families who hear those words with fore-boding. We know where Stephen's unit generally operates, so Marine casualty reports from other areas of Iraq don't throw us into anxiety.

"How do you do it?" a friend of my wife asked her. "Every day the news must set you on edge!"

"No," Cathy replied. "Don and I both lived in places where terrorists tried to blow us up. You just do the best you can and get on with life."

Then came December 2:

Ten Marines were killed yesterday and 11 were wounded by a road-side bomb near Fallujah, about 40 miles west of Baghdad, a U.S. mil-itary spokesman said today.

I write on my blog:

My son is based in Fallujah. Would I have heard by now that he is one of the ten? I don't know. I don't know how long notification takes. In the meantime I have to say that it sounds like the casualties were inflicted on a dismounted unit, that is, infantry. My son is in a mech-anized unit. But my heart skips beats anyway.

When there are casualties in a Marine unit the satellite phones are shut down for non-official business. The Marines rightly don't want to take a chance of a mom, dad or spouse learning of a loved one's death or serious wound except through official notification procedures. By the next evening the Marines have released the names of the killed and wounded. Later I learned that Stephen, who had been trained as a Com-bat Life Saver before deployment, was sent to the surgical center at Camp Fallujah to help out. He said it was sobering.

It's almost Christmas. I'll preach that day and hold a joyous worship service at my church. There is so much to celebrate along with the advent of the Christ child: the liberation of tens of millions of people from crushing tyranny, the steady improvement in Iraq's ability to stand on its own feet as a democracy, the fact our country has not suffered another attack. But our Christmas shopping has been simple and short this year. Our son is in harm's way on our behalf. Just getting more stuff cannot nourish our souls.

The prophet Micah wrote that God will judge between all the peoples and will settle disputes for strong nations far and wide. They will beat their swords into plowshares and their spears into pruning hooks. Nation will not take up sword against nation, nor will they train for war anymore. All people will be at peace, and no one will make them afraid, for the LORD Almighty has spoken (Micah 4:3–4).

Let us pray that day comes quickly. Until then may the Lord watch over those who serve, to make them instruments of justice, enablers of peace, and finally to see them safely home.

Semper fi, Lance Corporal Sensing, my eldest son. May God be with you 'til we meet again. You make us proud!

Pride in their military men and women is something that military families share. Erika S. blogs at *Military Bride* and writes of becoming the wife of a deployed soldier. Erika takes a look at the various stages of living through a deployment:

Military wives are like kindred souls. Even when Matt returns home and gets his honorable discharge—when I'm no longer a "military" bride, but rather, just a bride—I'll still have a connection to this phenomenal group of people. Though I will never truly understand all it entails to hold the title of a military wife, what it means to "keep the homefires burning" is exclusive to knowing how a deployment feels, how it feels to go to sleep alone night after night after night, how it feels to load the responsibilities of another person onto your own plate, how it feels to wish away a year more vehemently than you've ever wished for anything, how it feels to get "the rage" over an insensitive friend or coworker complaining over the weekend absence of a boyfriend or husband (and then later feeling really bad about "the rage").

It's funny to me now to look back over the "stages" one goes through in a deployment—the concept of which I could not even understand when Matt first left, but now seems so obvious. I was an emotional wreck when Matt first left. We were standing outside the armory drinking coffee, freezing cold, holding each other, crying, angry, sad, scared. Cameramen from the local news stations and photojournalists from the local newspaper were soaking up as many tears as possible with their lenses. The very first stage of the deployment was denial—it started the day we received word that Matt's unit was under alert for deployment; it stuck around when we received orders and the deployment became official. It pretty much didn't go away till that freezing January morning when I was suddenly hit with the full force of all that this entailed. Matt was really going away. For a really long time.

The second stage—which overlapped with the first for about a month—was fear. Not your typical phobia fears, but a really awful wrenching fear, the fear of the unknown. This fear is transcendent. There's no despair like it. It leaves you feeling worried, distraught, and incredibly scared. I was tormented with questions like What will it be like over there? How often will I hear from him? What is life going to be like without him? What if he falls out of love with me? What if I fall out of love with him? What if he doesn't come back? The fear started to subside after I got my first phone call from him. He's still WITH me, just not physically, and it was hard to grasp that right away, but when I did, the fear abated quickly. I was still worried about his well-being, his safety, but it's not the same as that initial egregious fear.

The third stage: sadness and loneliness. And the incredible clarity of just how long this journey's going to be. Matt's orders were for 545 days—I didn't think I'd be exhaling till June 2006. For me, it happened that I woke up one morning and it crashed down on me (much like an Acme Anvil colliding on the head of an unsuspecting Looney Tune). Matt wasn't going to be home for 18 months. A YEAR AND A HALF. We'd been together for 2 years (it'll be 3 years on December 12!!) and for the most part, joined at the hip for that entire time. We'd moved in together after being together only 6 months. Though he didn't propose till our 2-year anniversary, marriage was a frequent topic of conversation, and during that time, the longest we'd been apart was 2 weeks and that, at the time, seemed too long. Sure, we had leave to look forward to, but in the end, it's just the foreshadowing of another good-bye. It was hard for me to accept Matt's absence right away. Our dog would still get excited every time my roommate opened the garage door, thinking it was Matt. I'd still reach out for Matt in the middle of the night when I got cold, and it hurt like hell when I came up empty-handed. You wake up one night, from a nightmare or what have you, and instead of curling up against the warm body next to you, you lie awake staring at the ceiling, crying, hurting, and realizing that this is your life for the next year give or take. Stage three is really depressing.

I was so inconsolable during these first three stages, it was really difficult for me to believe that there would be any that followed. It was when I still went to FRG [Family Readiness Group] meetings because misery loves company. Karen and Jennifer were among the first military wives I met through blogging, and they were at the point I currently find myself—their husbands were so close to coming home. They both constantly consoled me that things would be all right, that I would make it okay, that things would get better. It was tough to believe it at stage three, and now I find myself writing the same things to girls who email me about their husbands and boyfriends who have just deployed or are about to—I tell them things will be all right, that they'll make it okay, that things'll get better. Some of them seem skeptical sometimes and seem incapable of believing me despite my reassurance, but then I think of what I was like during the months prior to the deployment and the first few months of the deployment—skeptical just the same. I was so envious of Karen and Jennifer because their husbands were coming home "sooner," but in reality, they'd just left sooner. They still had to withstand everything I withstood and just because their husbands had deployed earlier didn't make them "luckier." I feel like such a different person now than I was at the beginning of the deployment. For Christy, whose husband just came home, and Britt, whose husband will be home next month, I feel nothing but happiness. Making the transition from being in a deployment to becoming a deployment survivor is a HUGE accomplishment and it's so much easier for me to understand that now, it's easier for me to understand that everything Karen and Jennifer told me was true (you guys rock!).

As you could probably guess, stage four was acceptance. It's when you start to realize that dwelling on all the depressing aspects of a deployment isn't going to make the time go by any faster. Stage four is when you start taking advantage of the deployment—you use it to go back to school or to make new friends or to take on a new hobby, things you probably wouldn't have normally done otherwise.

Stage four is when you start to learn new things about yourself and you start to grow as a person, when you're proud of becoming Mrs. Fix-It and how adept you've becoming at balancing responsibilities that at one time seemed overwhelming. It's also when you start to realize how maintaining a relationship from opposite ends of the world has only helped your love to flourish and grow and strengthen. It's challenging to never see each other, to find new ways to communicate and express your love, but from what I can tell, it's well worth it. Stage four is awesome (all things considered)—take it for all it's worth!

Now that we know Matt's deployment is going to be more like 14 months rather than 18, I've started to move into the stage of anticipation. Next Tuesday (the 22nd), my countdown will officially have moved into the eagerly awaited double digits. I swear, I'm more emotional now than I was at the beginning of the deployment, and my visits to "la-la land" are much more frequent. It's not really irritating or aggravating, but rather hilarious how I forget to do the most mundane of things. I feel I've become completely bipolar—one minute I'll be laughing and happy, the next I'll be on the brink of tears, and the next, I'm ready to rip someone's head off over the simplest of comments. Really. I cry over On-Star commercials, it's that bad. I'm antsy and impatient and occasionally jump up and pace back and forth on whims, like my constant fidgeting will get Matt home to me sooner. It's like I expect everything to be in fast-forward; I even start to roll my eyes and sigh with disdain when my friends' stories seem to drag on too long, like they're not getting to their point fast enough. On the plus side, I'm constantly motivated and looking for things to keep me busy. I honestly don't know whether I should call this stage "anticipation" or "impatience."

To the wives, fiancées, and girlfriends out there whose soldiers have just left or are about to, it's a rollercoaster. I can pretty much guarantee that when it's all said and done with, you'll never look back on it with regret or wonder how things would've been different if he'd never deployed. The "what ifs" of a deployment are extremely irrelevant. Just keep your chins up and keep those homefires burning; you're already heroes.

CHAPTER SEVEN

THE FALLEN

In the beauty of the lilies Christ was born across the sea,
With a glory in his bosom that transfigures you and me;
As he died to make men holy, let us die to make men free,
While God is marching on.

—JULIE WARD HOWE, THE LAST VERSE OF
"THE BATTLE HYMN OF THE REPUBLIC"

Music has an enormous influence on our memories. On one early morning, I was on the way to work when music reminded me of a good friend. The first light of day had just peeked across the east horizon—the sky was still dark blue. Seventy-five degrees. *Beautiful.* I put the windows down and felt the cool morning wind off Lake Michigan. The radio station was playing Lynyrd Skynyrd's "Tuesday's Gone."

Tuesday's gone with the wind
But somehow I've got to carry on.

A few years ago, during a night much like that morning—75 degrees, the dusk sky purple and pink and blue, a cool breeze off Lake Michigan—my friend Cooter and I were in a beer garden watching a live band. Cooter was from East Kentucky and was visiting me in Chicago.

Cooter and I met about eight or nine years back. I was an officer and he wasn't. We shared some common hardships that would make us an oddball pair of friends. We became brothers.

So he came to Chicago not too long ago.

We were laughing over many beers when the band started playing "Tuesday's Gone."

Cooter, already well on his way to a hangover, jumped up on the picnic table and started singing along.

He yelled down at me, "Git up here, man!"

I jumped up on the table and noticed the crowd looking our way. I can't sing worth a damn and neither can Cooter. But that wouldn't stop us—one arm around the other's shoulders with the other extended, holding a plastic cup of beer sloshing all over the place—drunk and screeching at the top of our lungs.

Tuesday's gone with the wind
But somehow I've got to carry on.

And then I was back in the car and thinking of Coot and hearing that song and thinking of that night and thinking of his wife and wondering how she's doing and that I should call her.

That was the last time I saw Coot. He was killed in Afghanistan.

I remember that my eyes were a bit wet and the guy in the Lexus next to me had to be wondering, *What's up with the guy in the Ford, singing loudly and out of tune?*

Tuesday's gone with the wind
But somehow I've got to carry on.

As with music, there are other things that trigger our memories of loved ones lost in battle, or maybe they are signs. Heidi Sims blogs at *Learning to Live*, where she recounts her life before and after her husband, Captain Sean Sims, was killed in Fallujah, Iraq. Just a few days after learning of her husband's fate, Heidi runs across an article about Sean written by Tom Lasseter of Knight Ridder:

Today I was in the grocery store and could not help but think about signs from Sean. While in the grocery store, I was helping my grandmother find foods for her diabetic diet . . . we spent a lot of time on the "health" food aisle, which I am learning is not that healthy! So we are reading labels (seemed like all of them) when something caught my eye so I turned around. In the middle of the sugar-free cookies was a four-pack of Guinness cans . . . if you knew Sean you know how much he loved his Guinness beer. No matter where we traveled we always had to find an Irish pub so he could have a brew while I sipped tea.

I long for him to send me more signs. I must admit that I was never a believer before November 13, but that night changed my mind. I can't help but remember the letter I sent to my family and friends a few days after my world changed. It was the first sign Sean sent me so I am going to share a part of it. I am truly a believer and waiting for more.

Dear Family and Friends,

I just wanted to drop a quick (well, it did not turn out to be too quick) email to let you know how things are going in Germany. My parents arrived today so a big load was lifted off my shoulders. The days are still long and the nights short, but I am doing pretty good I think.

My friend, the "wife," has been staying with me 24 hours a day. We were talking at 4 this morning about signs from loved ones that have died. I told her that I just wish Sean would send me a sign to know that he is ok, and he was thinking of me. Today, I searched to see if there was a news article maybe giving some insight to what happened. I found two news articles . . . one contained very painful information especially from a soldier in his company and a quote that he made about the cause of Sean's death BUT I found the article below and in my mind I got a sign. Let me explain and then you can read the article.

A few weeks ago, Sean had asked me if there was anything that I might want from Iraq . . . he sent a few rugs but most of you know that I have an obsession with blue and white teapots. I told him to send me a blue and white teapot if possible or just a metal teapot. He said he would see what he could do. I don't think he ever had the time but as I read the article my sign appeared. It might seem odd to some of you but it was a great feeling, and I have had a happy after-

noon thinking about it and how much I love Sean and miss him tremendously!

Thanks for you prayers and support! I truly love all of you and know that I will get through this with all of your support! Enjoy the article. There is one sentence that is a little graphic.

With Love,
Heidi

AMBUSH STEALS LIFE OF TEXAS SOLDIER
By Tom Lasseter
Knight Ridder News Service
FALLUJAH, Iraq—Capt. Sean Sims was up early Saturday, looking at maps of Fallujah and thinking of the day's battle. His fingers, dirty and cracked, traced a route that snaked down the city's southern corridor. "We've killed a lot of bad guys," he said. "But there's always going to be some guys left. They'll hide out and snipe at us for two months. I hope we've gotten the organized resistance." Sims, a 32-year-old Texan from Eddy, commanded his Alpha Company without raising his voice. His men liked and respected him. When he noticed that one of his soldiers, 22-year-old Arthur Wright, wasn't getting care packages from home, Sims arranged for his wife, a schoolteacher, to have her students send cards and presents. Sitting in a Bradley Fighting Vehicle pocked by shrapnel from five days of heavy fighting, Sims figured he and his men, of the 1st Infantry Division's Task Force 2-2, had maybe three or four days left before returning to base. They were in southwest Fallujah, where pockets of hardcore gunmen were still shooting from houses connected by labyrinths of covered trench lines and low rooftops. A CNN crew came by, and

Sims' men led them around the ruins, showing them the bombed-out buildings and bodies of insurgents that had been gnawed on by neighborhood dogs and cats. The father of an infant son, Sims was still trying to get over the death of his company's executive officer, Lt. Edward Iwan, a 28-year-old from Albion, Neb., who'd been shot through the torso the night before. "It's tough. I don't know what to think about it yet," he said slowly, searching for words. Shaking off the thought, he threw on his gear and went looking for houses to clear. A group of rebels was waiting. They'd been sleeping for days on dirty mats and blankets, eating green peppers and dates from plastic tubs. When Sims and his men came through the front door, gunfire erupted. Two soldiers were hit. Crouching by a wall outside, Sgt. Randy Laird screamed into his radio, "Negative, I cannot move, we're pinned down right now! We have friendlies down! Friendlies down!" The 24-year-old from Lake Charles, La., crouched down on a knee, sweating and waiting for help. A line of troops ran up, taking cover from the bullets. They shot their way into the house. Sims lay on a kitchen floor, his blood pouring across dirty tile. An *empty teapot* sat on nearby concrete stairs. A valentine heart, drawn in red with an arrow through it, was on the cabinet. There was no life in his eyes. "He's down," Staff Sgt. Thorsten Lamm, 37, said in the heavy accent of his native Germany. "Shut the [expletive] up about him being dead," Sgt. Joseph Alvey, 23, of Enid, OK, yelled back. "Just shut the [expletive] up." The men sprinted to a rubble-strewn house to get a medic. The company's Iraqi translator, who goes by Sami, was waiting. "Is he in there? Is he there?" he asked. He tried running out the door, his AK-47 ready. As men held him back, he fell against a wall, crying into his hands. When the troops rushed back, they lifted Sims' body onto a pile of blankets and carried it to the closest Bradley. Six soldiers and a reporter piled in after, trying not to step on the body. In Baghdad, Qasim Daoud, interim minister of state for national security, had announced that Fallujah was under control. Back in Fallujah, a 2,000-pound bomb fell from the sky amid a storm of 155 mm artillery shells. A mosque lost half a minaret; its main building smoldered. In the back of the Bradley with Sims' body, no one spoke. The only sound was Wright sobbing in the darkness.

I often read the long version of this article and find the end results so hard to believe. He was so close to making it to the end. I struggle with this daily but am proud of what he did. Someday it will be a better place . . . I long to go find that house.

I finally got up the nerve to email this reporter to ask some questions. Apparently someone had already shared my email with him. I really appreciated that he took the time to answer all my questions. A few weeks after we traded emails, I got a box at the post office. I opened it and the tears began to fall. Mr. Lasseter sent me that blue and white teapot . . . I look at it every day. I wonder if he knows how much I appreciated it?

,   ,   ,

Marine Major Brian Kennedy is a Cobra Attack Helicopter pilot. Flying an armored and armed swift Cobra, he frequently pulled missions to protect slower and thin-skinned medical evacuation helicopters. His blog, *Howdy,* named for his call-sign, recounts his experiences in Iraq:

,   ,   ,

The bell rang. More like a garbage can lid being hit with a 2 by 4.

"Howdy, you got a mission!" yells the Battle Captain.

I sprint out the door and join the foot race of medical CH-46E Chinook helicopter pilots, crew chiefs, medical corpsmen, doctors and Cobra crews running to their helicopters.

Throw on your body armor, dive in, yell *"CLEAR!"* and crank it up. Get to 100% rotor RPM, arm up the missiles, rockets and 20mm cannon.

There is an urgent Casualty Evacuation (CASEVAC) in Ramadi. Time is crucial. The doctor and corpsman are on the CH-46. My Cobra is there to protect them so they can do their job.

We launch and "floor it" heading towards Ramadi. We are going as fast as we can get the aircraft to go.

Eight miles out from Ramadi we get a call on the radio that our mission is canceled.

Damn.

An urgent CASEVAC got canceled, meaning the individual that was supposed to get picked up lost their fight for life.

Turn around, land, de-arm, shut down, refuel, re-cock the aircraft, lay out your gear again just like a firefighter would and walk back to the ready room.

I don't know you or your name, but may God bless you and keep you.

,   ,   ,

Naval Reserve Lieutenant Scott Koenig wrote about his friend and college roommate, Kylan Jones-Huffman, on his blog *Citizen Smash—the Indepundit:*

,   ,   ,

Kylan didn't quite fit in at Annapolis. He was a nerdy kid from Aptos, a small town in California near Santa Cruz. While most of us were concentrating on manly studies like sciences and engineering, he was more interested in art, poetry, history, and foreign languages.

Kylan had an intellectual curiosity that bordered on true geekdom, and most of his classmates found his fascination in Nazi Germany a little bit creepy (I later learned that his interest in the Nazis was purely academic—Kylan's personal political views were somewhat to the left of most Annapolis midshipmen).

You don't get to pick your roommates during Plebe Summer, and I got stuck with Kylan and some football player, who would quit after a few weeks. But Kylan didn't drop out. Even in the darkest days of that first summer, the thought never seemed to cross his mind.

When we were juniors, Kylan introduced me to a girl from Mary Washington College in Virginia, whom I would date for several months. That relationship didn't work out, although it was through that girl that I met the Most Beautiful Woman on Earth, who would eventually become Mrs. Smash. (Hey, it was college!) Anyhow, Kylan is indirectly responsible for much of the happiness in my life, and for that he has my eternal gratitude.

Kylan's major field of study was history, and he was quite a gifted student. He enrolled in the honors history program, and had earned several credits towards his way to a Master's Degree in History by the time we graduated. After graduation, I went off to Newport, Rhode Island, for Surface Warfare Officers School, and Kylan went to the University of Maryland to finish up his Master's.

I didn't see him again until the following February, when he turned up in Newport to start the course just as I was finishing. In the interim, he had married Heidi, his high school sweetheart, and I had gotten engaged to the aforementioned Most Beautiful Woman on Earth. His bride had remained behind to finish school in California, so he stayed in my apartment for a couple of days while he was looking for his own place. A couple of weeks later, he returned the favor by allowing me to stay at his pad for a few days after my lease had run out—I only had a few days left in the course.

We had fun those last few days together, helping prop up the fragile winter economy of Newport by visiting the various drinking establishments that dot the waterfront. When I left for San Diego, and my first ship, at the end of February, we of course promised to keep in touch. But of course we didn't.

A couple of weeks ago, the selection message for Lieutenant Commander came out, and I spotted Kylan's name on it. "I wonder what he's up to these days," I thought.

Turns out that Kylan has been busy these many years. Always gifted at languages, he had learned to speak German, French, Arabic, and Farsi, the predominant language of Iran. This aptitude for languages had earned him a job with Naval Intelligence.

Kylan had returned to Annapolis to teach history for a couple of years, and had plans to earn a Doctorate in Turkish Studies at Johns Hopkins University. But before he could get started, his reserve unit got called up and he was sent to the Sandbox.

I never realized he was there.

On August 21, two days before I boarded my flight home from Kuwait, Lieutenant Kylan Jones-Huffman was shot and killed while riding in an SUV near the town of Al Hillah. His unit was stationed in Bahrain, and he was only supposed to visit Iraq for one week.

Rest in peace, shipmate.

,   ,   ,

Major Brian Delaplane blogs from Afghanistan, where he is an executive officer (second in command) of a battalion. His blog is *Fire Power Forward,* and he had the sad duty of escorting the remains of Special Operations soldiers and Navy SEALs to Germany on their way home to the States:

,   ,   ,

I found myself sitting in one of the canvas seats that lined the side of the C-17. Thirteen other people sat to my left and right and thirteen others sat in the seats on the other side facing us. Uncharacteristic of a flight headed out of a combat theater, there was no laughing or joking. All the normal yelling and good-natured taunts were replaced with a stoic silence as we gazed at the two rows of caskets between us, each meticulously covered with an American flag. The plane leveled out, and some began to shift in their seats to get comfortable for the long ride. One of the two Slovakian soldiers on the other side stared at the casket nearest him with an expression that was not irreverent but seemed to indicate that he couldn't comprehend something. Straight across from me, a young Sergeant wearing a Special Forces patch on his right sleeve sat ramrod straight gazing at the casket nearest him. We would accompany these warriors for the next seven and a half hours, the first leg of their final journey. We would each come to terms with it in our own way and wonder what it was that put us on this aircraft at this time.

I thought about how this had started just a few days ago. It was a Thursday. I had been assigned a mission of an administrative nature that not only promised to be tedious, distasteful, and time consuming, it would carry the added benefit of being my primary mission until completed. I waded in, and by the weekend I was so thoroughly immersed in this newly assigned duty that I barely took notice of the LTF commander's absence as he circulated the area of operations to see our soldiers in remote locations. I should have seen the omen. It seems that each time LTC Langowski departs, catastrophes emerge and crises erupt. The first time he left Salerno back in March, rockets rained down in the worst attack in over a year, and while the details escape me, the tradition has faithfully continued upon each of his departures. This time would be no different.

On Tuesday, as the commander was making his way to FOB Ripley in the south, and I was deluged with paperwork, LT Mahoney put his head in my office and asked, "Sir, are you aware of the Chinook that's down?"

What had been my primary duty seemingly evaporated.

"Precautionary landing?" I asked, hoping that a prudent aviator had sensed something amiss with the aircraft and chose to land, a fairly frequent and not very serious occurrence.

"No Sir, it was shot down near Asadabad. They're not sure how many are on board but we think there are at least 2 survivors."

My mind was whirling with questions. How do we know it was shot down? Where exactly was it? Can MEDEVAC land there? But the first one out of my mouth as we walked back into our operations center was "Do we have anyone flying today?"

LT Mahoney was answering me, but I wasn't paying attention. The question had been unnecessary. The screen was showing that it was an MH-47 that had been lost, a Special Ops version of the Chinook, and it was logically being reported by CJSOTF, the Combined Joint Special Operation Task Force. We wouldn't have had anyone on this aircraft. The initial sense of relief quickly dissipated, though. There were still troops on the ground out there, possibly badly injured and still in harm's way.

I read through the reports. Not much was known and I chose not to frustrate myself by staring at an immobile screen.

"Make sure that all our people are accounted for just in case," I told LT Mahoney as I began to leave, "and make sure that Mortuary Affairs is aware."

The Mortuary Affairs detachment, which has the sad and gruesome task of attending to the bodies of those lost here, recently was realigned to fall under the control of our task force. I sincerely hoped that they would be the only unit in the task force that never had to do their job.

As the day wore on, I repeatedly made my way back into the TOC to see any updates, but little changed. It was quickly verified that it was a Special Ops flight and that all our people were indeed accounted for, but the number of people on board ranged from 14 to 22 and the number of survivors was unknown. It normally takes a bit of time to piece all the details together from an incident like this but the information was painstakingly slow this time.

By nightfall, what we did know was that a formation of Apaches, Blackhawks, and Chinooks was traveling up a mountain valley north of Asadabad near the Pakistan border. As they approached their landing zone, the smaller Blackhawks slowed to allow the Chinooks to move ahead. A Blackhawk Crew Chief looking from his side window as the ill-fated Chinook moved ahead saw the smoke trail of an RPG from the trees below, then the explosion as the round hit the rear of the Chinook. Reports varied on whether the Chinook hit the trees wheels first or inverted, but it was very clear that it had then rolled to the bottom of the ravine. There were secondary explosions and there was fire. What we also knew by the time we went to bed that night was that there was no way to land an aircraft at the crash site, and we obviously knew that there were bad guys in the area. The terrain was brutal and inaccessible by vehicle. Help would have to come by foot from Asadabad. It would be a long time coming, and the question was how to protect the crash site until that help arrived without endangering more aircraft. These were special ops guys on the ground and they would have their own unique solutions to these problems, but all of them would take time.

What followed was waiting, no answers, and more waiting. By morning nothing new had developed. Predators had flown over the area all night and Apaches had over-watched from the ridgelines above, but news was maddeningly scarce and hope dimmed with each passing hour. The day crept by, and as it passed, the only thing we really became sure of was that there had been 16 people, SEALs and Task Force 160th Aviators, on board the Chinook.

By Thursday, word finally came from forces that had reached the aircraft that there were no survivors. The LTF Commander had also returned from his trek by this time, and I informed him that it was becoming increasingly clear that the mission I had been assigned was going to require me to return to Germany for a few days.

On Friday, the Mortuary Affairs unit was unfortunately employed and I was at the air terminal trying to figure out the best way to get to Germany. I had finally produced all the required paperwork and signed up for what I thought was the most expeditious route to Germany through Kuwait, when an announcement was made that a flight directly to Ramstein with seats available had just been scheduled. The delight over my good fortune of a flight directly to my destination was quickly tempered when I heard the PA announcement that the fallen comrade ramp ceremony was scheduled a half-hour before my flight was due to leave. It was going to be a somber ride.

At 9:00 P.M., for the fourth time since our return to Bagram, I found myself standing on the flightline as part of a long solemn line rendering respect as Humvees carrying our fallen comrades slowly rolled towards the mammoth aircraft. For three of these four times, it had been the CJSOTF colors that marched alongside our national colors leading these men who had made the ultimate sacrifice towards the beginning of their final journey. Only bits and pieces of the bagpipe rendition of "Amazing Grace" caught my ear over the wind before the rear doors of the C-17 clanged shut and the color guard made their way back into the darkness of the flightline.

A half-hour later, I was being led across the flightline with a group of 20 or so others towards the same C-17. As our group rounded the rear of the aircraft, en route to the side passenger door, we saw that there was still a large contingent of CJSOTF personnel milling about. Our Air Force escort asked us to stand fast and she disappeared into the aircraft.

From time to time CJSOTF people would disembark the aircraft alone, or in pairs, after having said their final farewells to their comrades, and walk somberly back to the group of people huddled in the dark. I was feeling like a plumber or mailman who had arrived at a house during a wake; decorum seemed to dictate that I divert my attention from the scene but it was impossible not to be drawn back to it.

Two people standing alone but very near me watched the procession, unmoving and in silence for the nearly 20 minutes I stood on that ramp. Instinctively, I knew that it was the CJSOTF commander and his Sergeant Major, and when our escort thankfully turned us around to return to the terminal for a few minutes, this instinct was confirmed when I caught a glimpse of their name tags and ranks.

Thinking back, I'm not sure why I did it or if I would do it again, but I was surprised to see my hand tugging at the commander's sleeve. When he turned to face me I saw the trails of tears glistening on his cheeks, and I could say only "Sir, I'm sorry for your loss." Words failed him but were unnecessary as he reached out and squeezed my shoulder before I started my walk back to the terminal. What I did know at this time was that this man had completed his tour and was scheduled to hand over his command. This couldn't have come at a worse time for him personally, but what I didn't know then was that the reason those aircraft had flown up that valley to start with was to search for four other SEALs who had gone missing. Though I'm not sure why I tugged at this man's sleeve, I knew that as I made the walk back to the terminal, I no longer felt like an intruder but rather a person who was fortunate to have been given the opportunity to express my condolences when it mattered most.

The lights illuminated in the cabin, stirring me from my slumber, and the crew chief announced that we would be landing at Ramstein in about 20 minutes. After zipping up my bag and tightening my seat belt I looked across the cabin to see the soldier with the Special Forces patch still sitting ramrod straight gazing at the two rows of flag-covered caskets, giving every indication that he hadn't moved for the past seven and a half hours.

When the door finally opened and I made my way to the front of the aircraft, I noticed something different about the last casket I would pass. There was something on the flag. Thinking that something had fallen from a rucksack on the way out the door, I reached to remove it before I saw that it was a dogtag with an inscription. I touched it briefly, then continued out the door, and standing on the ramp with the cool, early morning German rain streaming down my face I considered the inscription I had just read:

And I heard the voice of the Lord saying "Whom shall I send, and who will go for us?" Then I said "Here am I! Send me!"—Isaiah 6:8

, 	 , 	 ,

Coalition soldiers are not the only ones fighting and dying for a free Iraq. Iraqis are also making the ultimate sacrifice for their country. There are many military blog posts about the familial relationship that Americans have with their interpreters and Iraqi Army and Police counterparts. First Sergeant Patrick Cosgrove, the top noncommissioned officer in his artillery battery, blogs at *Six More Months* and writes about his Iraqi interpreter, Nabeel:

, 	 , 	 ,

Because the core of my job is controlling access to the camp, I have met thousands of Iraqis over the past 9 months. Many I speak to for a moment, just to determine what their business is and to make a quick decision about one-time access, most for about 10 minutes to interview them prior to granting them longer-term access. The Iraqis I know best are the interpreters, my own and those who work for other units here on the camp. They are wonderful people, with a diversity of backgrounds, education, and personalities. What they have in common is the ability to pass an English proficiency test and the guts to work side by side with U.S Troops, inside and outside the wire. As I have mentioned before, the job is incredibly dangerous.

When I first arrived here and began learning the ropes at the gate, the first Iraqis I came to know were our gate interpreters. Interpreters are mostly known by nicknames, for their own protection and for ease of pronunciation by Americans. We have a really hard time getting our tongues around Arabic names. They have nicknames like Doc, Navigator, Bulldog, Cowboy, and Caesar. Some speak what I call "Hollywood English," which they clearly learned watching American movies and TV, filled with slang and expressions they may or may not fully understand. These interpreters are always entertaining, not always for the reasons they think they are, and are very easy to get along with. New interpreters often speak very limited, literal English with little understanding of the subtleties of the language. Once they have spent some time around Americans, they grow into effective and trusted interpreters. Some, like Neo, speak fluent and proper English, sometimes better than the Soldiers they are interpreting for.

I met Neo the same day I met Fox and Junior, "my" interpreters. Neo, before he transferred to another job, worked the gate with about 12 other interpreters, and we considered him one of the best: intelligent, eloquent, and principled. He owned a jewelry business in Baghdad before the war and my predecessors introduced us quickly, advising me to talk to Neo before buying any jewelry, because he had the best quality at the most reasonable prices. After about a month, Neo left the gate to work at the base contracting office. This was the perfect match for him. His business experience and knowledge of the Baghdad economy allowed the contracting office to drive the hardest bargains and find the best suppliers. It also allowed him to get a little less face time in front of the other Iraqi workers, which he hoped would reduce the risk associated with working here and the constant threats he received. Neo moved his family four times since I arrived here to protect them from those threats.

I found out this afternoon that two days ago, Neo was driving to work when his car was stopped by terrorists. They pulled him from his car and shot him in the back of the head. They left his body lying in the ditch alongside the road. Neo's real name was Nabeel. Nabeel lived his life with more courage and honor than the cowards who murdered him will know in a thousand lifetimes.

Many times, fate or chance decides who lives and who dies in a war zone. Private First Class Trueman Muhrer-Irwin writes on *Rebel Coyote* about what happened on the day he switched places with his best friend, Specialist Robert Wise.

"Hey, would you mind riding in the turret today? I'm still feeling like shit."

"Yeah, no problem."

We were on our way to pick up a few things from our compound; if we were gonna spend the rest of the week at 1st AD [Armored Division] brigade HQ, we sure as hell were gonna have all our stuff. We were just gonna make a quick stop at the barracks then head over to Gunner Main where there was supposed to be some work for the EOD (Explosive Ordnance Disposal) guys we were escorting around.

As we were coming up towards River Road, I looked out at the street behind us pulling security from behind the .50 cal. I'd walked this road a hundred times so when it hit me, I couldn't understand what we could have driven under, what could have struck me so hard.

It took almost a full second to realize what had happened.

The smoke was all around us and there was no sound but the dull ringing in my head. All I could smell was the blood. I was doubled over the side of the turret and as I stared out into the gray haze that surrounded us, the fear and pain hit me like a second explosion. With each breath I screamed, the shrapnel inside me seared my muscles and my foot throbbed with pain. My tears were lost in the blood that poured down my face and clouded my vision. As I began to feel frantically around my throat for wounds, the voice of the vehicle's driver, platoon medic Matt Moss, pierced the silence.

"Get away from the vehicle!" he screamed. "Get away from the vehicle."

He was right, the gas tanks could go or someone could be waiting with an RPG for the haze to clear. I pulled myself out of the turret and rolled down onto the Humvee's hood. I could see out of my right eye now and the only thing I could still feel was the crushing pain in my left foot. While I lowered myself to the ground, onto my good foot, I looked through the missing windshield and saw Wise, still motionless in the passenger seat. His head was tilted back and his face was covered in blood.

"Oh no, Wise!" I shouted, as Matt ran to the side of the vehicle.

"Help me move him," he shouted. "Come on, help me get Wise!" His voice was edged with panic but he moved with the steady deliberation of a man concerned only with his duty.

"I can't," I yelled through a mouthful of blood, "I think my foot's broken." But it didn't matter, the guys from the other humvee had already run back to our vehicle. They helped Matt pull Wise out and lower him to the ground.

As I hopped off to the side of the road and sat down, I realized that my foot was not only broken but pouring a steady stream of blood from the left side. Through gritted teeth and shouts of pain I unlaced my boot and pulled it off. The smell of burnt flesh hit me instantly as I looked down at my foot. The left side of my sock was entirely soaked and dripping with blood but the right side was a large charred patch of indistinguishable skin, sock and shrapnel.

"I'm going to lose my foot," I thought between shouts of anger and pain. "I'm never going to skate again."

"Come on Wise, breathe!" Matt's voice broke through my self-absorbed agony. "Goddamnit, breathe, you're not going to die here!"

How could I be so obsessed with my own pain? I shouldn't be worried about my foot while one of my best friends is dying a few feet away from me . . . But it hurt so bad.

"Oh God, Wise, Ahhhh, my foot," I yelled and craned my neck to try and see them working on Wise behind me but I could only see his feet for all the people around him.

Now the QRF [Quick Reaction Force] was starting to arrive from the compound. They secured the area and, after about ten agonizing minutes of pain and uncertainty, Wise and I were loaded onto a Blackhawk and evac'd to the hospital at the palace. They'd gotten him breathing again, they said he was gonna be okay.

At the hospital they gave me morphine. It didn't do much for the pain, but Wise was gonna be okay and once the doctor pulled the piece of shrapnel out, he said I wasn't gonna lose my foot. I was in a good mood. Maybe it was just the drugs but I knew I was gonna be okay and I was in good spirits. The doctors put me under for surgery. They cleaned out my wound and cut away the dead, burned tissue. When I woke up, I didn't feel any pain. A general came and saw me and gave me a 1st Armored Division coin. I was gonna be back in the States in a week, and I found out that the guy I'd spent the last 9 months getting to know better than almost anyone else, Robert Allen Wise, died of massive head trauma while I was in surgery.

He'll be buried at Arlington National Cemetery next week.

,   ,   ,

Lance Corporal Eric Freeman completed two combat tours in Iraq. He left letters behind to be opened in the event of his death. He was killed in an automobile accident on his way to report for a third tour in Iraq. His last letter, to be read only if he died, was published on *Blackfive:*

,   ,   ,

Hi Everyone,

I'm sorry that I couldn't make it home to you and I'm sorry it took me so long to realize how great my family is. But enough of that. The best thing that anyone of you could do to honor me is not to pity any of us but rather remember the good times we shared. To remember all the goofy, fun and loving times we had will be what lets my life have value. I will not stand for sad faces every time I'm mentioned (I will haunt you meanly for that, LOL). But in all seriousness, celebrate my life and the love we had. Okay, everyone, I'm going to go now but remember that you all gave my life purpose and happiness and that is what I wish to give you.

Eric

Eric's letter to Tiara, his fiancée:

Tiara,

Heyya Hun. If you're getting this letter it's because I'm not coming home to you. Take heart though, Love, and please do not pity us. Be happy that we had the time we had and know that I died loving you. When you think of me don't think of what could have been but smile for me and remember the good times we had. I don't want you to be sad when you think of me, I want you to tell everyone about how much we loved each other and about how we laughed together. I did not live a life to be mourned, I lived it to make the people I love happy. I want you to know how wonderful you are, Tiara. You know, you made everything worth it. You were the most loving, supportive and amazing person for me. Only you could have made my heart sing the way you did. Okay, love, I'm gunna go now. I want only three things of you: Celebrate my life and our love, don't let the end of my life end yours, and remember that I love you still and nothing can take that away from us.

Eric

، ، ،

Sometimes, how we deal with the death of a loved one defines us more than how we live our lives. Heather McCrae writes of Erik, her husband, who died in Iraq, and how she now proposes to live her life. Her *Toast to Life* was published on *CaliValleyGirl*:

A lot has been going on in my life during the past two and a half months. The month of May felt like the world was coming to an end due to the endless memorial services and the inevitable approach of the one year of Erik's death. It was far worse than the previous 11 months. No longer numb, no longer in shock, I had to face this mile-stone sober, and the pain at times felt unbearable. And as some of you have come to learn, I had to do it my way, a.k.a. alone.

One week later, I was sitting in a motorcycle course learning how to ride. Amazingly enough, I passed, which meant I received my motorcy-cle endorsement and am legal to ride on the roadways. Though I am far from confident enough to do so. I spent the following week looking at bikes and decided in the end to have Erik's 1200 Sportster altered to fit my significantly shorter body. Learning how to ride just felt like some-thing I needed to do to help me in my grieving, and I was right. For the first time in a year I was excited about something and even felt a twinge of accomplishment.

The last week of June I went to Delta Company's first drill since they have returned. I had not seen any of the men since I was hiding in Europe when they returned and so I was extremely nervous. Nervous for what, I am not sure. Perhaps it was the finality of it all. If they were back and Erik wasn't, then the nightmare was confirmed. Instead of it being scary it was a relief to see them and gave me a peace I had yet to experi-ence. Two wise men (they would be patting themselves on the back right now if they were to read this) said something to me that weekend that planted a seed. They mentioned that though Erik's death is a part of my life it does not define it. I'm sure some of you have said this in those exact words or slight variations, but I was not ready at the time. And quite honestly, I believe only a soldier who was there with Erik could have said it in a way that could penetrate my thick Scottish skull.

That one comment made me start thinking about my life. I realized that a year has gone by and I had nothing to show for it except an indentation in my couch and an increasingly "grumpy" disposition. It was now up to me to decide what to do with my life. I could either sit and continue to be a cranky old lady and allow Erik's death to define me, or I could get up, start living life, and allow Erik's death to be a part of who I am. With memories of my Great Grandma Carlson coming to mind—my hero—I chose the latter.

Though some of you might think this was the "only" choice or the "easiest" choice, you couldn't be further from the truth on either account. It is not the only choice. I have examples in my life of family members who chose the first route. And as far as it being the easy one—wow. Being grumpy and sticking to yourself means you don't have to be around happy couples and families with kids. Choosing to live means choosing to be around those very things that make me the saddest, because those are the things I was supposed to have with Erik. And more than anything, choosing to live means learning how to love again. I don't just mean another man but love in general. Love has not been something I have been capable of feeling or accepting over the last year. True I may have said it to family members, but I never really meant it. To love means you put your whole self out there, you are vulnerable to pain and loss, and over the last year I was diligently working on building a wall to protect me from that kind of pain and loss again. But as I told Erik in Scotland as he grappled with the idea of giving me the boot as he prepared himself for the inevitable deployment, God said it best, "And now these three remain: faith, hope and love. But the greatest of these is love."—1 Corinthians 13:13.

So here I go in the only way I know how to do things—100%. I'm ready to live and love again. Please do not misinterpret this as Oh good, Heather is finally "moving on." "Moving on" indicates leaving behind, forgetting and going on to something better. I am not, as most say, moving on, I am instead continuing to play the game just like you do after you are sent to jail in Monopoly, or sent home in Sorry or rolling the dice again after sliding down a slide in Chutes and Ladders. You start out at a new position impacted by the previous play but still in the game.

So here is a toast to life. May we all have a summer filled with laughter and love to get us through those trials that we cannot avoid. One

last thing before I go: I owe you all a great thank you for putting up
with the cranky me.

,   ,   ,

Below is "Taking Chance," the powerful account of U.S. Marine
Corps Lieutenant Colonel Michael Strobl, who escorted the remains
of a Marine, Lance Corporal Chance Phelps, home to Wyoming.
Phelps was killed in action from a gunshot wound received on April 9,
2004, during combat operations west of Baghdad. He was buried in
Dubois, Wyoming, on April 17, 2004. "Taking Chance" was published
on *Blackfive:*

,   ,   ,

Chance Phelps was wearing his Saint Christopher medal when he was
killed on Good Friday. Eight days later, I handed the medallion to his
mother. I didn't know Chance before he died. Today, I miss him.

Over a year ago, I volunteered to escort the remains of Marines
killed in Iraq should the need arise. The military provides a uniformed
escort for all casualties to ensure they are delivered safely to the next
of kin and are treated with dignity and respect along the way.

Thankfully, I hadn't been called on to be an escort since Operation
Iraqi Freedom began. The first few weeks of April, however, had been a
tough month for the Marines. On the Monday after Easter I was review-
ing Department of Defense press releases when I saw that a Private
First Class Chance Phelps was killed in action outside of Baghdad. The
press release listed his hometown—the same town I'm from. I notified
our Battalion adjutant and told him that, should the duty to escort PFC
Phelps fall to our Battalion, I would take him.

I didn't hear back the rest of Monday and all day Tuesday until 1800.
The Battalion duty NCO called my cell phone and said I needed to be
ready to leave for Dover Air Force Base at 1900 in order to escort the
remains of PFC Phelps.

Before leaving for Dover I called the major who had the task of
informing Phelps's parents of his death. The major said the funeral was
going to be in Dubois, Wyoming. (It turned out that PFC Phelps only

lived in my hometown for his senior year of high school.) I had never been to Wyoming and had never heard of Dubois.

With two other escorts from Quantico, I got to Dover AFB at 2330 on Tuesday night. First thing on Wednesday we reported to the mortuary at the base. In the escort lounge there were about half a dozen Army soldiers and about an equal number of Marines waiting to meet up with "their" remains for departure. PFC Phelps was not ready, however, and I was told to come back on Thursday. Now, at Dover with nothing to do and a solemn mission ahead, I began to get depressed.

I was wondering about Chance Phelps. I didn't know anything about him, not even what he looked like. I wondered about his family and what it would be like to meet them. I did pushups in my room until I couldn't do any more.

On Thursday morning I reported back to the mortuary. This time there was a new group of Army escorts and a couple of the Marines who had been there Wednesday. There was also an Air Force captain there to escort his brother home to San Diego.

We received a brief covering our duties, the proper handling of the remains, the procedures for draping a flag over a casket, and of course, the paperwork attendant to our task. We were shown pictures of the shipping container and told that each one contained, in addition to the casket, a flag. I was given an extra flag since Phelps's parents were divorced. This way they would each get one. I didn't like the idea of stuffing the flag into my luggage but I couldn't see carrying a large flag, folded for presentation to the next of kin, through an airport while in my Alpha uniform. It barely fit into my suitcase.

It turned out that I was the last escort to leave on Thursday. This meant that I repeatedly got to participate in the small ceremonies that mark all departures from the Dover AFB mortuary.

Most of the remains are taken from Dover Air Force Base by hearse to the airport in Philadelphia for air transport to their final destination. When the remains of a service member are loaded onto a hearse and ready to leave the Dover mortuary, there is an announcement made over the building's intercom system. With the announcement, all service members working at the mortuary, regardless of service branch, stop work and form up along the driveway to render a slow ceremonial salute as the hearse departs. Escorts also participated in each formation until it was their time to leave.

On this day there were some civilian workers doing construction on the mortuary grounds. As each hearse passed, they would stop working and place their hard hats over their hearts. This was my first sign that my mission with PFC Phelps was larger than the Marine Corps and that his family and friends were not grieving alone.

Eventually I was the last escort remaining in the lounge. The Marine Master Gunnery Sergeant in charge of the Marine liaison there came to see me. He had Chance Phelps's personal effects. He removed each item: a large watch, a wooden cross with a lanyard, two loose dog tags, two dog tags on a chain, and a Saint Christopher medal on a silver chain. Although we had been briefed that we might be carrying some personal effects of the deceased, this set me aback. Holding his personal effects, I was starting to get to know Chance Phelps.

Finally we were ready. I grabbed my bags and went outside. I was somewhat startled when I saw the shipping container, loaded three-quarters of the way into the back of a black Chevy Suburban that had been modified to carry such cargo. This was the first time I saw my "cargo" and I was surprised at how large the shipping container was. The Master Gunnery Sergeant and I verified that the name on the container was Phelps's, then they pushed him the rest of the way in and we left. Now it was PFC Chance Phelps's turn to receive the military—and construction workers'—honors. He was finally moving towards home.

As I chatted with the driver on the hour-long trip to Philadelphia, it became clear that he considered it an honor to be able to contribute in getting Chance home. He offered his sympathy to the family. I was glad to finally be moving yet apprehensive about what things would be like at the airport. I didn't want this package to be treated like ordinary cargo, but I knew that the simple logistics of moving around a box this large would have to overrule my preferences.

When we got to the Northwest Airlines cargo terminal at the Philadelphia airport, the cargo handler and hearse driver pulled the shipping container onto a loading bay while I stood to the side and executed a slow salute. Once Chance was safely in the cargo area, and I was satisfied that he would be treated with due care and respect, the hearse driver drove me over to the passenger terminal and dropped me off.

As I walked up to the ticketing counter in my uniform, a Northwest employee started to ask me if I knew how to use the automated boarding pass dispenser. Before she could finish, another ticketing agent interrupted her. He told me to go straight to the counter, then explained to the woman that I was a military escort. She seemed embarrassed. The woman behind the counter already had tears in her eyes as I was pulling out my government travel voucher. She struggled to find words but managed to express her sympathy for the family and thank me for my service. She upgraded my ticket to first class.

After clearing security, I was met by another Northwest Airline employee at the gate. She told me a representative from cargo would be up to take me down to the tarmac to observe the movement and loading of PFC Phelps. I hadn't really told any of them what my mission was but they all knew.

When the man from the cargo crew met me, he, too, struggled for words. On the tarmac, he told me stories of his childhood as a military brat and repeatedly told me that he was sorry for my loss. I was starting to understand that, even here in Philadelphia, far away from Chance's hometown, people were mourning with his family.

On the tarmac, the cargo crew was silent except for occasional instructions to each other. I stood to the side and saluted as the conveyor moved Chance to the aircraft. I was relieved when he was finally settled into place. The rest of the bags were loaded and I watched them shut the cargo bay door before heading back up to board the aircraft.

One of the pilots had taken my carry-on bag himself and had it stored next to the cockpit door so he could watch it while I was on the tarmac. As I boarded the plane, I could tell immediately that the flight attendants had already been informed of my mission. They seemed a little choked up as they led me to my seat.

About 45 minutes into our flight I still hadn't spoken to anyone except to tell the first-class flight attendant that I would prefer water. I was surprised when the flight attendant from the back of the plane suddenly appeared and leaned down to grab my hands. She said, "I want you to have this" as she pushed a small gold crucifix, with a relief of Jesus, into my hand. It was her lapel pin and it looked somewhat worn. I suspected it had been hers for quite some time. That was the only thing she said to me the entire flight.

When we landed in Minneapolis, I was the first one off the plane. The pilot himself escorted me straight down the side stairs of the exit tunnel to the tarmac. The cargo crew there already knew what was on this plane. They were unloading some of the luggage when an Army Sergeant, a fellow escort who had left Dover earlier that day, appeared next to me. His "cargo" was going to be loaded onto my plane for its continuing leg. We stood side by side in the dark and executed a slow salute as Chance was removed from the plane. The cargo crew at Minneapolis kept Phelps's shipping case separate from all the other luggage as they waited to take us to the cargo area. I waited with the Soldier and we saluted together as his fallen comrade was loaded onto the plane.

My trip with Chance was going to be somewhat unusual in that we were going to have an overnight stopover. We had a late start out of Dover and there was just too much traveling ahead of us to continue on that day. (We still had a flight from Minneapolis to Billings, Montana, then a five-hour drive to the funeral home. That was to be followed by a 90-minute drive to Chance's hometown.)

I was concerned about leaving him overnight in the Minneapolis cargo area. My ten-minute ride from the tarmac to the cargo holding area eased my apprehension. Just as in Philadelphia, the cargo guys in Minneapolis were extremely respectful and seemed honored to do their part. While talking with them, I learned that the cargo supervisor for Northwest Airlines at the Minneapolis airport is a Lieutenant Colonel in the Marine Corps Reserves. They called him for me and let me talk to him.

Once I was satisfied that all would be okay for the night, I asked one of the cargo crew if he would take me back to the terminal so that I could catch my hotel's shuttle. Instead, he drove me straight to the hotel himself. At the hotel, the Lieutenant Colonel called me and said he would personally pick me up in the morning and bring me back to the cargo area.

Before leaving the airport, I had told the cargo crew that I wanted to come back to the cargo area in the morning rather than go straight to the passenger terminal. I felt bad for leaving Chance overnight and wanted to see the shipping container where I had left it for the night. It was fine.

The Lieutenant Colonel made a few phone calls, then drove me around to the passenger terminal. I was met again by a man from the cargo crew and escorted down to the tarmac. The pilot of the plane joined me as I waited for them to bring Chance from the cargo area. The pilot and I talked of his service in the Air Force and how he missed it.

I saluted as Chance was moved up the conveyor and onto the plane. It was to be a while before the luggage was to be loaded so the pilot took me up to board the plane, where I could watch the tarmac from a window. With no other passengers yet on board, I talked with the flight attendants and one of the cargo guys. He had been in the Navy and one of the attendants had been in the Air Force. Everywhere I went, people were continuing to tell me their relationship to the military. After all the baggage was aboard, I went back down to the tarmac, inspected the cargo bay, and watched them secure the door.

When we arrived at Billings, I was again the first off the plane. This time Chance's shipping container was the first item out of the cargo hold. The funeral director had driven five hours up from Riverton, Wyoming, to meet us. He shook my hand as if I had personally lost a brother.

We moved Chance to a secluded cargo area. Now it was time for me to remove the shipping container and drape the flag over the casket. I had predicted that this would choke me up but I found I was more concerned with proper flag etiquette than the solemnity of the moment. Once the flag was in place, I stood by and saluted as Chance was loaded onto the van from the funeral home. I was thankful that we were in a small airport and the event seemed to go mostly unnoticed. I picked up my rental car and followed Chance for five hours until we reached Riverton. During the long trip I imagined how my meeting with Chance's parents would go. I was very nervous about that.

When we finally arrived at the funeral home, I had my first face-to-face meeting with the Casualty Assistance Call Officer. It had been his duty to inform the family of Chance's death. He was on the Inspector/Instructor staff of an infantry company in Salt Lake City, Utah, and I knew he had had a difficult week.

Inside I gave the funeral director some of the paperwork from Dover and discussed the plan for the next day. The service was to be at 1400 in the high school gymnasium up in Dubois, population about 900, some 90 miles away. Eventually, we had covered everything. The CACO had some items that the family wanted to be inserted into the casket and I felt I needed to inspect Chance's uniform to ensure everything was proper. Although it was going to be a closed casket funeral, I still wanted to ensure that his uniform was squared away.

Earlier in the day I wasn't sure how I'd handle this moment. Suddenly, the casket was open and I got my first look at Chance Phelps. His uniform was immaculate—a tribute to the professionalism of the Marines at Dover. I noticed that he wore six ribbons over his marksmanship badge; the senior one was his Purple Heart. I had been in the Corps for over 17 years, including a combat tour, and was wearing eight ribbons. This Private First Class, with less than a year in the Corps, had already earned six.

The next morning, I wore my dress blues and followed the hearse for the trip up to Dubois. This was the most difficult leg of our trip for me. I was bracing for the moment when I would meet his parents and hoping I would find the right words as I presented them with Chance's personal effects.

We got to the high school gym about four hours before the service was to begin. The gym floor was covered with folding chairs neatly lined in rows. There were a few townspeople making final preparations when I stood next to the hearse and saluted as Chance was moved out of the hearse. The sight of a flag-draped coffin was overwhelming to some of the ladies.

We moved Chance into the gym to the place of honor. A Marine Sergeant, the command representative from Chance's battalion, met me at the gym. His eyes were watery as he relieved me of watching Chance so that I could go eat lunch and find my hotel.

At the restaurant, the table had a flier announcing Chance's service. Dubois High School gym, two o'clock. It also said that the family would be accepting donations so that they could buy flak vests to send to troops in Iraq.

I drove back to the gym at a quarter after one. I could've walked— you could walk to just about anywhere in Dubois in ten minutes. I had planned to find a quiet room where I could take his things out of their pouch and untangle the chain of the Saint Christopher medal from the dog tag chains and arrange everything before his parents came in. I had twice before removed the items from the pouch to ensure they were all there—even though there was no chance anything could've fallen out. Each time, the two chains had been quite tangled. I didn't want to be fumbling around trying to untangle them in front of his parents. Our meeting, however, didn't go as expected.

I practically bumped into Chance's stepmom accidentally and our introductions began in the noisy hallway outside the gym. In short order I had met Chance's stepmom and father, followed by his stepdad and, at last, his mom. I didn't know how to express to these people my sympathy for their loss and my gratitude for their sacrifice. Now, however, they were repeatedly thanking me for bringing their son home and for my service. I was humbled beyond words.

I told them that I had some of Chance's things and asked if we could try to find a quiet place. The five of us ended up in what appeared to be a computer lab—not what I had envisioned for this occasion.

After we had arranged five chairs around a small table, I told them about our trip. I told them how, at every step, Chance was treated with respect, dignity, and honor. I told them about the staff at Dover and all the folks at Northwest Airlines. I tried to convey how the entire Nation, from Dover to Philadelphia, to Minneapolis, to Billings, and Riverton expressed grief and sympathy over their loss.

Finally, it was time to open the pouch. The first item I happened to pull out was Chance's large watch. It was still set to Baghdad time. Next were the lanyard and the wooden cross. Then the dog tags and the Saint Christopher medal. This time the chains were not tangled. Once all of his items were laid out on the table, I told his mom that I had one other item to give them. I retrieved the flight attendant's crucifix from my pocket and told its story. I set that on the table and excused myself. When I next saw Chance's mom, she was wearing the crucifix on her lapel.

By 1400 most of the seats on the gym floor were filled and people were finding seats in the fixed bleachers high above the gym floor. There were a surprising number of people in military uniform. Many Marines had come up from Salt Lake City. Men from various VFW posts and the Marine Corps League occupied multiple rows of folding chairs. We all stood as Chance's family took their seats in the front.

It turned out that Chance's sister, a Petty Officer in the Navy, worked for a Rear Admiral—the Chief of Naval Intelligence—at the Pentagon. The Admiral had brought many of the sailors on his staff with him to Dubois to pay respects to Chance and support his sister. After a few songs and some words from a Navy Chaplain, the Admiral took the microphone and told us how Chance had died.

Chance was an artillery cannoneer and his unit was acting as provisional military police outside of Baghdad. Chance had volunteered to man a .50 caliber machine gun in the turret of the leading vehicle in a convoy. The convoy came under intense fire but Chance stayed true to his post and returned fire with the big gun, covering the rest of the convoy, until he was fatally wounded.

Then the commander of the local VFW post read some of the letters Chance had written home. In letters to his mom he talked of the mosquitoes and the heat. In letters to his stepfather he told of the dangers of convoy operations and of receiving fire.

The service was a fitting tribute to this hero. When it was over, we stood as the casket was wheeled out with the family following. The casket was placed onto a horse-drawn carriage for the mile-long trip from the gym, down the main street, then up the steep hill to the cemetery. I stood alone and saluted as the carriage departed the high school. I found my car and joined Chance's convoy.

The town seemingly went from the gym to the street. All along the route, the people had lined the street and were waving small American flags. The flags that were otherwise posted were all at half-staff. For the last quarter mile up the hill, local Boy Scouts, spaced about 20 feet apart, all in uniform, held large flags. At the foot of the hill, I could look up and back and see the enormity of our procession. I wondered how many people would be at this funeral if it were in, say, Detroit or Los Angeles—probably not as many as were here in little Dubois, Wyoming.

The carriage stopped about 15 yards from the grave and the military pallbearers and the family waited until the men of the VFW and Marine Corps League were formed up and school buses had arrived carrying many of the people from the procession route. Once the entire crowd was in place, the pallbearers came to attention and began to remove the casket from the caisson. As I had done all week, I came to attention and executed a slow ceremonial salute as Chance was being transferred from one mode of transport to another.

From Dover to Philadelphia; Philadelphia to Minneapolis; Minneapolis to Billings; Billings to Riverton; and Riverton to Dubois, we had been together. Now, as I watched them carry him the final 15 yards, I was choking up. I felt that, as long as he was still moving, he was somehow still alive.

Then they put him down above his grave. He had stopped moving.

Although my mission had been officially complete once I turned him over to the funeral director at the Billings airport, it was his placement at his grave that really concluded it in my mind. Now, he was home to stay and I suddenly felt at once sad, relieved, and useless.

The chaplain said some words that I couldn't hear and two Marines removed the flag from the casket and slowly folded it for presentation to his mother. When the ceremony was over, Chance's father placed a ribbon from his service in Vietnam on Chance's casket. His mother approached the casket and took something from her blouse and put it on the casket. I later saw that it was the flight attendant's crucifix. Eventually friends of Chance's moved closer to the grave. A young man put a can of Copenhagen on the casket and many others left flowers.

Finally, we all went back to the gym for a reception. There was enough food to feed the entire population for a few days. In one corner of the gym there was a table set up with lots of pictures of Chance and some of his sports awards. People were continually approaching me and the other Marines to thank us for our service. Almost all of them had some story to tell about their connection to the military. About an hour into the reception, I had the impression that every man in Wyoming had, at one time or another, been in the service.

It seemed like every time I saw Chance's mom she was hugging a different well-wisher. As time passed, I began to hear people laughing. We were starting to heal.

After a few hours at the gym, I went back to the hotel to change out of my dress blues. The local VFW post had invited everyone over to "celebrate Chance's life." The post was on the other end of town from my hotel and the drive took less than two minutes. The crowd was somewhat smaller than what had been at the gym but the post was packed.

Marines were playing pool at the two tables near the entrance and most of the VFW members were at the bar or around the tables in the bar area. The largest room in the post was a banquet/dining/dancing area and it was now called "The Chance Phelps Room." Above the entry were two items: a large portrait of Chance in his dress blues and the Eagle, Globe, & Anchor. In one corner of the room there was another memorial to Chance. There were candles burning around another picture of him in his blues. On the table surrounding his photo were his Purple Heart citation and his Purple Heart medal. There was also a framed copy of an excerpt from the *Congressional Record.* This was an elegant tribute to Chance Phelps delivered on the floor of the United States House of Representatives by Congressman Scott McInnis of Colorado. Above it all was a television that was playing a photo montage of Chance's life from small boy to proud Marine.

I did not buy a drink that night. As had been happening all day, indeed all week, people were thanking me for my service and for bringing Chance home. Now, in addition to words and handshakes, they were thanking me with beer. I fell in with the men who had handled the horses and horse-drawn carriage. I learned that they had worked through the night to groom and prepare the horses for Chance's last ride. They were all very grateful that they were able to contribute.

After a while we all gathered in the Chance Phelps Room for the formal dedication. The post commander told us of how Chance had been so looking forward to becoming a Life Member of the VFW. Now, in the Chance Phelps Room of the Dubois, Wyoming, post, he would be an eternal member. We all raised our beers and the Chance Phelps Room was christened.

Later, as I was walking toward the pool tables, a Staff Sergeant from the Reserve unit in Salt Lake grabbed me and said, "Sir, you gotta hear this." There were two other Marines with him and he told the younger one, a Lance Corporal, to tell me his story. The Staff Sergeant said the Lance Corporal was normally too shy and modest to tell it but now he'd had enough beer to overcome his usual tendencies.

As the Lance Corporal started to talk, an older man joined our circle. He wore a baseball cap that indicated he had been with the 1st Marine Division in Korea. Earlier in the evening he had told me about one of his former commanding officers, a Colonel Puller.

So, there I was, standing in a circle with three Marines recently returned from fighting with the 1st Marine Division in Iraq and one not so recently returned from fighting with the 1st Marine Division in Korea. I, who had fought with the 1st Marine Division in Kuwait, was about to gain a new insight into our Corps.

The young Lance Corporal began to tell us his story. At that moment, in this circle of current and former Marines, the differences in our ages and ranks dissipated—we were all simply Marines.

His squad had been on a patrol through a city street. They had taken small arms fire and had literally dodged an RPG round that sailed between two Marines. At one point they received fire from behind a wall and had neutralized the sniper with a SMAW [Shoulder-launched multipurpose assault weapon] round. The back blast of the SMAW, however, kicked up a substantial rock that hammered the Lance Corporal in the thigh, missing his groin only because he had reflexively turned his body sideways at the shot.

Their squad had suffered some wounded and was receiving more sniper fire when suddenly he was hit in the head by an AK-47 round. I was stunned as he told us how he felt like a baseball bat had been slammed into his head. He had spun around and fell unconscious. When he came to, he had a severe scalp wound but his Kevlar helmet had saved his life. He continued with his unit for a few days before real-izing he was suffering the effects of a severe concussion.

As I stood there in the circle with the old man and the other Marines, the Staff Sergeant finished the story. He told of how this Lance Corporal had begged and pleaded with the Battalion Surgeon to let him stay with his unit. In the end, the doctor said there was just no way—he had suffered a severe and traumatic head wound and would have to be medevaced.

The Marine Corps is a special fraternity. There are moments when we are reminded of this. Interestingly, those moments don't always happen at awards ceremonies or in dress blues at the Marine Corps Birthday Balls. I have found, rather, that they occur at unexpected times and places: next to a loaded moving van at Camp Lejeune's base hous-ing, in a dirty CP tent in northern Saudi Arabia, and in a smoky VFW post in western Wyoming.

After the story was done, the Lance Corporal stepped over to the old man, put his arm over the man's shoulder and told him that he, the Korean War vet, was his hero. The two of them stood there with their arms over each other's shoulders and we were all silent for a moment. When they let go, I told the Lance Corporal that there were recruits down on the yellow footprints tonight that would soon be learning his story.

I was finished drinking beer and telling stories. I found Chance's father and shook his hand one more time. Chance's mom had already left and I deeply regretted not being able to tell her good-bye.

I left Dubois in the morning before sunrise for my long drive back to Billings. It had been my honor to take Chance Phelps to his final post. Now he is on the high ground overlooking his town.

I miss him.

CHAPTER EIGHT

HOMECOMING

———

I love war and responsibility and excitement. Peace is going to be hell on me.

—GENERAL GEORGE S. PATTON JR.

After a long year, my friend Chief Warrant Officer Steve Arsenault made it home in one piece. Here's the e-mail I received from Steve's wife, Sue:

✦   ✦   ✦

Hard to believe but our long separation is finally over! Words can't really describe how wonderful it is to have him back safe, back where he belongs (he's headed for work with a stop at daycare and a grocery list in his back pocket!).

We had a wonderful surprise when we finally did get home. Our friends, the Small family and the Johnson family, had decorated the house with banners and helium balloons, adorable handmade cards from the kids, and . . . 2 coolers full of Steve's favorite kind of beer (how did they remember that?). It was such a great surprise. And, while we were admiring the house, our neighbor came over with a beautiful balloon bouquet that had been delivered earlier.

Just when Steve thought it couldn't get any better, Krissie gave Steve tickets to the Chiefs–Patriots game next month!

I continue to be astounded at the thoughtfulness and outstanding support from our friends and family. I am welling up just thinking about it. I don't know how we would have got through the last year without all of you.

THANK YOU!

And, at the end of the day, Steve was on his couch giving his baby a bottle, a cold beer on the table in front of him with his football tickets safely in his back pocket, and a big smile on his face.

Our love,
The Arsenault family
(complete again)

⸙ ⸙ ⸙

When loved ones come home, relief and elation are the two emotions most commonly displayed. Parties and reunions commence. Delayed birthdays, Christmases, and anniversaries are finally celebrated.

But coming home is more than just surviving the war; it's surviving the changes that have happened to your life.

Sergeant Michael Durand, of *This Is Your War,* is a California Army National Guard soldier who spent a year in Iraq. He writes about trying to be normal again after coming home:

⸙ ⸙ ⸙

I sat looking out the large window facing Howe Avenue. The door to the office was to my right, the window to my left front, Sandy sat to my direct 12 o'clock. Beyond the blinds traffic rushed past, cars, vans, Comcast cable trucks, a H&D motorcycle rumbled past.

Normal traffic. Cars. People on their way to and from work. Mothers driving their kids home from school. Nothing would explode. There were no VBIEDs here. No IEDs. This was The World. This place was safe from Death.

Bullshit.

"So, Mike, what do you want out of this?" Sandy asked me.

I was at the Vet Center in Sacramento. A week ago I had come in for my first appointment. The "In Brief." This was my first contact with *my* counselor. Sandy had been in Iraq. She was a mental health professional, an E-7 that had worked at one of the two Combat Stress wards In Country.

After Duplantier was killed and I returned from my four-day R&R in Qatar, I was sent to Baghdad. "Don't worry, Sgt Durand, everything will be the same when you get back." Both the LT and SFC B told me. That was before they took my Fire Team away from me.

Sandy had worked in Balad.

It was all the same, though.

It didn't really matter.

I needed to *fix* myself and so here I was. A month-plus after I had arrived back home. Out of Iraq. I looked long and hard out the window, past the blue blinds, my mind blank. Just what do I want out of this?

Images flashed through my mind.

Doc with a pistol in his mouth. Duplantier laying in the black body bag in the CASH, his eyes glazed over, like dead fish in the supermarket. The medics had tried to intubate him, to save his life, knowing he was already dead the second the sniper's bullet shattered his heart. I threw up into my hand as I staggered over to the trash can, bent over. My flight gloves smelled of vomit and stomach acids for the rest of the mission.

The old man as he got out of the red BMW I had destroyed with the M240, his left arm flopping beside him, the elbow blown away—by me—he must have walked a dozen steps before he crumpled to the asphalt, the sun hot, the light intense and bright in the Middle Eastern sky, like the F-stop on the world's aperture had been set too high.

Sara, the last time I had seen her alive, berating a teenage Iraqi girl for selling Joe's gum in front of the CASH the night Doc and I worked on the Iraqi with the sucking chest wound.

"She should be home with her mother," Sara told me. Sara. Thick dark hair down to her waist. We were both in our thirties. Sara, no husband, no children, she had worked for Saddam as a Terp.

Well, I thought to myself, *she will be sucking Joe's cock for fifty bucks this time next year.* I never would have said that to Sara, though. Sara had her face and both feet blown off by an IED meant for us days later.

"What do I want out of this?" I finally respond as an eighteen-wheeler Jake-braked down the road. Moving from right to left as I considered the question. In my mind, I watched the IED explode near the LT's truck again, engulfing the vehicle in a brown cloud of dust tinged with black.

"I want to be, you know, normal again. Whatever the fuck that means . . . Like I was ever normal."

The front of Sandy's desk was decorated with various pictures of Soldiers posing with Camel Spiders. In one, a 1SG held up two, maybe they were mating or just eating each other, gripped in the jaws of a Gerber Multi-Tool. The other photo showed what I can only guess was a senior NCO with a spider on his head. Other printouts and flyers proclaimed "Welcome Home Iraq Vets!" all posted at jaunty angles. I imagined Sandy on her hands and knees one slow afternoon—a roll of Scotch Tape in her hand—considering which angle to post the photos at. What would be most pleasing to the eye?

What I didn't want was this to be another bullshit-feel-good-I-have-problems-please-feel-sorry-for-me headshrinker deals. I have had enough of those.

"Just don't fuck with me, ok? Let's start with that," I told her. "Look, I know I have shot more goddamn people than you ever have. So don't bullshit me about 'Duty, Honor, and Country.' Been there and done that . . . And you know what? It ain't there, man. It's just War, and War don't give a good Godddamn what the fuck."

I looked out the window again. Except it wasn't Howe Avenue, it was Route Vernon I was seeing. The route we used to go on day after day, trolling for IEDs, waiting for them to explode, to kill or wound us.

Over and over again.

I used to get so pissed off that I would take off my helmet and throw it against the Humvee windshield, wanting an IED to go off just to end the suspense.

Kill me, motherfuckers, I would think, *fucking kill me and get the waiting over with.*

. . . And now what?

"I want to go home."

First Lieutenant Lee Kelley writes at *Wordsmith at War* from the heart of the Al Anbar Province in Iraq. Kelley wants to ensure that, although the combat soldiers have certainly changed, America remains the same in "A Letter to the Republic for Which We Stand":

,   ,   ,

Americans, we remain your constant and faithful servants.

Satellites that hover 23,000 miles above the planet in geospatial orbit feed down into our little dish and we get to see sports and current events and news. We know what you're up to. We might watch the news for 10 minutes after a long shift outside the wire, just enough to get the highlights, or read it on the internet, or have friends mail us copies of newspapers, or monitor CNN just as the insurgents do, for breaking news. Maybe you know one of us personally, or maybe we're nothing more to you than nameless faceless soldiers on the news. Either way, we still know about the hurricanes down South, the newest movies, the earthquakes in Pakistan, and the latest football scores.

You populate our dreams.

Your state of affairs is still part of our thought processes, however hard it may be right now to recall exactly what it felt like to stand within those borders. The mind and eyes play tricks on you when you live in this environment, always on guard, ready to kill if needed.

Yes, we're soldiers, but who wants to live this way? What man enjoys being threatened all the time? Show me that man and I'll show you a fool. But ask me to show you a person who is willing to live like this so that Americans back home can live more safely, and we'll show you a couple hundred thousand.

You can drive your comfy cars to work. We want you to. It makes you the personification of our daydreams. As you're giggling at the immature humor of local morning radio comedy, sipping a vanilla latte from Starbucks, oblivious of the gunshots and explosions in Iraq, and tailgating the car in front of you, we're trying not to get blown up. We are not complaining—we raised our hands and swore to serve. But we do envy the ease with which you can walk out of your door and take a casual stroll through streets that are not your own in that soft suburban streetlight safety.

We wouldn't expect you to alter your lives for us—you're not soldiers. You don't have to travel 7,000 miles to fight a violent and intelligent enemy. We'll take care of all that. You just continue to prosper in the middle class, trade up on your economy-size car, install that new subwoofer in the trunk, and yes, the red blouse looks wonderful on you—buy it.

Remain the same embodiment of our fading memories, the portal to our daydreams, the catalyst for hope when hope eludes us, a land of winding roads and fishing holes, pretty pictures in frames, postcard lives, fields of wheat, skyscrapers made of glass, a woodshop, a fireplace, a patriotic song. Be you a mantle full of family photos, a smiling face at a convenience store, a dog that follows us around the yard, someone we meet spontaneously and get along and laugh with, the feel of grass on our bare feet as we walk out to get the morning paper, a parade or a fair or a swap meet.

Be you a pool table in a dimly lit room, a candle in a window, a Christmas tree, a scarecrow at Halloween, a hug after a hard day, a bowl of chicken noodle soup when we have a cold, the feel of our own steering wheel in our hands, gravity tugging at our calves as we walk up a mountain trail, the thrill of water running over rock, a stone thrown from a bridge or skipping across a lake, someone to call on a cell phone just because, or our favorite band coming to play a show in our hometown at an outdoor amphitheater. Be you the faces of strangers at that concert, laughing, smiling, silhouetted in light and smoke amidst the energy of musical celebration, or be Chris Cornell's CD, *Euphoria Morning*, which has some lyrical moments that put chills down my spine.

Be all of these things and more, as we know you can.

Just be what you will, Americans, with your goods and bads, your lights and darks, your jerks passing at 100 mph in the slow lane (Believe it or not, I miss you jerks—I will relish the next opportunity I have to give you the finger), your wrong change and bad attitude because you don't like your job at the drive thru, your high school boy with braces handing us that delicious movie theater popcorn (extra butter please), your mall food courts, your egg-drop soup, your soft shell taco for 49 cents on Tuesdays, your dryer sheets that make the pillowcase smell so damn fine, your beautiful face the first thing we see in the morning, your crying children, and yes, your diapers that need changing.

Remain a perfect parody of yourself by having a midlife crisis and listening to tribal meditative music on a state of the art CD player that you ordered online from SharperImage.com, buy that Porsche and drive it to yoga class, or be the guy in Wyoming whom I cursed because he won the Power Ball and he was already a millionaire.

Be whatever you choose. Let fate and destiny and blind luck and synchronicity guide you.

But please remain constant as well, because we have changed.

Don't move the continent. Don't sell the house. Don't lose the dog.

Just be Americans with all your ugliness and beauty, your spectacular heights, and your flooded cities, climbing the corporate ladder or standing in the welfare line. Live your lives and enjoy your freedoms. We're not all walking idealist clichés who think your ability to work where you want and vote and associate with whomever you want are hinged completely on our deployment to Iraq. But you know what? Our work here is a part of that collective effort through the ages that have granted you those things.

So don't forget about us, because we can't forget you.

I, for one, am a walking paradox. I believe in my fellow soldiers, and I am proud to serve. I don't even like country music, but I'll tell you what, being in this environment, if I heard "Proud to Be an American" or that one Toby Keith song right now I'd probably cry like a baby and get those big patriotic goose bumps kind of like the ones you can't help getting at your Basic Training graduation ceremony when you've just entered the military culture and been eating, sleeping and drinking it for eight weeks.

But I don't think I'll do this to my kids again. I may be done. When this is over, I just might go back to school and aggressively pursue my writing career and grow a goatee and sit in my living room like an armchair quarterback the next time America goes to war, and write a blog for the soldiers I see on the news, and sponsor one, and join the VFW, and examine the political process, and explain it to my children, and protect them, and live on in that bittersweet, but oft taken for granted blind bliss of democracy, in liberty and justice for all.

Yes, that's my plan for the moment. But like everything else, it changes.

I'll keep you posted.

Thanks for caring, Americans.

,   ,   ,

Staff Sergeant Fred Minnick led a team of combat photographers and journalists in Iraq. His blog, *In Iraq for 365,* focused on his responsibility both as a journalist and as a leader. He writes of his last days in the Army and of the things that he won't forget:

,   ,   ,

The two duffel bags were filled with my equipment collection of nine years. Cold weather mittens. Goggles. Kevlar. Canteens, canteen cups and canteen covers. Pistol belt. First aid kit. It was all there. Except for a camelback that was lost in Iraq.

Any equipment not turned in, even after a decade of service, the soldier is responsible for. I signed a statement of charges for a little over $30 for the item and I was done. I wrote a typical military memo, dry and free of inspirational thought, indicating my intentions of getting out.

I wanted to write that I planned to grow my hair to the length of my butt and not shave for two years, but I didn't. I wanted to say that my final day of Army service was one of the happiest days of my life, but I didn't. I wanted to thank the Army for losing my medical records three separate times, causing me to receive more vaccinations than a rabies patient, but I didn't. I wanted to write about how the Army's health insurance, TriCare, failed to pay for multiple bills it was responsible for while I was hospitalized with Lyme disease, leaving my credit rating a wreck, but I didn't. I wanted to ask how some officers ever received promotions while several more-deserving candidates were passed up because they were not good-old boys, but I didn't. I wanted to demand an answer for why we need to fill out 25 pieces of paperwork to use a toilet in a government building, but I didn't.

See, I don't measure my years of service by the Army's inadequacies or the people I want to forget. Rather, I will remember the important moments.

I'll never forget the 25-mile road march in basic training. My feet were raw and my arms, back and thighs were sore as sore can be. After the march, we turned Blue, meaning we received the infantry's coveted Blue Cord. I felt like a man that day.

I'll never forget my first drill in Wisconsin. The majority of the unit was women. Being an infantryman transferring to a public affairs unit, I felt out of place and in the past harbored ill feelings toward female soldiers. But the females made me feel comfortable and the commander encouraged my creativity. I reenlisted after one year of service in Wisconsin.

I'll never forget the day I received the "call." It was Valentine's Day, 2003. We were placed on alert and the only girls I called on this day of love were those I called soldiers.

I'll never forget the time I spent in the hospital. My most frequent visitors were fellow soldiers.

I'll never forget when we boarded the plane to leave the U.S. Joe and I placed towels on our heads and we laughed the flight away.

I'll never forget the smell of my first patrol. The mixture of sewage and burning trash is a unique smell.

I'll never forget our first night in NCO alley, where we learned to leave the war behind and just laugh. We learned the only way we can get through Iraq is by leaning on one another. By laughing more than crying.

I'll never forget meeting Sergeant Mitts. His smile, his soft-spoken words and his heart impacted me in unmatched ways. At his memorial, I didn't cry. I smiled in his memory.

I'll never forget the day Samir bought me a vase from the Mosul market. He tried for a week to find one nice enough for my mother. "For you, sergeant, only the best." The man made me laugh more than any-body and to this day, I can't stop thinking about him.

I'll never forget hearing the National Anthem as we walked off the plane. Shaking hands with politicians and seeing American soil for the first time.

I'll never forget the battle within my mind with readjusting. The nightmares. Fears. And how I overcame them all without medications or drinking. How it was tough and will continue to be a challenge, but I got through it and will continue to do so with the help of special people.

I'll never forget my last drill. We had two new soldiers, both of whom wanted me to stay in.

"You can't leave, man, you're so funny."

I'll never forget Sammy's face as I walked down the long hallway to our office for the last time. Tears filled his eyes as if he were at a funeral. He and I are close.

I'll never forget opening my car door on the last day and I saw Sammy walking toward me.

"Dude, are you stalking me?"

"No, I got to go across the street to turn in some paperwork."

I'll never forget how red his eyes were. They were visible even under his thick magnifying glasses.

I'll never forget my last salute as a soldier.

Near my car in the Wisconsin Guard headquarters, I snapped to attention, looked in the direction of Staff Sgt. Brian P. Jopek, aka "Sammy," raised my right hand, touching the brim of my soft cover and simply said, "Take care, brother."

He didn't respond and just kept walking. See, NCOs don't salute NCOs. Technically, you're only supposed to salute officers and in cere-monies. But out of respect, I was saluting Sammy.

"Dude, I'm serious. I'm saluting you."

He returned the salute and held it.

"Take care, Sammy. I love you, man."

He didn't respond. "Hey, aren't you going to say something?"

"The last time I said something like that, you called me a faggot."

"I was joking then; I'm serious now."

"OK, I love you too." He dropped his salute and proceeded on.

As he left, I yelled, "Faggot. I can't believe you said you love a man."

I'll never forget Sammy's laugh. After all the ridicule I've given him over the years, including my in-jest faggot remark, he still laughs at every stupid thing I do. It was this laugh that got the gang in NCO Alley through many tough times.

I'll never forget my military career. Through all the bad, there was plenty of good. And more laughs than on Comedy Central.

,　　,　　,

First Lieutenant Rusten Currie is the intelligence officer for a California National Guard air assault infantry battalion. His blog, *Sic Vis Pace, Para Bellum,* chronicled his time in Iraq. Rusten posts a final message as he prepares to depart Iraq and resume his life in America:

,　　,　　,

December 15, 2005, was one of the greatest days of my life—I was witness to the birth of democracy in Iraq. It is a rarity to be a part of such an historic event. Despite any and all arguments about why we are here, by some accounts 75% of Iraqis registered to vote did so. (Imagine who, or groups of who, would not be in office if 75% of American voters turned out!) Despite threats (very real threats) of violence Iraqi men and women lined up and waited, some for hours, to vote. They waited patiently in lines that would have driven me mad! They have never before had such an opportunity to vote and have a say in their own nation. None of these candidates (nearly 8,000 of them) will share the overwhelming 99.9% landslide victory Saddam Hussein (former dictator, tyrant, and poet) once enjoyed. The day passed without incident, save for the aforementioned self-determination of the nation by its citizens. All was quiet on virtually all fronts of the war in Iraq. In fact, I can honestly say I was bored. Being bored in war is a good thing, and as of late, I have been blissfully bored to no end. Which is why I have not posted for some time. I simply had nothing to say.

Our battalion awards ceremony was on the 17th and I am now, at long last, a 1st Lieutenant. Odd, I never imagined I'd ever be a 1LT, and now like some magic wand was waved, the often comical look of confusion that plagues most Second Lieutenants is gone from my face. In its place is a grimace of a combat veteran, a sort of permanent scowl with my cover pulled down over my eyes and a frown etched on my face. I move about the base walking briskly and as of late avoiding most unnecessary conversation. I have not been in a particularly bad mood, but save for time left here in Iraq, the mind has distanced itself from much around me. Funny, I don't feel any different. It was a great moment in my life. I stood with 2 other officers and we were promoted together. Our battalion commander asked us to address the battalion and I was caught so off guard by it I couldn't think of a thing to say. Oh, and the microphone wouldn't bend down so I had to stand on my toes to speak clearly into it. It reminded me of my speech for Student Council back in 1985. All I could think to say was that we'd seen our last full moon in Iraq. I hope that is true. At the ceremony promotions and medals were awarded for our time here and for some very courageous young men, the medals were well deserved. For others . . . well perhaps another time.

Looking back at the last year, I remember so much and so many people I have met and had the honor of serving with. I have seen some wonderful things here and I have seen some of the worst violence, and the darkness of the human soul. I have seen vicious acts of hatred, and I have seen selflessness I never thought possible. This war is different from other wars . . . this war is exactly the same as every other war. War devours everything in its path; there is no mercy to it. There is no reason in it, it exists to destroy, and as long as there are governments run by mortals there will always be war. Yet, even in war the brighter side of humanity can shine through. I have seen it. Average Iraqis handing me a bottle of cold water in the blistering heat, a little girl holding the hand of a grieving soldier whose friend had been mortally wounded in an IED attack. Defiant Iraqi civilians standing in line to vote, so that their voice is heard.

How do I explain this place to those who will not listen? We are winning here. Of that, there is no doubt. The cost is high, but as Heinlein asserts, "Something given has no value." A free Iraq has cost us more than I ever wanted to spend, in time, lives, friends and blood. For the soldier there is no politics (at least there shouldn't be), for the soldier if there is to be war, then we destroy the enemies of our nation. War, as horrific as it is, is simple. Everything else is hard.

I have been afforded the honor of being an Army Officer in time of war, and I have served with the very best that our nation has to offer. When this is over and I move on to other things, it will be from this perspective that I move forward. Simplicity. Occam's Razor suggests we not add anything unnecessary to a problem to solve it. In short, keep it simple; when you find a problem, fix it. I will miss the men I have served with here. When you spend nearly 16 hours a day with the same people every day for 18 months, like them or not they become family. I see that now, again perspective, and a healthy amount of time spent apologizing to myself for being such a miserable SOB at times in my life. A healthy amount of time spent reaching out to old friends I'd slighted years and years ago, and saying I'm sorry. A healthy amount of time spent not talking but listening, and I mean really listening to what people had to say. I have met some great people through emails, and in meeting them, I have been presented with some great opportunities for life after "this war." Like I said 11 months ago, there are only two days here, the day you arrive and the day you leave (yes, like prison). Soon it will be tomorrow and I will leave. Not that this hasn't just been a blast (often quite literally), but I'll be glad to kick the dust of Southern Baghdad from my boots and focus on tomorrow, walk my dog, and hug my wife, and move past the only life I have known for nearly a year. Soon I'll be whole again.

I am not certain if I'll post again. Not being dramatic, but this blog (in its current form) has nearly run its course. I would like to thank everyone who has written me, even those who attacked me and lashed out with anger and at times apparent insanity. Interesting at times, and often downright hilarious. Those of you who sent me comfort items, thank you so very much, your kindness and consideration truly lifted my spirits (AFSister!!). Those of you who shared pictures of your families and children, I appreciate your sharing what "normal" is with me. Those of you who think of me as a friend, I am always an email away.

Those of you who thanked me for doing my job, well again, all I can say is that sometimes the extent of my patriotism was putting my boots on, especially when I didn't want to. So, I humbly thank you for reaching out to me and expressing your gratitude, thank you, thank you, thank you! Those of you who engaged in healthy and heated debate with me over our different political views, I thank you as well. Soon we'll see one way or the other, won't we. Those of you who continue to question this war, and why we are here, good for you; without different opinions, there is no debate. Without debate and open discussion, our perspective is skewed and we can ill afford to lose any more of who we are because of a lack of perspective. Seek reason, find common ground, and never be afraid to stand up for what is right.

Finally, to my wife—my angel, my best friend and my compass. It has been so long since I watched you drive away from the Airport on April 21, 2005. It has been so long since my cheeks were stained with tears as I watched you pull away and felt as if I'd just died. At times, I thought it was the last time I'd ever see you, and at that thought my heart grew cold. We have been apart for 9 months now, and soon we will be together again. The one and only wish I have had since I saw you last was that I could see you again. To see you smile at me is the best present I could ever hope for; it is in fact the only thing I have let myself hope for, for months now. When this is over and I hang up this faded uniform I hope to spend the rest of my life with you. And when we grow old together, and reflect on this war and our time apart, as with soldiers in all wars I'll be able to smile and say, "I was there . . ."

What will I miss about Iraq? Nothing . . . everything.

Until the next . . .

꘎   ꘎   ꘎

Rachelle Jones is an Army wife whose husband was deployed with the Arkansas National Guard in Iraq. She blogs about her life at *ArmyWifeToddlerMom* and recounts her feelings of being reunited with her husband:

꘎   ꘎   ꘎

I am still feeling "separate" from Dear Husband.

Eighteen months of different day-to-day existence can do this. So I stand on the outside now and try and imagine his life.

He is a "rules" kind of guy, he doesn't tell, and I don't ask.

The other day we were in the truck on the way to the bookstore and I asked, "Does it feel weird driving your truck?"

I got a small glimpse into his head. He said, "I still don't like driving under the overpasses and over bridges. Random garbage on the shoulders makes me edgy."

That small glimpse was enough for me that day. I haven't asked another question. Maybe later.

That first night alone in the hotel, when the children finally fell asleep, I clung to him and cried. I am not a big crier—try not to be, anyway. Reunion is frightening, and you feel lucky, blessed, cheated, alone, and guilty.

You want to hear "the story" that proves you have every right to feel lucky and blessed, but you don't want to hear it.

So you lie on a bed in a dimly lit hotel room, and you watch your babies sleep in peace. You put your head on your husband's chest, and you hear his heart beating, and you can smell him for the first time in months, and you can feel his hands on your back, and you cry as quietly as you can.

The tears come . . . and you try and stop them. All of the worry, gratefulness, sorrow, and love. You cry for him, and his lost brothers, and for the widows that must cry in the shower, so their children can't hear them.

You feel guilty for the tears on his chest, and he pulls you to his mouth and tries to kiss your tears away. No one says a word, and you swear you can hear your tears dropping onto his flesh, and you can hear his heart beating . . .

. . . And it is the best sound in the World.

EPILOGUE

Although the view you've just had into the military world has been open and direct, military blogging is changing rapidly and will never quite be the same again. To protect information and the safety of its troops, the military is changing its formerly liberal rules midstream. Once open to the idea of solders with Internet access as a morale enhancer, the military has realized that it has opened its own Pandora's Box by allowing unfettered access to the Internet—hundreds of thousands of soldiers posting stories on blogs and Web sites and e-mailing photos and stories to family and friends. In response, the U.S. Army has created an amendment to its Operational Security (OPSEC) Regulation (Policy) that includes blogging and restricts certain content for security reasons.

General Peter J. Schoomaker, the chief of staff of the Army, sent this message out in mid-2005:

OPSEC IS A CHAIN OF COMMAND RESPONSIBILITY. IT IS SERIOUS BUSINESS AND WE MUST DO A BETTER JOB ACROSS THE ARMY. THE ENEMY AGGRESSIVELY "READS" OUR OPEN SOURCE AND CONTINUES TO EXPLOIT SUCH INFORMATION FOR USE AGAINST OUR FORCES. SOME SOLDIERS CONTINUE TO POST SENSITIVE INFORMATION TO INTERNET WEBSITES AND BLOGS, E.G., PHOTOS DEPICTING WEAPON SYSTEM VULNERABILITIES AND TACTICS, TECHNIQUES, AND PROCE- DURES. SUCH OPSEC VIOLATIONS NEEDLESSLY PLACE LIVES AT RISK AND DEGRADE THE EFFECTIVENESS OF OUR OPERATIONS.

The effect of the guidance has been to restrict the majority of military blogs and put an end to some blogs altogether. Many have gone "dark," letting their blog registrations expire and the content disappear—bits and bytes no more—rather than face censorship. Others have followed the new OPSEC guidance and continue to blog but no longer post photos or stories about their experiences. And still others ignore the new rules, hoping to fly under the radar and not be noticed by those searching for violators.

So where are the authors now? As of April 2006, some are still in Iraq or Afghanistan. Others have made it home. Some have been visibly scarred, and others have wounds that you can't see. And some will return to the fight. Here is the current information about the authors:

CHAPTER ONE: SOME MUST GO TO FIGHT THE DRAGONS

Marine Corporal Stephen Wilbanks (*Red State Rants*), who opened this book with his reasons to rejoin the Marines, is in Fallujah, Iraq. He started his own blog, *Green Again*, at http://www.greenagain.type pad.com. *Red State Rants* can be found at http://redstaterant.com/.

Scott Koenig (*Citizen Smash—the Indepundit*) returned home to his wife in California and was promoted to lieutenant commander in the Naval Reserves. He now organizes pro-military rallies to counter antimilitary protests at marine and naval bases around the Southern California area. You can find him at http://www.lt-smash.us/ and http://indepundit.com/.

American Soldier was a team leader of Army snipers working with the Marines in Ramadi, Iraq. He was given a new assignment as an infantry squad leader in spring 2006 when he suffered shrapnel wounds from an IED. Now on the road to recovery in a hospital in the United States, *American Soldier* is in good spirits, supported by his wonderful wife and family. You can find him at http://www.soldierlife.com/.

Jay Czaja, Caelestis of *Makaha Surf Report*, returned from his third tour of Iraq in November 2005. He is currently planning on making weekly podcasts about the war and politics. He is very happy to be back in Hawaii with his dolphin-trainer wife, four dogs, and one

dogs, and one very demented cat. You can find Jay at http://www
.themakahasurfreport.com/.

Navy Hospital Corpsman Sean Dustman (*Doc in the Box*) returned
home from his second tour of duty. He found a wonderful girl and
married her, and is preparing for a third tour in Iraq. You can read
Sean's blog at http://docinthebox.blogspot.com/.

Greyhawk (*The Mudville Gazette*) returned home from Iraq to his
family at a base in Germany and continues to blog along with his
wife. *The Mudville Gazette* was a finalist for Best Blog in the 2005
Weblog Awards. You can find Mudville at http://www.mudville
gazette.com/.

Sarah Walter's (*Trying to Grok*) husband, First Lieutenant Russell Walter, an officer in the 1st Infantry Division, made it back to Germany
and will be returning to duty stateside soon. They are enjoying
being reunited and visiting their families. *Trying to Grok* is at
http://www.tryingtogrok.com/.

CHAPTER TWO: LIFE IN A WAR ZONE

Specialist Alex Barnes (*Blog Machine City*) returned home to his wife
in Minnesota. He's pursuing a college degree in 2006. You can read
Blog Machine City at http://bl0g.delobi.us/.

Staff Sergeant Fred Minnick (*In Iraq for 365*) now lives in Louisville,
Kentucky, with his girlfriend and her two cats. The cats do not like
Fred. He is the managing editor for two national trade magazines.
You can find *In Iraq for 365* at http://desert-smink.blogspot.com/.

Major Brian Delaplane (*Fire Power Forward*) was reunited with his
wife, Pam, and they returned to Germany in February 2006. Brian
was selected for promotion to lieutenant colonel and will complete
at least one more assignment before retiring. He is working on a
novella loosely based on his experiences over the past several
years. *Fire Power Forward* is located at http://bdelapla.typepad
.com/firepowerforward/.

First Sergeant Jeff Nuding (*Dadmanly*) returned with his company to New York on Veterans' Day 2005. Jeff thoroughly enjoyed his reunions with his wife, son, daughters, and many supportive neighbors and friends. He resumed work as a project management professional, consulting with a division of the New York State government, and continues to serve in the New York Army National Guard. Jeff plans to gather a book together from his blog at http://dadmanly.blogspot.com/.

Sergeant Taylor Allen Smith (*American at Heart*) returned home safely. In fact, his whole unit returned home healthy. Taylor stopped military blogging due to the new OPSEC rules. He is in college pursuing a political science degree with minors in Spanish and Arabic and plans on trying out for Special Forces. *American at Heart* is at http://simplesmith.blogspot.com/.

Sergeant Elizabeth A. Le Bel is "Sergeant Lizzie" of *New Lives*. She recovered from her wounds but not enough to remain on duty. She was married in October 2005 and medically discharged as of November 2005. As of spring 2006, Lizzie is living in Arizona, working, going to school, taking care of her garden, and living with her husband and cat. *New Lives* can be found at http://sgtlizzie .blogspot.com/.

First Lieutenant Micah Bell (*Courage without Fear*) was the mayor of his FOB in Iraq and returned to the United States in late February 2006 to be reunited with his wife and son. Micah works for the National Park Service as a wildland firefighter. His blog is at http:// couragewithoutfear.typepad.com/courage_without_fear/.

Sergeant Joshua Salmons (*Talking Salmons*) is serving as a combat journalist in Iraq. He will return to Fort Hood, Texas, in September 2006. He will resume pursuing his MBA from Baker College in Michigan and doesn't know what he wants to do with his life except to try to make people a little happier. *Talking Salmons* is at http://thesalmons.typepad.com/.

Master Sergeant Patrick Cosgrove (*Six More Months*) left Iraq on Christmas Day, 2005, and returned home with his National Guard artillery battery on January 1, 2006. He returned to his career as an investment representative for a major brokerage firm and, in the Guard, is currently the fire support operations sergeant for the 34th ID Aviation Brigade. His primary focus is on getting to know his family again and savoring every moment of normalcy that he can. *Six More Months* is located at http://topmustang.blogspot.com/.

Staff Sergeant CJ Grisham of *A Soldier's Perspective* returned home in November 2003. He was promoted to sergeant first class while in Fallujah, Iraq. He was sent to the National Training Center at Fort Irwin, California, to train our troops deploying to Iraq to work effectively with civilians and to counter the IED threat. CJ received the Bronze Star for his valor during the invasion. He is now stationed in the Washington, D.C., area and has been visiting the wounded at Walter Reed Army Medical Center and publishing their stories. You can find CJ of *A Soldier's Perspective* at http://www.soldiersperspective.us/.

Sergeant Mike Durand was given the choice to shut down *This Is Your War* or to have his commander read every post prior to publication. His commander was exercising his authority to filter Durand's writing. Durand chose to shut down his blog with this message:

> *I am nothing special, I'm not unique. You pass people like me every day on the streets of your cities and towns, sometimes they are so close you can't even see them—and sadly enough normally you wouldn't even speak to them. But we are all around you, we always will be, too. Past, present, and future. Some of them are reading these words right now. We protect you while you sleep.*
>
> *Don't ever forget that . . .*

Sergeant Durand returned home from Iraq in early 2006.

CHAPTER THREE: THE HEALERS

Lieutenant Commander Heidi S. Kraft (*Blackfive*) left active duty in March 2005 and currently works as a Navy contractor in international military HIV prevention. She continues to see patients on a part-time basis. She lives in Southern California and is married to a former Marine Corps Harrier pilot, Mike. They have twins, Brian and Megan. Heidi has become a friend of Jason Dunham's mother.

"Major Pain" (*Magic in the Baghdad Café*) returned home to Virginia and is going to retire from active duty soon. She stopped blogging, but her blog remains at http://bear.typepad.com/magic_in_the_baghdad_cafe/.

Shot eleven times in Fallujah, Navy Hospital Corpsman James Pell (*Pull on Superman's Cape*) was determined not to let his wounds keep him from caring for his Marines. Lance Corporal James Powers saved his life. Doc Pell recovered from his wounds and returned to San Diego for a time. He volunteered to go back to Iraq and returned exactly one year after he was wounded. As of March 2006, he is busy training Iraqi Army forces as part of a Marine Embedded Training Team. *Pull on Superman's Cape* is at http://pullonsupermanscape.typepad.com/.

Chaplain (Captain) Brad Lewis (*Training for Eternity*) has stopped blogging due to OPSEC guidance. He returned from Afghanistan and continues his work ministering to the Special Operations community. December 25, 2005, was the first Christmas that he spent at home with his wife and kids in three years. His blog remains at http://chaplain.blogspot.com/.

Army Specialist Nick Cademartori's (*The Questing Cat*) combat life-saving skills saved the life of his friend, who made a complete recovery. Contrary to Nick's thoughts that day, he did not make any mistakes. And contrary to his wishes, he was "awarded" for it. Because of him, his friend made it home alive. As of August 2006, Nick is slated to be in Iraq for his second combat tour. After the new

OPSEC guidance was issued, he shut down *The Questing Cat* to avoid any trouble from the Army.

Dr. (Major) Kevin Cuccinelli (*Blackfive*) returned home to Colorado and married Tara, the head nurse of the ER of the 28th Combat Support Hospital. He separated from the Army and is pursuing his civilian medical career. He is applying his medical skills in rural areas of Colorado and Kansas that don't have easy access to medical care. Kevin and Tara's first son was born in February 2005, and their second child will be born in June 2006. Kevin's one stipulation for being included in this book was that all 113 soldiers that helped to save Specialist Roy Alan Gray were included.

CHAPTER FOUR: LEADERS, WARRIORS, AND DIPLOMATS

Captain Danjel Bout (*365 and a Wakeup*) brought his company of air assault infantry home to California in January 2005. He has reunited with his wife. You can read Captain Bout's war journal at http://thunder6.typepad.com/365_arabian_nights/, which was a finalist for Best Military Blog in the 2005 Weblog Awards.

Colonel Austin Bay (*austinbay.net*) retired from the U.S. Army Reserves upon returning home in 2004. He was awarded the Bronze Star for his work in Iraq. He continues to write his successful syndicated column, teach at the University of Texas, and publish occasional commentaries on National Public Radio's Morning Edition. You can find Austin's blog at http://austinbay.net/blog/.

Major E (*Powerline*) returned home to his native California in 2005. He and his wife were blessed with their first child, Noah, in 2005. Inspired by the courageous Iraqi voters and their stand for democratic freedom on January 30, 2005, Major E and his wife founded Mission Freedom (http://www.missionfreedom.org/index.php), a nonprofit dedicated to promoting religious freedom in the Middle East. *Powerline* is at http://www.powerlineblog.com/.

First Lieutenant Neil Prakash (*Armor Geddon*) returned home with one Silver Star for his valor in the Battle of Baqubah and a Bronze Star for his bravery during the Battle of Fallujah. He returned to Germany and was married. Promoted to captain, he and his wife (also an Army officer) were deployed to Iraq with the 4th Infantry Division in 2006. You can read Neil's 2004 war journal at http://avengerred six.blogspot.com/.

First Lieutenant Jason Van Steenwyk (*CounterColumn*) returned to Florida after a year in Iraq. He continues to blog and serve in the Florida National Guard. *CounterColumn* is at http://iraqnow.blog spot.com/.

Corporal Michael Bautista (*Ma Deuce Gunner*) returned home to Idaho in November 2005 and was reunited with his wife. After a vacation in Hawaii, they've purchased their first house and Mike is busy making repairs and getting them settled. I met a very tough wounded soldier at Walter Reed Army Medical Center who knew Mike and described him as a "badass." *Ma Deuce Gunner* is located at http://www.madeucegunners.blogspot.com/.

First Lieutenant Scott Langlands (*Medicine Soldier*) returned to the States and is resuming his job with the American Red Cross Blood Services. He is pursuing his master's degree in public health and preparing to take command of his Army Reserve company. His blog is at http://medicinesoldier.blogspot.com/.

First Sergeant James Thomson (*Sergeant Hook*) was promoted to sergeant major. He returned home to his family in Hawaii from Afghanistan and is now attending the Army's Sergeant Major Academy at Fort Bliss, Texas. Sergeant Major Thomson's blog is at http://www.sgthook.com/.

Specialist Mark Partridge Miner (*Boots in Baghdad*) returned home to Florida after his year-long tour with the Louisiana National Guard in Iraq. He volunteered for another tour in Afghanistan but the tour was cancelled. You can read his blog at http://www.bootsinbagh dad.blogspot.com/.

Sergeant Michael (*A Day in Iraq*) survived his tour as an infantry team leader in Baghdad and returned home to Fort Stewart, Georgia, in 2006. Michael's blog is at http://www.adayiniraq.com/.

CHAPTER FIVE: THE WARRIORS

Sergeant Robert Florkowski (*Sniper Eye*) returned home to the United States after a year in northern Iraq. He took part in many major combat operations, including the offensive in Samarra. Rob is currently creating a book about his missions in Iraq and pursuing a degree in business administration. His blog site is http://www .snipereye.blogspot.com.

Army Captain Chuck Ziegenfuss (*From My Position . . . On the Way!*) was severely wounded by an IED in Iraq. The explosion sent him flying headfirst into a deep canal, where the weight of his armor had him sinking quickly. His second-in-command, Captain Jason Spencer, dove after his commander and saved his life. Chuck is recovering at Walter Reed Army Hospital as of February 2006. He will recover from his wounds to his hands, arms, face, and legs, and he has started a project to get the patients at Walter Reed Army Medical Center who can't type due to their wounds laptops with voice recognition software so that they can stay in touch with family and friends. His project has expanded to include patients in all military and Veterans Administration hospitals. Chuck blogs at http:// tcoverride.blogspot.com/.

Marine Lance Corporal Eric Scott Freeman (*Blackfive*) kept a journal of his second tour in Iraq. Eric graduated from high school at age sixteen and completed almost two years of college before joining the Marines. He wanted to become a published author when he was finished with his military commitment. Eric Freeman was killed in an automobile crash on January 3, 2005. He was on his way to report for duty—his third tour of duty in Iraq.

Marine Gunnery Sergeant Nick Popaditch (*Blackfive*), the "cee-gar Marine," recovered from wounds he received in Fallujah, Iraq, but, with the loss of one eye and hearing in one ear and damage to the other eye, he has been medically retired. He received the Silver Star for his valor:

> While on patrol in Al Fallujah, Iraq, Fox Company came under heavy enemy fire and without hesitation, Gunnery Sgt. Popaditch surged his two tanks into the city to support the Marines under fire. He led his tank section several blocks into the city, drawing fire away from the beleaguered Marines. His decisive actions enabled Fox Company to gain a foothold in the city and evacuate a critically wounded Marine.
>
> For several hours, enemy forces engaged his tank section with withering rocket propelled grenade fire until they were destroyed by accurate machinegun fire. Acting as the forward observer for an AC-130 gunship, Gunnery Sgt. Popaditch directed fire onto enemy targets, effecting their annihilation. On the morning of April 7th, Gunnery Sgt. Popaditch was severely wounded by a rocket propelled grenade blast while fighting insurgents. Blinded and deafened by the blast, he remained calm and directed his crew to a medical evacuation site.

Nick is still 100 percent Marine, receiving top grades in his college classes despite his vision and hearing disability. Nick recently gave the keynote speech at the 230th Marine Corps Birthday Ball at the Marine Corps Ground Combat Center, where he was regarded as a hero of his generation. He would have none of that, however, instead directing the praise to the Marines who had fought by his side. He still smokes cigars.

Retired Major John Donovan (*Argghhh!*), who wrote about Raven 42's engagement during an ambush, is currently a government contractor. His military blog focuses on the more ballistic issues of military history as well as military humor and contemporary military topics. Raven 42 suffered casualties but was regarded as an amazing success. Staff Sergeant Timothy Nein and Sergeant Leigh Ann Hester were awarded the Silver Star for their heroism. Hester is the

Hester is the first female soldier since WWII to be awarded the Silver Star. You can find *Argghhh!* at http://www.thedonovan.com/.

CHAPTER SIX: HEROES OF THE HOMEFRONT

Tim Fitzgerald's (*CPT Patti—The Sweetest Woman on the Planet Goes to Baghdad*) wife, Captain Patti, also made it back home, after 427 days in Iraq, and was promoted to major ahead of her peers. After vacationing in Italy and Bavaria, Tim and Patti were moved to Washington, D.C., where Patti serves in the Human Resources Command. As of March 2006, Patti's brother, Sergeant Dan, is patrolling Iraq in his Stryker somewhere on the Syrian border. Tim has ceased blogging to spend more time in adoration of his wife. His blog remains at http://gatorsix.blogspot.com/.

Britt (*CaliValleyGirl*) was reunited with her boyfriend in Germany in March 2006 after his year in Afghanistan. She received her master's degree from the University of Cologne and is just enjoying her boyfriend's not being deployed. *CaliValleyGirl* is located at http://calivalleygirl.blogspot.com/.

Carla Meyer Lois (*Some Soldier's Mom*) is retired and following the travails of her son's unit as they redeploy back to the United States. Her son, Noah, is almost completely recovered and is still in the Army. He's taking college classes in pursuit of a degree in criminal justice. *Some Soldier's Mom* is at http://www.somesoldiersmom .blogspot.com/.

Wendy Marr (*Biting Their Little Heads Off*) was reunited with her husband, Parrish, in June 2005. She gave him a homecoming gift: a brand-new Harley-Davidson motorcycle. Wendy and Parrish now operate their own construction company. Wendy is just glad to have him home—until his next deployment. *Biting Their Little Heads Off* is at http://www.bitingtheirlittleheadsoff.blogspot.com/.

Reverend (and retired Major) Donald Sensing (*One Hand Clapping*) continues to watch the news for signs of his son, a Marine in Iraq.

Stephen will return from Iraq in March 2006. Donald focuses on his church and family and continues to blog at *One Hand Clapping*, located at http://www.donaldsensing.com/.

Erika S. (*Military Bride*) was reunited with her fiancé, Matt, in March 2006 after 415 days apart. Erika is pursuing her degree in accounting while working and planning their wedding. *Military Bride* is at http://militarybride.blogspot.com/.

CHAPTER SEVEN: THE FALLEN

Heidi Sims (*Learning to Live*) continues to write about her life as a single mom and dealing with the loss of her husband, Sean. She lives in Texas raising her son, Colin. Heidi wants to make sure that Colin knows who his daddy was and what he died doing. Heidi is teaching part time and will puruse her master's degree. Heidi's blog, *Learning to Live,* can be found at http://heidijournal.blogspot.com/.

After a very successful second tour in Iraq, Marine Cobra Pilot Major Brian Kennedy (*Howdy*) came home in July 2005 to a transfer to Washington, D.C. He will be promoted to lieutenant colonel in 2006 and looks forward to getting back to flying Cobras again. Brian continues to write at http://www.camelspider.typepad.com/howdy/.

Private First Class Trueman Muhrer-Irwin (*Rebel Coyote*) returned home to Florida. Because he was hospitalized, Trueman missed the memorials for his friend, Robert Wise. Two years after Robert was killed in action, Trueman was able to visit his grave at Arlington. *Rebel Coyote* is at http://rebelcoyote.livejournal.com/.

Heather McCrae (*CaliValleyGirl*) is still embracing life as much as she can after the loss of her husband, Erik.

Marine Lieutenant Colonel Michael Strobl (*Blackfive*) is serving with the Marines as the head of the Officer Distribution Section for Manpower and Reserves Affairs of the U.S. Marine Corps Headquarters in Quantico, Virginia.

CHAPTER EIGHT: HOMECOMING

First Lieutenant Lee Kelley (*Wordsmith at War*) returned home in spring 2006 after serving for a year in Ramadi, Iraq. He is very happy to be a full-time dad again and is aggressively pursuing his writing career. He works full time in the Utah Army National Guard as a communications officer and still updates his blog at http://www.wordsmithatwar.blog-city.com/.

First Lieutenant Rusten Currie (*Sic Vis Pace, Para Bellum*) returned home to his wife in early 2006 and is contemplating a career in politics; he might run for Congress in Southern California. He also will be putting his writing skills to work as cowriter for a Showtime series and work as a military advisor for some movie and television projects. But before he will do all that he wants to spend time with his wife and travel "like Jules in *Pulp Fiction*, just walk the earth for a while . . ." More than likely Rusten will start a new blog in the future. His wartime journal blog, *Sic Vis Pace, Para Bellum*, can be read at http://currierd.typepad.com/centurion/.

Rachelle Jones (*ArmyWifeToddlerMom*) continues to write about supporting her Army husband and raising two very interesting toddlers at http://armywifetoddlermom.blogspot.com/.

GLOSSARY

.50 cal Browning M2 .50 caliber (12.7mm) machine gun

155mm Refers to either the 155mm artillery cannon or the 155mm (diameter) artillery round

1SG First sergeant; senior enlisted soldier in a company or battery; responsible primarily for logistics

550 cord Parachute cord used for multiple purposes

5-ton Military transport truck with a 5-ton cargo capacity

7-ton Military transport truck with a 7-ton cargo capacity

A-10 U.S. Air Force A-10 Thunderbolt II aircraft used for close air support of ground forces; also known as the Warthog for its less than graceful appearance

AAR After-action review: an assessment of strengths and weaknesses exposed during an operation

Abrams M1A1 Abrams main battle tank

AC-130 AC-130H Spectre: a U.S. Air Force C-130 converted from a cargo plane to a gunship

AIF Anti-Iraqi forces; refers to insurgents trying to stop Iraq from forming a democracy

AK-47 An automatic rifle that fires a 7.62mm round; most commonly made by Russia and China

Ali Baba Iraqi jargon for thief or insurgent

AO Area of operations

Apache AH-64 Apache: the Army's primary attack helicopter

APC Armored personnel carrier

AR Armor regiment or tank regiment

Armory Either a secure location for weapons storage or an assembly center for National Guard soldiers

ASR Alternate supply route

AT-4 A light antitank weapon that fires a rocket with an effective range of about 250 meters

Battalion A unit with at least two company-size units and a headquarters, usually commanded by a lieutenant colonel

Battery The basic firing units of artillery battalions; the artillery branches' company-size unit, usually commanded by a captain

BC Battalion commander, usually a lieutenant colonel

BDA Battle damage assessment

Bde Brigade

BFV Bradley fighting vehicle: provides mobility and protection to an infantry or cavalry squad; sometimes referred to as a Brad or Bradley

Blackhawk UH-60 Blackhawk utility helicopter: used for transport of troops or for Medevac

Blog A Web log or online diary

BN Battalion

Bradley Bradley fighting vehicle; sometimes referred to as a BFV or Brad. See BFV.

Brigade A unit with at least two battalion-size units and a headquarters, usually commanded by a colonel

BRT Brigade reconnaissance troop: a company-size unit responsible for providing intelligence and surveillance for a brigade; usually an armor force

C-130 C-130 Hercules: a U.S. Air Force cargo airplane

C-17 C-17 Globemaster: a U.S. Air Force cargo airplane

C-4 Composition C4: a block demolition charge; commonly referred to as plastic explosives

CA Civil Affairs

CASEVAC Casualty evacuation aircraft (normally transport helicopters) not configured as Medevac aircraft; usually litters are added to the aircraft configuriation. See Medevac.

CASH A Combat support hospital; a mobile hospital. See CSH.

CH-46 CH-46 Sea Knight helicopter: a Marine transport and Medevac aircraft

CH-47 CH-47 Chinook helicopter: an Army transport aircraft

Chinook CH-47 Chinook helicopter: an Army transport aircraft

CLS Combat lifesaver: a member of a nonmedical unit the unit commander selects for additional training beyond basic first aid procedures

CO Commanding officer

Company A unit with at least two platoon-size units and a headquarters, usually commanded by a captain

COSCOM Corps Support Command: provides logistics support to the corps (more than one division)

Counterfire Attacking enemy artillery (indirect fire), usually after tracking their incoming rounds

CP Command post or headquarters

CSH Combat support hospital

CSM Command Sergeant Major

CVC Combat vehicle crewman's helmet, worn in tanks and Bradley fighting vehicles

D-9 A T-9 or D-7 armored bulldozer

DCU Desert combat uniform or desert camouflage uniform

DFAC Dining facility, commonly known as a mess hall

Division A unit with at least two brigades and a headquarters, usually commanded by a major general

DSN Defense Switched Network, the military telephone system

Dust-off Jargon for a Medevac helicopter or calling a Medevac helicopter

EMEDS U.S. Air Force Expeditionary Medical Support: a medical station or facility

EOD Explosive Ordnance Disposal; the military's bomb squad

EPW Enemy prisoner of war

ER Hospital emergency room

First sergeant The senior enlisted soldier in a company or battery; responsible primarily for logistics; abbreviation is 1SG

FNG Fucking new guy

FOB Forward Operating Base

Fobbit Someone who doesn't leave the safety of the FOB

FRG Family Readiness Group

HE High-explosive round

HEAT High-explosive antitank round

Hellfire An antitank missile carried by aircraft

HEMMT See HEMTT

HEMTT Heavy expanded mobility tactical truck: an eight-wheeled transport truck used to deliver cargo and fuel

HMMWV High mobility multipurpose wheeled vehicle, more commonly known as a Humvee: the light tactical vehicle for our armed forces

Hooch Jargon for living area

Hummer High mobility multipurpose wheeled vehicle, more commonly known as a Humvee: the light tactical vehicle for our armed forces

Humvee The high mobility multipurpose wheeled vehicle: the light tactical vehicle for our armed forces

IA Iraqi Army

IBA Interceptor body armor

ICU Hospital intensive care unit

IED Improvised explosive device; homemade bomb

Indirect Indirect fire: artillery or mortar fire (indirect because the gunners usually can't see their targets)

IP Iraqi Police

ISF Iraqi Special Forces (soldiers)

IZ International Zone of Baghdad, Iraq, also known as the Green Zone; the heavily guarded diplomatic and government area of central Baghdad

JDAMS A GPS-guided bomb dropped by U.S. Air Force or Navy aircraft

KBR Kellog, Brown and Root: contractor providing many services in Iraq

Kerlix First-aid gauze

Kevlar Aramid fiber used in body armor and helmets for American forces

KIA Killed in action

LD Line of departure

LMTV M1078 standard cargo truck

LOGPAC Logistics package; usually everything needed to resupply a unit

LOL Laugh out loud

LRAS Long-range advanced scout surveillance system; used to detect enemies at extended ranges

LT Lieutenant; when used without a name, pronounced "el-tee"

LTF Logistical task force

M1114 An armored HMMWV or Humvee

M16 The standard military automatic rife (5.56mm round)

M1A1 M1A1 Abrams main battle tank

M203 A 40mm grenade launcher, attached to an M16 rifle

M24 A sniper rifle that fires 7.62mm rounds

M240 A medium machine gun that fires 7.62mm rounds

M249 M249 light machine gun: a light automatic rifle more commonly known as a SAW or squad automatic weapon; fires 5.56mm rounds

M4 The carbine (shorter barrel) version of the M16 rifle

M9 M9 Beretta pistol: semiautomatic, fires a 9mm round

Medevac Medical evacuation by aircraft

Mess Dining facility, more commonly known as the mess hall

MH-47 Special Operations version of the CH-47 Chinook helicopter

MI Military Intelligence

MilBlog Military blog or Web log

MK19 A 40mm grenade machine gun with a range of about 1,600 meters

MOS Military occupational specialty

MOUT Military operation in urban terrain

MP Military Police

MRE Meal ready to eat

MWR Morale, welfare, and recreation

NCO Noncommissioned officer: corporal and above in the Army and Marines, petty officer in the Navy

NCOIC NCO in charge

OPS Operations

OR Hospital operating room

Paladin M109A6 Paladin: a 155mm self-propelled artillery gun

PKM Light machine gun made in Russia, fires a 7.62mm round

Platoon A unit with at least two squad-size elements

Platoon leader Officer in charge of a platoon, usually a lieutenant

Platoon sergeant The senior NCO of a platoon

POO Point of origin

PT Physical training

PX Post Exchange (store)

QRF Quick Reaction Force

R&R Rest & relaxation (or recuperation)

Red Zone The area outside of the safety of the International Zone (IZ) of central Baghdad, Iraq

ROE Rules of engagement

RPG Rocket-propelled grenade

RPK Light machine gun made in Russia, fires 7.62mm rounds

S-2 Either the Intelligence Section of a headquarters element of a unit or the intelligence staff officer in charge of the Intelligence Section

S-3 Either the Operations (and Training) Section of a headquarters element of a unit or the operations staff officer in charge of the Operations Section

S-4 Either the Logistics Section of a headquarters element of a unit or the logistics staff officer in charge of the Logistics Section

SAM Surface-to-air missile

SAW Squad automatic weapon. See M249.

SITEMP Situation template: the prediction of enemy actions (usually on a map)

Sitrep Situation Report

SMAW Shoulder-launched multipurpose assault weapon: primarily used against armored vehicles and bunkers

Snivel gear Any gear that provides comfort

SP Start point

Squad A unit with at least two teams, usually led by a staff sergeant

Task force A temporary (temporary can be a long time) grouping of units under one commander for a specific mission

TC Tank commander (also used to refer to vehicle commander)

Team The smallest unit, usually made up of at least two soldiers; more commonly referred to as a fire team

Terp Interpreter

TIC Troops in contact; soldiers engaged by enemy forces

TOC Tactical Operations Center, where a commander and staff gather and analyze information and control subordinate units (via orders)

TOW Tube-launched, optically tracked, wire-guided missile; primarily an anti-tank weapon

VBED Vehicle-borne explosive device; commonly known as a car bomb

VBIED Vehicle-borne improvised explosive device; commonly known as a car bomb. Same as VBED

VC Vehicle commander

Web log A Web site usually posting items in a diary format

WIA Wounded in action

XO Executive officer; refers to the officer that is second in command of a military unit, usually coordinating staff actions

ACKNOWLEDGMENTS

First, thank you to my wonderful wife, Jennifer, for standing by me and my crusades over the past decade (she *must* love me). She's lived with this book project for a while now and I couldn't have asked for a greater supporter or friend. A big thank you to my wonderful children, Jack and Gracie, for making me laugh and smile. Every day they do something amazing to make me believe that my world is good. My mother and step-father, Mary Ann and John Gee, and my in-laws, Jim and Carol Kolar, helped proof the book and generate ideas. Their support, enthusiasm, knowledge, expertise, and love were a godsend.

A huge thank you to the professionals who helped to craft this idea into a book. Over the past few years, many literary agents had approached me about a book, but they didn't really understand bloggers, let alone military bloggers. Bob Mecoy of Creative Book Services sent me one letter that outlined our contributions so well I called him and this book was born. Thanks, Bob.

Thank you to our editor, Bob Bender, Senior Editor and Vice President at Simon & Schuster, who has been our guide, expertly helping us find the right path for our words.

No thank you would ever be complete without a personal note of thanks to my former sergeants. They are responsible for much success in my life: Sergeants Casiano, Williamson, Zinc, Reddick, Love, Wilson, Grant, Haubner, Snodgrass, Jackson, Arsenault, Gary, Christianson, Wojick, Adamson, Hassan, Sternberg, Thompson, Keel, Tesar, Armstrong, Smith, Bond. Thank you for taking care of me and our troops.

I owe a humongous thank you to those who've supported *Black-five.net* and military bloggers. To Lieutenant Colonel (Ret.) Buzz Patterson, Hugh Hewitt, Michelle Malkin, John Hockenberry, and Glenn

Reynolds, thank you so much for bringing attention to military bloggers and the good work that our Armed Forces are doing around the world.

Thank you to Master Sergeant (Ret.) James Hanson, Uncle Jimbo of *Madison.com*; Subsunk of the U.S. Navy's silent service; Cassandra of *Villainous Company*; Blake Powers of *Laughing Wolf*; and Grim of *Grim's Hall* for helping out with *Blackfive.net* while I worked on this book. I really owe you folks a few drinks (or twenty) sometime!

To Marine veteran Seamus Garrahy (and his *thousands* of All Hands); USMC Master Sergeants (Ret.) Glen Evans, Alan Johnson, and Curt Gustafson; Watt Keller; Carrie Constantini; Amy King; Deb and the Marine Corps Moms; and the Airborne Moms (Bobby Carrasquillo Sr., too!), thank you for including me in your groups of friends and family. You all are a big reason behind the success of *Blackfive.net*.

Last, but certainly not least, thank you to the authors for sharing your experiences with us. Thank you for giving me your friendship, trust, and compassion—especially while producing this book.

You are all heroes.

INDEX

ABOUT THE AUTHOR

Matthew Currier Burden enlisted in the military when he was seventeen. He left the military as a major in the U.S. Army Reserve in July 2001. During his last assignment as executive officer of an intelligence detachment for the Defense Intelligence Agency, Burden's unit received the Joint Meritorious Unit Award from the secretary of defense for their work in modernizing military intelligence gathering and analysis. He has a master of science degree (computer science) from the University of Chicago, where he received the Faculty Award. After the death of his friend in Iraq, Burden started *Blackfive.net* in mid-2003 to support the troops fighting the War on Terror and tell their stories. *Blackfive.net* quickly became one of the most visited and linked blogs and has won consecutive Best Military Blog titles in the Weblog Awards.